D0906207

Stumbling
Toward Justice

The Penn State Series in Lived Religious Experience

Judith Van Herik, General Editor

The series publishes books that interpret religions by studying personal experience in its historical, geographical, social, and cultural settings.

Lee Hoinacki, *El Camino: Walking to Santiago de Compostela*

Suzanne Selinger, *Charlotte von Kirschbaum and Karl Barth: A Study in Biography and the History of Theology*

Lee Hoinacki, *Stumbling Toward Justice: Stories of Place*

Lee Hoinacki

Stumbling Toward Justice

Stories of Place

The Pennsylvania State University Press
University Park, Pennsylvania

Excerpts from "The Second Coming," by William Butler Yeats, reprinted with the permission of: Simon & Schuster from *The Poems of W. B. Yeats: A New Edition*, edited by Richard J. Finneran, Copyright © 1924 by Macmillan Publishing Company, renewed 1952 by Bertha Georgie Yeats; and A. P. Watt Ltd., on behalf of Michael B. Yeats.

Excerpt from "At a Country Funeral," by Wendell Berry, from *The Country of Marriage*, reprinted with permission of the publishers, Harcourt Brace, and the author. Copyright © 1973 by Wendell Berry.

Excerpt from "Traveling Home," by Wendell Berry, from *Collected Poems, 1957–1982* (New York: North Point Press, 1994), reprinted with permission of Farrar, Straus & Giroux, Inc.

Excerpts from *Cantares Mexicanos* reprinted from *Cantares Mexicanos: Song of the Aztecs*, translated from the Nahuatl, with an Introduction and Commentary, by John Bierhorst, with the permission of the publishers, Stanford University Press. Copyright © 1985 by the Board of Trustees of the Leland Stanford Junior University.

Library of Congress Cataloging-in-Publication Data

Hoinacki, Lee, 1928–
    Stumbling toward justice: stories of place / Lee Hoinacki.
        p.   cm.
    Includes bibliographical references and index.
    ISBN 0-271-01940-9 (cloth : alk. paper)
    1. Life.   I. Title.
    BD431.H525   1999
    973.92'092—dc21   99-22617
                                                              CIP

It is the policy of The Pennsylvania State University Press to use acid-free paper for the first printing of all clothbound books. Publications on uncoated stock satisfy the minimum requirements of American National Standard for Information Sciences—Permanence of Paper for Printed Library Materials, ANSI Z39.48-1992.

For Mary, Ben, and Beth

Contents

Preface		ix
Acknowledgments		xi
1	In Search of Patriotism	1
2	New Beginnings in Illinois	19
3	Life at the Margins	43
4	The Last Farms in America	63
5	From Science to Poetry	81
6	Word Roots	97
7	The Beauty of Saying No	113
8	To Die My Own Death	133
9	Childhood as Addiction	149
10	A Job to Find	167
11	The Stars of Mexico	185
12	An Economy of Vision	203
13	Yet Another War	217
Notes		235
Index		247

Preface

> . . . [O]ne sometimes wishes to be a stone breaker.
> There's no doubt about breaking a stone. But there's
> doubt, fear—a black horror, in every page one writes.
>
> Joseph Conrad

These words were on my desk while I thought about and wrote this book. I have done work similar to breaking stones; I, too, have felt what Conrad experienced. Diffident, then, I completed the manuscript, a collection of stories. With Roger Shattuck, I believe that "the best set of records we have about ourselves" are stories. He goes on to say that "[w]e need ideas to reason logically and to explore the fog of uncertainty that surrounds the immediate encounter with daily living. Equally, we need stories to embody the medium of time in which human character takes shape and reveals itself to us." I have been privileged to live in a queer time; I have witnessed the possibilities of both transcendence and horror. Beneath the mélange of comely and loathsome, I found a hope hidden in contemporary existence: one can set out on a quest, a search for the truth of the whole, the good of one's life. In spite of the stumbling, the errors, the moral lapses, indeed, because of the disarray, I came to see that only a teleological odyssey makes sense, quiets the need for meaning. The end not only illumines the journey, it also permits one to live with the shame of failure.

Such language implies moral reasoning, an explicit notion of the good, perhaps a daily reflection on perceptions and actions. One needs to stop, to examine how the ongoing narrative, the chronicling of connections, fits the journey. Did I stray from the path? Have I reached a dead-end? Dare I acknowledge an advance?

The stories I relate here are highly selective, both in their content and in what I have taken from the available record. My principal interest is to illustrate a fundamental insight: The promise of progress is a lie, a terrible and cruel trap. My words can have only one justification: they sow doubt.

Lee Hoinacki
Corvallis, Oregon
November 1997

Acknowledgments

I started writing some of these chapters almost twenty years ago, trying to make sense of experiences that questioned the places in which, seemingly, I had settled. Some comments, then, may at times appear dated.

The dedication and text name many of the persons whose affection and generosity have enriched my life and, I hope, this book. Among these persons, one stands out: Ivan Illich. For nearly forty years, his friendship has repeatedly moved and clarified my spirit.

With pleasure, I thank Rustum Roy, Carl Mitcham, and Héctor Flores of Penn State University, for generously giving me office space and privileges. Karen Snare, of the same institution, was unfailingly helpful with bureaucratic conundrums.

I never needed to apply for foundation grants to support me during writing, since I enjoyed the gracious hospitality of Barbara Duden in Germany and Valentina Borremans in Mexico.

I am particularly thankful to friends in Canada, the United States, Mexico, Ireland, Spain, Germany, and India, who through their conversations on the themes of this book, helped me to sharpen my thoughts. Further, students at Penn State University and at the University of Bremen, many of whom have become close friends, challenged me to strive for arguments that exhibit both logic and life. Mother Jerome, O.S.B., a cloistered nun at the Abbey of Regina Laudis, offered apposite criticisms of the last chapter.

All the people at Penn State Press impressed me with their competence and friendliness. But I am especially grateful to Philip Winsor, my initial editor at the Press, for his confidence and encouragement; Peter Potter, who ably took over as my editor after Philip's retirement; Patricia Mitchell, for the graceful knowledge of her editing; and Judith Van Herik. In my attempts to write, I am privileged to enjoy the perceptive remarks of this dear friend.

For the dust jacket, I want to thank Beth Hoinacki, Barbara Withey, and Ray Liddick Jr. Historically, Icarus is taken to symbolize someone who exceeded the measure, the middle (from Aristotle's verb μεδεο). Hence, he suffered the fate of such presumption, falling into the sea and drowning.

Today, Aristotelian virtue may not be enough; some have to go to extremes, for example, quitting their mainline job, taking their kids out of school, refusing medical care, and so on. But persons acting thusly must be prepared to pay the price. They may experience a kind of double irony. For them, the audacity of Icarus is not foolhardy; it may be the courage demanded of them by the times. They must not fear to be judged loony, to fall into the sea and drown.

In an earlier and different version, Chapters 4 and 8 first appeared in *The Catholic Worker* (New York). Chapter 9, in an edited form, appeared in the *Journal of Family Life*; a section of Chapter 11, in the *Bulletin of Science, Technology & Society*. Chapter 12 was published in a Spanish translation in *Ixtus* (Mexico City).

1

In Search of Patriotism

> . . . [J]ust as religion is a certain profession of faith, hope and charity, by which man is primordially ordered to God, so piety is a certain profession of charity, which one holds toward his parents and native land.
>
> Saint Thomas Aquinas

I stopped filling up the Blue Book with words; I was tired; I needed to rest my hand. Could there ever be some conceivable relationship between answering these examination questions and a life devoted to study and teaching? But if I wanted to set out on that life, I must first get an official piece of paper, the Ph.D., and to obtain this I had to jump through the requisite hoops. So I found myself, on an unusually clear morning in the spring of 1970, sealed up on the third floor of an air-conditioned building in Westwood, covering page after page of my Blue Book.

Somewhere in the middle of writing on the last question, I seemed to sense an unusual movement outside the tightly-closed windows. Rising, I walked over to look out. Disturbed at first by what I saw below, I then began to feel a vague fright. Groups of frantic students dashed by, as if trying to escape some dreadful pursuer. The malignant threat soon appeared: a whitish haze—tear gas. Under the cloud, riot police, waving what seemed like monster clubs over their heads, chased the scattered students.

Later, the scenario repeated itself, but in a different direction. Obviously, a lot of people were moving about over the campus, confused—but angry and frustrated, too. How protest this awful war, several thousand miles away, in Vietnam? How dream of stopping the senseless killing? The last weeks' student demonstrations exploded in a climactic flash, a violent confrontation with the police, the very morning scheduled for my quiet, academic exercise. Three years' orderly progression of course work and field research, study and reflection, writing and reporting, were brutally interrupted. Could I continue to ignore what my government wantonly—it appeared—inflicted on a distant, unknown people? But I was already forty, impatient now to begin a new career as an academic. If I were younger, I could indulge the luxury of sharing in the excitement and zeal of militant student action. However, my history seemed not synchronous with the history of the times. When I was a young college student, a benign and fatherly Eisenhower, a man "above" politics, presided over the domestic stillness. A short tour of duty with the U.S. Marines in China had not been enough of a culture shock to sensitize me to the ominous importance of the Rosenbergs' execution as atomic spies. Now I felt too old to participate in riotous protests. More important, I had an immediate and clear obligation to a wife and two small children. I had to prepare for a lifetime of employment; I had no time to lose.

I returned to the table to face my dull Blue Book, and stared at the lifeless words. Up there, high above the swirling mass of chased and chasers, I had nothing to worry about, no need to be apprehensive. But something knotted up inside me; I felt queer deep in my gut. Repeatedly, I attempted to continue phrasing my answer to the question . . . but could not. An examination in political science appeared more and more cold, distant, surreal, while the real drama of my country's politics unfolded unseen (by me) under my feet. Finally, I briefly described what I had seen from the window, and explained that I was unable to continue with the exam. The faculty judges would have to take what I had already written and, extrapolating from that, make an inference as to what I was capable of finishing in quieter circumstances. As in a daze, I got up, left the room and walked out of the social sciences building. That day I did not notice the new plaque on the wall. To honor an American UN diplomat, and Nobel laureate of 1950, the building had recently been named "Ralph J. Bunche Hall."

The comfortable world I had constructed for myself precipitously collapsed that morning. My stomach told me that something must change in my life. Returning to the United States in 1967, after about seven years working in Latin America, I married and immediately entered graduate school. A strict academic schedule rigidly defined the years since then. During that time, I kept one proximate goal constantly before my eyes: to get my working papers as soon as possible. Somewhere on the periphery of my awareness, Angela Davis was on campus, fighting to retain her academic appointment. After completing her graduate work at U.C. San Diego, under Herbert Marcuse, she was hired to teach philosophy at UCLA. An articulate and outspoken self-professed card-carrying member of the Communist Party, she enraged the Regents, reigning stalwarts of California's *haute bourgeoisie*. Apparently, they had vowed to get rid of her by any means possible. Mario Savio and the Free Speech movement at Berkeley were somewhere, dimly, in the past. The Days of Rage during the Democratic National Convention in Chicago in 1968 were far, far away—too distant to affect my world. A short visit up the coast did nothing to disturb my academic slumbers.

Some reports in the media had portrayed Haight-Ashbury, in San Francisco, as a new Eden of heightened awareness and experience. Venturing out of the affluent enclave of Westwood, my wife and I decided to take a look for ourselves, to see firsthand. Walking up and down the street, we were immediately affected by what we saw, indeed, seized with pity—young people, spaced-out, lost to themselves, to the other, to any real world . . . a pathetic sight. In one short hour of observation, I concluded that the drug scene could take you out of today's arid boredom, only to deposit you as a burned-out wreck of disheveled senselessness.

Leaving those dreary lower depths, we went to visit a dear friend, John, at Santa Cruz. He had begun a graduate program there when I entered UCLA. That evening, we had dinner in the student cafeteria, the first time I entered such a place since my distant undergraduate days. I was shocked—choices of entrées, vegetables and deserts, seconds simply as a matter of course. At the end of the serving line, I was surprised to find a number of different liquids to drink. But I was even more perplexed by a young student who was filling pitchers at one spigot. I asked her, "What is that drink and why are you filling the pitchers?" It was some kind of fruit punch and they were having a party in her dorm that night. No restrictions prevented her from taking as much as she wanted out of the dining hall.

Was this the principal effect of all the student rebellions and movements? . . . a hugely enlarged menu in a genuine cafeteria. I wondered. . . . Did the calls for academic reform achieve any more serious changes?

The State of California had obviously invested a great deal of money and thoughtful restructuring of the curriculum at this, the newest of its university campuses. From what John told me, the faculty and administration had made serious efforts to get rid of artificial and meaningless divisions and categories in study and teaching. But I was uncertain about their so-called constructive replacements. Did the changes involve something more substantial than trivial variations played out on entrenched privilege and narrow specialization? I was not there long enough, however, to explore the question, and left Santa Cruz with a more immediate, more sensible reaction to what I had seen and heard—a *feeling* of unease. The students were given a campus of unusual natural beauty, a faculty of outstanding talent. However, so much seemed to be taken for granted, so much appeared to be unexamined complacency. The public authorities provided a graceful setting revealing a remarkably generous indulgence. What *more* could they give their children? But what kind of learning can occur in such a place? Does California-bourgeois radicalism allow truly troubling questions to arise? I had the sensation of seeing guilty innocence, something like professional sports.

My questions are aptly illustrated by a story John told us. The students, influenced by what was occurring at the other campuses, especially nearby Berkeley, were looking for some issue, some example of arbitrary administrative authority they should protest. This was extremely difficult, since everything about the place, from physical arrangements to intellectual offerings, was designed to make university life exciting and attractive to the students. But one day a good cause finally presented itself. The administration planned to situate a new building in a place that would restrict a certain "scenic view." This assault on the students' aesthetic sensibilities should be opposed! One night, some concerned students seriously damaged a bulldozer parked there to begin the excavation for the building.

The next day, an administrator called a meeting and explained the facts about the bulldozer to the students. The man doing the excavating did not own his machine; he rented it. He had no money to repair it, nor could he get another bulldozer. With a family to support, he was now deprived of his only source of income.

University authorities, I suppose, would argue that the institution is not designed to prepare students for intelligent and mature social activism. And one could also maintain that the students themselves are, in a sense, merely children. They are not responsible for the affluence of their social background, for having been reared in a profusion of privilege, removed from the experience of being rooted in a community, a soil. I could not help thinking, however, that there is an idea in recent intellectual history that throws light on what I had witnessed at Santa Cruz—the questions that tormented Wittgenstein: What are the connections? How see them? How *show* them? I had the feeling that the institution was only trying to *say* something, that the faculty were unaware of Wittgenstein's opinion that *the* cardinal issue in philosophy today is to know the difference between what can be said and what can be shown. The social atmosphere and political intent of the place *showed* one thing; the teaching *said* something else. What the urbane humanists in that lovely forest on the Pacific wanted to say could only be shown. The enterprise was inevitably self-defeating.

Shortly after our excursion to reputed centers of enlightenment, another experience planted unobtrusive seeds that would eventually sprout into further questions, threatening my academic comfort. Conscientious and frustrated liberal activists started meeting, making plans to form a national political movement—the Peace and Freedom Party—to drastically change the direction of the country's national and international policies, seen as racist and imperialistic, respectively. Mary, my wife, was elected as a delegate to the party's founding convention in Oakland. I accompanied her and found that the delegates were housed in the working-class homes of party members, not in hotels. At the Oakland auditorium, which seemed a fitting place for radical political stances and speeches, I was greatly impressed by the raw and slashing eloquence of Eldridge Cleaver, but troubled by what appeared to be white self-hatred. Between the anguished cries and demands of the Black Panthers, and the tortured guilt of liberal-minded whites, I smelled the erupting pus of old suppurating sores—the injustices of American society. In both domestic and foreign policy, there was no conception of a common good to be sought. Elite interests were preoccupied with other priorities: a confused mishmash of irrational fears and volatile hatreds . . . home-grown black revolutionaries destroying law and order, and distant yellow Communists threatening the American Way of Life. On balance, I was impressed by the Peace and Freedom Party people. In spite of their interior pain and self-doubt, their historical innocence and naive rhetoric, they were reaching out beyond their narrow selves, stumbling toward the agonizing questions of injustice in the world around them. I felt I had to learn something more about them. Having been out of the country so long, I was confused about their origins and the specific character of their concerns.

Among the documents and sources I found when I returned to UCLA, one especially impressed me, the Port Huron Statement. Shortly after the founding of Students for a Democratic Society (SDS), Tom Hayden and fellow activists met in Port Huron, Michigan, in 1962, to draw up a declaration of their thought and aims. These white middle-class students, predominantly male, hoped to begin a movement of social change that would result in a truly participatory democratic society. Anxious young people, painfully aware of the horrors hanging over the world, they expressed themselves with the ingenuousness of ahistorical innocents: "Our work is guided by the sense that we may be the last generation in the experiment with living." But they were caught in a limiting and confining paradox. They admitted that "our experience in the universities [has not] brought us moral enlightenment." Nevertheless, they hoped that the social change they envisioned could begin in the university through an alliance of students and faculty. "Social relevance, the accessibility to knowledge, and internal openness—these together make the university a potential base and agency in a movement of social change." Reflecting a clear ideological position, the statement was firm in its rejection of violent means. "We find violence to be abhorrent because it requires generally the transformation of the target, be it a human being or a community of people, into a depersonalized object of hate."

But a manifesto by these young idealists had little effect on American violence, ultimately rooted in a shadowy and somber tradition that reached back before history to Cain and Abel, and that was to burst out into more heinous forms both here and abroad after the SDS meeting in Michigan. The well-known victims of this violence, such as John F. Kennedy, Robert F. Kennedy, Martin Luther King Jr., and Malcolm X, by their very prominence, obscured the awful crimes against countless others who were also killed. The youthful dreamers who founded SDS were unable to launch a national social movement of peaceful change. Presciently, however, they wrote, "If we appear to seek the unattainable, as it has been said, then let it be known that we do so to avoid the unimaginable." Now the blight of the unimaginable appeared to have spread throughout the nation, and to have been concentrated on faraway poor countries.

In spite of my reading and these experiences, I was still uncertain about what to make of my feelings that spring morning in Ralph Bunche Hall. How unravel the complexities? For example, the police were in no danger of mistakenly hitting one of their own children with their clubs. Their kids, if they were in college at all, enrolled at a place like Long Beach State. The students at UCLA did not generally come from blue-collar homes. The young protesters in Los Angeles, like their peers in Santa Cruz and Berkeley, represented the solidly affluent sectors of the California economy. Were all these young people, therefore, foolishly quixotic, perhaps spoiled, and to be dismissed? Or did they stand for, bear witness to, some deep malaise in the society, some festering disorder that I could not clearly see because of the comforting layers of intellectual and social isolation?

One day the killing-fields world of Vietnam touched my sheltered life more directly. Daniel Berrigan, just back from a trip to Hanoi, came to Los Angeles to give a talk. He found that no Catholic Church or institution had a hall available for him, although he was a priest in good standing with his society (the Jesuits) and the Church. Finally, a liberal rabbi at the edge of West Los Angeles offered Berrigan his synagogue. I had met Dan in Mexico, when he spent some days with us in Cuernavaca. I drove him to the synagogue, and we caught up on each others' lives since our last meeting. For me, the conversation, together with the poetic power of his public appearance, was deeply troubling.

Berrigan had gone to Hanoi with Howard Zinn to accept three American prisoners of war set free by the North Vietnamese. In his book describing this mission, he wrote,

> It occurs to me beyond any doubt that Americans are "prisoners of war," locked in dungeons of illusions, of fear, of hatred and contempt and joylessness; all of us hearing the closure in our faces of the hinge of fate, strangers to our own history, to moral passion, to the neighbor, strangers to the immense and vagrant and splendid mysteries of life itself, the forms of community that await the "trial of peace," men who advocate formal and legalized murder as a method of social change.

The gifted poet was also a discomfiting prophetic witness.

After Berrigan had left the city, I found myself forced to justify myself to myself. I tried to convince myself that I had some kind of vocation to do a certain kind of research in Latin America: to sort out the ideological sources, the "spiritual" origins of Copei, the Christian Democratic party in Venezuela. Similar parties existed in many Latin American countries, and in several Western European ones, too. The idea of a "Christian" political party struck me as perilously anomalous, both for the Church and for politics. In a long history of ambiguity and abuses, the Gospel was being used yet again to legitimate a temporal kingdom on earth. This time, it was claimed, for a good cause—social justice. On close examination, however, I found the reasoning to be ideological and, finally, another expression of idolatry. It seemed important to do the research that these dangers be exposed, so people could see that such a party may not be good for politics, and is most certainly noxious for the religious life of a people. But a lot of empirical work, informed by clear thinking, would be necessary before such conclusions could be adequately tested. Since I saw no one else researching these issues, I felt a strong urge to attempt a contribution, albeit modest, to contemporary discussions of such questions.

Years earlier, when I was an undergraduate, wartime austerity was eagerly replaced by apparently limitless consumption. It was a time to relax, to enjoy the fallout from military technology. But among some intellectuals, high level civil servants, and politicians, McCarthyism spread terror and fear. There were not many courageous public figures, like I. F. Stone, who understood and spoke clearly about the ambiguities and risks in this sort of fanatical irrationalism at home, and questionable crusades abroad. As Stone saw, Korea and other "hot spots" of the world might be distant, but they were real, and government policy needed to be questioned; indeed, both overt and covert actions demanded serious and sustained public debate. All of my attention, however, was absorbed by the excitement of my immediate studies—I hugely enjoyed my college years. James Joyce revealed realms of expression I never dreamed possible. In a very different mode, Jacques Maritain invited me to experience the adventures awaiting me in metaphysics. I will never forget the thrill I experienced when I came upon T. S. Eliot. During my first trip to New York, I gorged myself with a Sadler-Wells production of *Sleeping Beauty*, the riveting presence of Leonard Bernstein conducting at the newly opened Lincoln Center, the—for me—confusing dialogue of Luigi Pirandello's characters in a Village theater. I treated myself to a summer in Cambridge—classes on Dostoyevsky each morning, a different play at the Brattle Theater each weekend, an occasional picnic on the Charles River or canoeing at Walden Pond, with an acquaintance who became a dear and respected friend. Except for nominal membership in the ACLU and SANE, I tended to ignore the "larger" issues of national and international affairs. And this stance did not change until I arrived in Latin American in 1960.

That day in 1970, in Los Angeles, I was acutely and painfully conscious of being an *American* citizen. I was treated to a vast prodigality, just by living in a country whose government was cruelly and callously destroying and poisoning other peoples and their lands. In my complacent position of considerable comfort, I did nothing, I was silent. Was it not time to rethink my goals? To look more deeply into the apparent order of my life? To see how I fit the history of my times?

Back in college I had been introduced to the thought of Thomas Aquinas. Now, confronted with the wasting of Southeast Asia and the violent protests at home, I wondered if this thirteenth-century thinker could help me get through the intellectual posturing and public disarray and, finally, the troubling doubts of my own mind. I had a suspicion that, to figure out where I was standing and where, perhaps, I *should* stand, my thought had to be characterized by two qualities: distance and order. I needed to get back from the mêlée around me, and to discover principles of order. With about seven hundred years between us, Aquinas was certainly distant enough, and I knew of no other thinker in the Western tradition whose conception and presentation of arguments could show greater order.

To see Aquinas, one must look at him in his tradition. In this tradition, I am not really independent, not a modern individual. Rather, I am a member of a community, bound to its members. The question I must ask is: How do I love them? This is primary, the beginning of any human response to a known other. How do I love my country? Conventionally, the word to denote this is patriotism. But, among the people who *seemed* to occupy the moral high ground, patriotism was almost an obscenity. That presented no obstacle for me, however, since even the best words in our tradition were now sometimes distorted or perverted. For example, some young people, along with their elders, engaging in mutual sexual self-seeking and exploitation, incongruously named their behavior "making love."

How did Aquinas talk about patriotism? I found that the subject occurs in his treatise on the virtue of justice—roughly, the habit of giving to some other what I owe them. Connected with justice, there is another virtue called piety—also a problematical term today. For Aquinas, however, piety is important, and one tough virtue. If I am strong (good) enough, the practice of piety enables me to pay the debt I owe that, however, I can never fully pay, to the three sources of my existence: God, parents, and my land. I attempt to discharge this debt through the virtues of religion, filial respect, and patriotism, respectively.

The distance of Aquinas from recent historical developments and current ideological fashions is also a great help. Patriotism, as a virtue of justice, long preceded the appearance of the modern state and fundamentalist nationalism. To be patriotic, I did not have to acknowledge any allegiance to the State, nor wrap myself in the flag. Quite obviously, my land was the physical and cultural source of my life. Further, its history included enough heroic and noble chapters to inspire any citizen, and enough cruelty and injustice to move that person to action.

It is not too difficult for a modern person to acknowledge the fact that, in some way, one's existence is owed to his or her native land. One of the principal traditional ways of expressing this is to say that I love my country, my place. Aquinas points out that this love is not a sentimental feeling, nor a commitment one discharges in a singular, even heroic, act. This love is a habit; it is a *habitual* way of thinking, feeling and acting. Further, it is a binding obligation in justice; there is no way to deny or escape it; it expresses the very nature of reality; its practice allows one to become real. After listening to Berrigan, it seemed that first I had to clear up and settle the question of this debt. I might then discover that other considerations, with respect to my way of life at that time, were only mystifications or specious rationalizations.

With the exception of Berrigan's witness, which was *sui generis*—specific to his gifts and vocation, the kinds of protest I had seen or heard about had little or no appeal for me. Actually, I knew very little about these protests. During my years in Latin America, I had scant knowledge of or contact with what occurred in the United States. When I returned, I immersed myself completely in my graduate studies. But now I seemed to face a crossroads. Something more than the war was at issue here. I felt it necessary to confront my country directly. Further, my action would have to be a permanent disposition, a way of being, not the enthusiasm of a moment. But, if what Berrigan and the protesters said was true, then the government and the political regime, maybe the entire society, were deeply corrupted. How love this land if it were transformed into a moral monster?

To answer these questions, I had to go back even further in history, until I came to the Greeks of Aristotle's time. For them, the most unnatural punishment, the most painful affliction of the gods, was to be cut off from one's native ethos, from the community that made it possible for one *to be* human. There was no virtue, no friendship, no good life possible apart from living in one's own land. Here, too, the Greeks had something to teach a contemporary person: the most extreme action open to me was permanent exile.

By voluntarily turning my back on the source of my existence, on my good—because that good had become seriously defiled—I would be able truly to serve my country, to practice the virtue of patriotism. By this irrevocable action, I would raise a serious objection, a continuing cry of dissent: The nation has betrayed its founders; it has abandoned its ideals, its raison d'être! My life itself might continue to be quite ordinary, unknown, but I would place my body as a silent witness, speaking to the injustice and disorder that was America. It was necessary, then, to go into exile; I appeared to have no other choice. Discussing the situation and my reasoning with Mary, I discovered that she was even more ready to act than I. Her taste of radical politics had helped prepare her for decisive action.

But we would not have to set out on an open and possibly unfriendly sea in a leaky boat with only a pair of oars; we would not have to suffer any truly disagreeable privations. I was offered a job with a modest salary in Venezuela. Earlier, we had been in the country one summer, while I studied firsthand the social, political, economic, and religious background for my research questions. During that time, we had made good friends and numerous acquaintances in Caracas. I would now enjoy the opportunity to finish gathering data and speaking with Venezuelans, to write up the dissertation and, if all went well, get the degree. I would then possess a meal ticket for life.

As a married graduate student living on a fellowship, I had few possessions to dispose of. We sold our car to friends, gave the Salvation Army furniture to other friends who were about to found a Catholic Worker house in Los Angeles, said good-bye to our respective families, and departed for Venezuela. I did not contemplate a future return to my country.

After the dreary smog of Los Angeles, the brilliant sky of Caracas was an ever-changing delight. The sun seemed always to shine, but masses of cumulus clouds also moved from horizon to horizon, almost continually. Looking at the summit of the mountains that separated the city from the sea, we could see a hotel perched there, often engulfed in a cloud. The story I heard—but I never checked to see if it was completely true—related that the deposed dictator, Marcos Pérez Jiménez, had built it as a kind of hide-out (!) for his cronies and their girl friends. It was accessible only by cable car, and one of the thrills of the city was to ride this to the top, then get in another that dropped precipitously down the other side of the mountain to the beach, far below.

We set out to make a new beginning in a foreign but not altogether unknown country. The older architecture of Caracas—for example, the small, classical building housing the legislature, and the lovely colonial structure containing the national library—conferred a charming suggestion of a slower pace of life. Except for three years in Los Angeles—interrupted by a summer in Caracas—I had lived in various countries of Latin America since 1960. In some ways, I had come to feel more "at home" south of the border than in the land of my birth. And it was undoubtedly a region of great excitement, even hope. Although the United States had conspired to overthrow the reformist Arbenz government in Guatemala (1954), Fidel Castro had ridden in triumph into Havana (1959). Although Che Guevara was killed in Bolivia in 1967, the Frei government cautiously had moved forward with land reform and national participation in Chile's copper mines beginning in 1964.

Within the Church, several outstanding bishops—for example, Manuel Larraín in Chile, Helder Camara in Brazil, Sergio Méndez Arceo in Mexico—manifested unmistakable charismatic gifts, while theologians and numerous pastoral workers labored to foster a religiosity more directly based on biblical reading and reflection. Only a few people then foresaw that the Alliance for Progress, which began in 1961, and other such initiatives would have as their principal results the creation of a solid, affluent consumption-oriented minority in every country, together with a huge majority ever more deeply mired in *modernized* poverty. Thinkers like Ivan Illich pointed out that the North exported expensive, large packages to the South. These goods and services, supposedly designed for peoples' "needs," were beyond the reach of the majority in every Latin country—but they were attractive. The rich became addicts of consumption, the poor, addicts of envy. Economic and social development, as conventionally understood and practiced, was a recipe for social disaster.

In Venezuela, a certain optimism ruled, in spite of the country's turbulent and melancholy history. Simón Bolívar, the most famous leader among the men who fought in the hemisphere-wide independence movements of the nineteenth century, was from Venezuela, but the country experienced seemingly insurmountable difficulties in producing other public statesmen who could match him in political vision and probity. A major change in the country's politics promised to institute new methods of leadership selection a few years before I arrived. The regime of Pérez Jiménez, a rather corrupt and unscrupulous opportunist, fell. A democratically elected government, under the leadership of Rómulo Betancourt, was installed. His party, Acción Democrática, later lost national elections to Copei—the Christian Democrats —led by Rafael Caldera, reputedly an honest and honorable politician. A democratic and peaceful change of government had occurred—a highly significant event for Venezuela.

Caldera and his friends were the founders of Copei. On one side, party leaders strongly stressed ideology—the intellectual rationale of the party, derived partly from the writings of people such as Jacques Maritain, and partly from ecclesiastical documents such as *Rerum novarum* of Pope Leo XIII (1898). On another side—which was not a side, but a spirit or inspiration or ambition—the founding members were strongly motivated by their sense of themselves as Venezuelan *Catholics*, as men belonging to this religious orientation. Their public actions, I suspected, were an attempt to define themselves *and* their nation, as Catholic.

If I could understand how this occurred, I might learn something about religion and political culture in Latin America. For example, does a certain form or structure of religiosity translate into a corresponding pattern of political behavior? a more "worldly" religion into a more honorable politics? But I had to probe more thoroughly, and ask more nuanced questions. These, finally, were to be the goal of my research. In terms of political reform—understood as seeking the community's *common* good, not one's own advantage in a war of all against all—Venezuelan history was singularly troubled and murky. The Copeyanos seemed to embody a hopeful movement toward a more just society. Was this true? And, if so, why? Did the religious beliefs of the party's founders inform the ideology and practice of their politics? And, if so, how?

Reading documents, talking with representative figures in the social, economic, political, academic, religious, and artistic worlds, I gradually settled myself into life in Venezuela. Mary and I laughed over some curious anomalies: We did not have enough money to completely furnish the house we had rented, but we could just barely afford a maid to help with the children. She wanted to know where our furniture was. We told her it was "on the way." Eventually, I found an Englishman who was leaving the country and I was able to buy cheaply what we still lacked. For a wedding anniversary, we decided to look for an inexpensive drawing or painting. It took a long time searching through the galleries of Caracas before we discovered an artist whose work could *not* just as well have come from New York or Paris. Frequently, we had to look closely to find cultural expressions that appeared to result from specifically Venezuelan sensibilities.

Among the people I met, the two who had the greatest impact on my life in the country were not native Venezuelans. The first, an American, invited me to lunch one day at his club. He had been working in the country for about twenty years as the director of a foundation distributing money—for educational, social and cultural projects. He was about to retire and return to the States and, over a long lunch, reflected on his life in Venezuela. One item of his story stuck in my memory. He liked the country and enjoyed the people; he felt that he had accomplished much good in his time here. But one lingering sadness gnawed at him, gave him no rest. In conversation with Venezuelans, he noticed that when a certain point would almost be touched, a certain subject almost broached, unobtrusively but unquestioningly, a curtain would drop. A barely perceptible change would occur in the direction of the talk, leading away from the delicate subject, a possibly embarrassing opinion, or deeply-felt but unmentionable accusation. He, as a foreigner, as an American, was decisively cut out. After all these years, he remained the alien outsider, the uninvited guest, perhaps the unwelcome intruder.

That night, recounting the luncheon conversation to my wife, I could not help but muse . . . was his life, then, some kind of failure? Is this part of the price one pays for exile? Why did he invite me to lunch? Why did I hear that story today? Does it have some meaning for my life? Or is he just an American who didn't fit in? I well knew that, apart from questions of individual personality, it is extremely difficult for a person from the North to be accepted in the South. This was one of the clearest and most certain truths I had learned while living in Latin America. Willy-nilly, by our tone of voice and manner of stating opinions, body movements, and gestures, we project a certain superiority, condescension, and it is almost impossible to shed this attitude. With great and continual effort, perhaps one can control its expression or soften its impact.

A short time later, I met one of the most distinguished and respected men in the country, Dr. Pedro Grases. Like others I had met in Latin American countries, especially Mexico, he had been forced to flee Spain at the end of the Civil War, and had now been in Venezuela many years. Next to his home in Caracas, he housed his large library in a separate building. A historiographer, he had gathered together the primary documents and books for the study of Venezuelan history. At that time, this was probably the most important collection of such items in the country—or the world. Periodically, he published other works based on these materials.

Every Saturday morning, in the library, he presided over a *tertulia*, a frank and civil conversation, with coffee. His invited guests might include, on any particular Saturday, a cabinet minister, a leading industrialist, an army general, a writer, or academic. In certain respects, Venezuela seemed a small country; in terms of total population, it was.

One could say that those at "the top" were not so many. In the library, I was surprised at the open and candid character of the conversation. Later, I learned that these men observed an unwritten rule: What was said in that room on Saturday was not to be *used* on Monday morning. Although these men might not be close friends, or friends at all, Dr. Grases was able to impart a certain tone to the *tertulia*, a certain trust, so that all were moved to listen to one another with respect. I had the feeling that one could be fairly candid in voicing his considered opinion; it would not be used against him later. This was a gathering of gentlemen.

Pedro Grases, originally a foreigner, had come to occupy a unique place in the country's intellectual and social life. His work as a historian was internationally known and admired. But I was even more impressed by his personal contribution to the creation of a civic culture, heretofore fragile or nonexistent in Venezuelan history, through his organization of an amiable conversation among elite male actors. He thereby worked to restrain universal tendencies to barbarism, tendencies that intermittently appear among almost all social and political leaders of every society. He understood the importance of conversation in the western tradition for the creation and maintenance of a peaceful community. For example, Rafael Caldera, as a young man, apprenticed himself for a time to Dr. Grases, working with him in his library, recognizing that this exercise in a humanistic formation could not be obtained anywhere else in the country. A friend told me that the older man's influence was truly important in terms of such qualities as honor and wisdom in Caldera's public life. Now, Caldera was president of the country.

One day when Grases and I were alone in the library, he talked of his life's work. Waving his arm across the rows of book shelves he asked rhetorically, "Who will carry on these studies? My children are not interested in such bookish work. And I have found no disciples here . . . Several universities in the States want to buy the entire collection—and ship it up there; they've made generous offers. But it should stay here. These are the sources of this people's history. These documents should remain in the country, accessible to local scholars and students. How else will the people come to know their own history, except through a study of the sources? In Venezuela, however, I see no one interested enough to pay even a modest sum for the library, much less to keep up the continuing costs of maintenance."

That night I returned home a very confused person. The American and the Spaniard had both come here as young men. Both had dedicated their lives to the good of this country. And each, in his distinct way, felt that his life was wrapped up in failure. Did their examples say something about my life after, say, twenty-five years in Venezuela? To what had I brought our children?

At that moment, maybe with greater clarity than before, I thought especially of the children. What was my duty toward them? Was it proper to bring them to a foreign country, to a country that, in the estimation of historians, was among the poorest in pre-Columbian culture, and among the richest in post-independence violence. All four grandparents were still alive; all four abundantly manifested that kind of affection for the children that one usually associates with grandparents. But no one of them had dared to object when we announced our decision to leave the country. As far as any of us knew, this meant that they might never again see these grandchildren. Had I been led by some vain self-righteousness in abandoning the country? Had I considered myself only as a modern individual? And, as some accurately name the creature, a modern *possessive* individual? Did I really understand the nature of *pietas*, patriotism, at all? Many evenings, Mary and I sought to clarify our thinking, our motives. The more we talked, the more uncertain we were of our position. The practice of patriotism did not appear as clear-cut as we had believed when we left Los Angeles.

I was bothered by the specific character of these men's stories. Why had they shared *these* details of their lives, intimate revelations of collapsed hopes, with me, a person who, actually, was a stranger to them? Why had *these* stories come into my life, seemingly seeking a place in *my* story? What sense or meaning should I see in the meeting and crossing of these personal histories? How to read the signs? How practice this version of the discernment of spirits?

One evening, picking up a newspaper sent by someone from the States, I was startled to see the place, Springfield, Illinois, mentioned in an article. This city was fewer than thirty miles from where I grew up. My parents were still there, in my hometown, Lincoln. The writer argued that something genuinely exciting in higher education was occurring at a new, experimental university called Sangamon State. The founders had instituted changes already discussed for some years, such as the elimination of conventional academic departments. But they had also ventured much further. There seemed to be a genuine effort to involve all—students, faculty, townspeople, and administrators—in the actual governance of the university. A structured conversation was put in place so that the interested parties might determine the shape and, to some extent, the content of their common learning. With an open admissions policy and an emphasis on the formation of *public* persons, the institution appeared to move significantly beyond those academic elite sectors that promoted the unbridled advancement of self, or that were often helpless before the attraction of solipsistic soul massage via hallucinogens.

Obviously, no new institution, no matter how imaginative and courageous its founders, was going to be a fitting response to the ills that infected the country. It would be naive to think that modern persons, often weak or shallow in their grasp of Western history, and largely lacking a systematically critical view of the social sciences—the sandy foundation for so much of their thinking—would be able to create an institution adequate to respond to the destructiveness of humans as expressed in twentieth-century hubris. But a certain gestalt, based on the little I had read, formed in my mind. I somehow felt that the parameters of this place might be such as to allow the practice of patriotism. Perhaps I could honorably begin to pay my debt to America by working there. I had to mull over this information and these thoughts, to discuss them with Mary, to see where they would lead.

Each day I continued to visit the libraries, research institutes, government offices, people, making my notes, gathering the documentation I needed for the dissertation. But each day I also tried to rethink my position. In some sense, was I running away in coming here? Had I found an easy way out? Was my action a washing of the hands? Was I mostly intent on perfecting a sterile purity? A continuous tradition of ambiguous import exists in the Church—the desire for purity. Some propose that this desire is the source of all heresies. They point out that the human condition is not one of purity; people are sinners; everyone stinks, at least a little. I had thought I was taking a principled stance. Yes, that was true. But perhaps love of one's country is like love for one's friend. It can seldom be expressed in grand stands, but rather through the daily, messy, tiring, often trivial actions of attention, loyalty, thoughtfulness. Perhaps it was time to return home and, in the words of an old cliché, "face the music."

Learning to slow down and enjoy the more relaxed atmosphere of conversation in a Latin country, we had made good friends; we shared their hopes for their families and country. Their humor was easy, often gently self-mocking. To return to the States would mean cutting off so many warm human ties again—to begin all over. But this is what it means, I suppose, to be a modern person: to be attentive to the signs, to reflect continually, and then coldly set the outlines for the next move, whether across town or beyond the horizon. If I see the world well, the move's necessity will impose itself. My parents really were a different generation—their narrative was largely written for them; I must discover and improvise my own story as I go along.

2

New Beginnings in Illinois

Above those institutions which are concerned with protecting rights and persons and democratic freedoms, others must be invented for the purpose of exposing and abolishing everything in contemporary life which buries the soul under injustice, lies, and ugliness.

Simone Weil

S cientifically tested hybrid seed mixed with friable Illinois loam, enriched by a generous infusion of chemicals, produced endless fields of tall corn on the prairie, hiding the university buildings until we were right on top of them. Sangamon State University, yet another American experiment in educating the young, had gobbled up quite a few acres of Midwest farmland to plant a novel form of civic engineering in the state's capital, Springfield. Nevertheless, the emphasis, I read, centered on the student. Faculty were expected to dedicate themselves primarily to teaching, and to be available as friendly advisors to students. The library was consciously designed, and the staff carefully trained, to facilitate the students' learning. Fourteen years after Sputnik, which threatened a research-deficient America, the institution boldly proposed to put student growth in learning before faculty climbing in careers. Just one year before I arrived, Sangamon State had welcomed the first students, with an open-admissions policy.

We had come to Illinois (shortly after arriving in Los Angeles from Caracas) so that my parents might see their grandchildren again. But immediately after leaving the children with the family in Lincoln, we drove to Springfield to investigate Illinois' institutional response to nationwide student protests that had originated with Berkeley's Free Speech movement in 1964. In terms of historical precedent, this was an astonishingly rapid answer to the student complaints. Other states also acted; several new institutions had already begun, or were in the process of opening their doors to young people. I was eager to see what the bureaucrats in educational administration in the state of Illinois had designed for the youth of this state. Immediately, of course, I needed a job, for my Venezuelan salary had ended. But another concern lay quietly in the recesses of my awareness: I wanted to work in a situation that would enable me to be a patriotic American, that is, one facing squarely the corruption of my society and government.

The idea of a private person is a contemporary conceit. I had been born into a society; I was part of that society's history. Paradoxically, the government of that society had paid for the degree that I could now turn into a position from which to criticize both society and government. But such is the task of a privileged person in a free society. Now I had to learn the virtues proper to this task. Could such be accomplished in this modest collection of temporary-appearing buildings, almost swallowed up by the surrounding cornfields?

Virtue is a habitual disposition, an ingrained mode of acting, and each virtue has its characteristic practices. For example, the virtue of teaching would have as its practices those actions that lead the students to the truth of the questions or subject matter under investigation. To the extent possible, the actual arrival at this truth would be the work of the students themselves, not the result of being fed by the teacher. Further, the teacher would seek these goods, the goods of the students' learning, over the external goods of salary and career advancement. Such an action assumes that there is "the good," that the search for the good is an integral part of what is called education. Soon one comes, of necessity, to discuss the character of a common good. Through the entire matter, a question insistently surfaces: What is the good life? This university, as any, could be judged by the prominence and clarity with which these issues are addressed.

The goal of virtuous teaching, however, and the encouragement to seek the internal goods of teaching's practice, require some kind of institutional support. Many other factors are either necessary or important, but institutional support is the condition *sine qua non*, the foundation of the entire edifice. Therefore, I had to determine the character of this institution.

We walked around the campus, then into one of the buildings, and found that the office doors of faculty members contained information about them—where they were from, where they went to school, their interests, their family. I knocked at the door of a man who had received his degree at the University of Chicago, since I had a vague feeling of respect for this school. Years earlier, I had been impressed by the ideas and initiatives of Robert Hutchins when he was president of that university. Knocking, I found the faculty member in his office, and he graciously took time to talk with us about Sangamon State. It turned out that the founding president was also a graduate of Chicago. Doug, the man we met, described the school's first year of operation, something about the faculty already recruited, and the ideas behind the experiment. The more he talked, the more the place took on the contours of the institution I had vaguely dreamed about in Venezuela.

There was great openness, and much yet to be defined and accomplished. As someone who had been brushed by the academic criticisms of the 1960s, I tended to believe that if administrators gave them the freedom, faculty and students could work out a "relevant" curriculum with an appropriate style of teaching and learning. At Sangamon State, the specific mandates appeared to be solid: to teach students *in this place*. Although faculty would come from distant and strange regions, they were expected to dedicate themselves to this place, to take real part in community activities, to insert themselves here, to become members of this group of people in Central Illinois. Ideally, their loyalty was to be shaped in terms of their students, principally young people living in this area, *not* in terms of an abstraction called a discipline, or a self-elected elite called a profession. In other words, their lives were to be grounded here, to become embedded in this soil.

Faculty were asked, in their conception and expression of self and in their research, to reverse one of the historical processes that defines modernity, disembedding. Although they were educated in various academic disciplines, that is, in disintegrated knowledge compartments, probably accepting the disembedding of specialized knowledge from the matrix of wisdom without protest, they were now expected to question this situation in light of Karl Polanyi's research in economic history. In order to be good teachers in Springfield, Illinois, they had to reexamine their reception of today's conventional academic assumptions. They were asked to look back to Plato, and to seek out the tradition of learning that finds its roots in his Dialogues. The pretensions of professionalism and carved out disciplinary fiefdoms were recent innovations. This institution would seek to be more traditional, more rooted in the past, historically, and in the present, physically.

I had come to believe that the uprooted intellectual—perhaps the French term, *déracinée* (literally, torn up out of the earth by the roots), is more forceful—is one of the curses of our age, of modernity. Even one of the greatest visionaries to propose a specifically American identity, Thomas Jefferson, was infected by this sickness. The dream that impelled him to send Lewis and Clark on their remarkable expedition contained the shadow of a territorial hubris. In uprooted and unscrupulous adventurers, this temptation would directly result in violently tearing out numerous native nations from their rooted places and, when they objected or resisted, in killing them.

On that hot, late summer afternoon, I was introduced to an institution whose basic philosophy—if one dare speak so grandly of this recently born enterprise—clearly implied a reversal in uprooting, one of the most destructive and corrupting ideas to come out of the Enlightenment. The bloody crusade in Vietnam was, in part—or so I firmly believed—the result of the disordered delusions of uprooted intellectuals. The opportunity to participate in an initiative that asked academics to turn their gaze away from limitless horizons and cosmopolitan universals, away from ahistorical assumptions and linear progress, and to look directly and fixedly at the people in front of their eyes appeared wonderfully attractive to me. To seek the good in a circumscribed place, to see the beautiful in my immediate surroundings, to search for the truth in staying put seemed to me a possible expression of a genuine love of my country. Sangamon State appeared to be an institutional setting that did not prevent me from seeing the other. I would be free, here, to ground myself in a way that allowed me to act in terms of the other. What would I do, I asked Doug, if I wanted to come work here?

He took me to the office of the faculty recruitment director. This man introduced me to the vice-president for academic affairs, who, in turn, led me to the president's office. Conversations with these three men were impressive in the sense that each appeared firmly grounded in his academic field yet not afraid to look further—not afraid to extend himself but willing to rethink the place where he stood. Each had meditated on his own academic formation, on the raison d'être of this training in view of what was happening in today's world, and in light of Western intellectual history. We discussed my background and current interest in the institution. Since I had to return to Los Angeles almost immediately, they arranged for a faculty interview committee to meet with me in a couple of days. A few weeks later, after they had received and read my documents from UCLA, I was offered a position, to begin teaching that fall. Our immediate economic worries were resolved.

And so we set out to make yet another new beginning. But in place of the spectacular setting of Caracas, where mountains cradled the city, we now looked out at the plain American prairie all around us— decorated with perfectly manicured crops. After more than twenty years' absence, I had to become intimately familiar with this land so that I might learn to embrace it, to love it.

At first it appeared monotonously prosaic, almost dull. But I was so busy with my new duties that I had little time to reflect on landscapes. In terms of the job, three tasks confronted me: finish writing the dissertation, participate in constructing this new institution, and teach. The excitement of the last was immediate and continual. I already had some experience teaching in Latin America, and I always found it a pleasure. Therefore, every aspect of course preparation and interaction in the classroom was an absorbing and rewarding affair. The first day of a new semester was especially thrilling. I would meet a new group of people eager, I assumed, to listen and speak. And I was prepared—keyed up—to speak and listen. If I listened carefully and looked directly, I would come to know something about them, and perhaps be able to help them make some steps forward: to recognize the truths of the past and to question the assumptions of the present. My degree was in political science, and I was asked to teach in this general area. With the students, I examined the pragmatic and symbolic goals, the peculiar sources and frustrations of politics, north and south of the border.

As with the field research, so with the writing, I enjoyed working on the dissertation. It was soon finished, and I returned to Los Angeles for the defense. When I appeared before the five-person committee, one asked me to summarize what I had done. What a marvelous opportunity! Since I was interested in the subject—the ideological/religious origins of the Christian Democratic Party in Venezuela—and knew more about it than anyone present, I confidently set out to lecture my audience. After a half hour or so, an older, more senior member of the committee, interrupted me. "May we ask some questions?"—spoken with a certain tone of frustration, or perhaps even annoyance.

Clearing this final hurdle was no concern or worry. I was vain enough to believe that the exam would be nothing other than an interesting, maybe slightly challenging, several-hour performance. And so it turned out. But there was a further, more serious matter about the entire project that bothered me. In a certain sense, I had *used* Venezuela. I had taken advantage of the friendly way in which almost everyone I approached for help in either the research or living arrangements received me. I had turned these people and their historical experience into material for my entrée into the world of well-paid and prestigious employment, thereby incurring a serious debt. How to repay it? It was possible that I would never return to their country, never see any of these familiar faces again. I arranged to send a copy of the dissertation to the library of the Universidad Central, the principal institution of higher education in the country at that time. But the nagging feeling of an unpaid debt remains with me to this day. I received so much from the people in that country. . . .

At the university in Springfield, I faced a troublesome and tough task: to participate in the creation of a new institution. This was a goal that, I feel today, was never successfully reached. Perhaps the enterprise was doomed from the start. Is it given to extremely fallible academics "to create" *anything*? And who presumes to understand the use of the adjective "new" in relation to higher learning? Scattered throughout the history of the West, there exist thousands of years of experience. Why is it so difficult for the very persons who have come out of this tradition to consult the record? There are mountains of documents, innumerable witnesses. Why is it so hard to learn from them? I ask these questions because, looking back, I see that we—the faculty and administrators during those first years—expended enormous amounts of time and intellectual/emotional energy in this work of building, and I wonder about the quality of the results. Did the taxpayers of the State of Illinois get an honest return on their dollar? Did we academics act justly—render competent and honorable work for the rewards and respect we received? I cannot answer the questions, for I was never able to see beyond the modest place I occupied, and I have never returned to look at the institution after I left. I've learned, however, that Sangamon State University no longer exists. The school is called the University of Illinois at Springfield, and is a branch campus of the University of Illinois in Champaign-Urbana.

I now believe that important issues lay behind the student protest and rioting of the 1960s. But we—faculty and administrators at Sangamon State—did not understand them very well then. The disorderly turmoil of youthful revolts was a gangling but truthful witness to a nationwide social pathology. Americans had built a country on the basis of a maxim taken as a command: conquer and exploit. Native peoples were indiscriminately "relocated" or savagely eliminated, and the rich earth greedily mined. Sacralizing their experiment in democracy, many found it all too easy to demonize political opponents. If the Reds, for example, were evil, a sick morality could justify any means to eliminate the devils, wherever on earth a fevered imagination saw them. Many students vaguely sensed that the sins of the New World had to be faced and acknowledged. Injustices inflicted on peoples of color, at home and abroad, had to be addressed. A university should do something more than prepare young people for the available employment opportunities.

Today, as the century ends, both students and society are relatively quiet, not because the original distemper was ever correctly recognized and healed, but because many have been bought off; the society's institutions offer generous rewards to the talented who toe the line. Others are busy, busy, busy . . . or distracted to enervation. As we see with Thoreau, the one who acts resolutely with courage is often a solitary misfit. The issue of reform in higher education, however, presses as insistently today as thirty years ago.

In 1987, a single book by a professor of philosophy, selling more than a million copies in a few months, threw down a dramatic challenge to all involved in higher education. Allan Bloom, the renowned translator of Plato's *Republic*, claimed that students no longer learn to read, that the curriculum has become incoherent, that there is no dedication to reasoned thought, nor a belief in truth. Bloom made the failings of the academy a public issue. Ten years after its publication, *The Closing of the American Mind* remained in print, and continued to be discussed. But it appears that its actual impact on serious reform in the colleges and universities is essentially nil: action is confined to discussion. Studies continue to be published every year addressing problems. But as the historical situation becomes more desperate, the suggested reforms appear more ephemeral.

Student turbulence, basically, was a *cri du coeur*. Without going deeply into the sources of their feelings, young people in the 1960s were genuinely upset about themselves in the *kind* of society they had inherited. With few exceptions, their teachers were not facing the historical cul-de-sac of the academy, nor the internal contradictions of other mainstream institutions. If one were to push educators and keep asking, until the most fundamental response to the question "What are you doing?" was reached, it might sound something like this: "We are trying to teach students to think or, more expansively, to think critically, in terms of the western notion of thought." The answer, however, is incomplete, because it is colored by what might be called a Cartesian error. There is no such thing as thinking occurring independently or in some kind of isolation, abstracted from the whole person, from that person's place physically, and in history, social and personal. But the source of the mistake must be sought many years before Descartes.

As Ivan Illich and Alasdair MacIntyre show, in nicely complemented studies (*In the Vineyard of the Text*, and *Three Rival Versions of Moral Enquiry*, respectively), certain innovations were made in the twelfth and thirteenth centuries that determined the subsequent personal mode of study and the institutional arrangement of a curriculum—how people read and the structure of universities. Prior to the twelfth century, reading was a kind of activity very different from what obtained in the thirteenth. The old way was incarnate, one read aloud, more often in common; the action was done in such a way as to enflesh the words read—one hoped to become the sense of what one read. Study was both intellectual and sensual, one needed to acquire *both* the intellectual and moral virtues to be able to do it. The activity engaged the whole person; it demanded a way of life, assumed a community. This kind of reading went under the name of *lectio divina*.

Because of seemingly simple technological insertions on the page, which Illich describes and analyzes, reading changed. In one of the effects, reading was split into two very different acts that came to be named *lectio scholastica* and *lectio spiritualis*. Scholastic reading, fitting well the social and intellectual needs of commerce, law, government, and ecclesiastical administration, enabled what we now call a university to flourish. In the initial flush of academic excitement emanating from the creation of this new institution, Thomas Aquinas produced (in the *Summa theologiae*) his great synthesis, bringing together two very different traditions, the Aristotelian and the Augustinian.

But almost immediately after Aquinas's death, his method and doctrine were distorted. The bishop of Paris, Stephen Tempier, condemned 219 theses of Aquinas's teaching in 1277, barely three years after the scholar's death. But this was only part of the rejection of Aquinas's attempt to integrate (Aristotelian) philosophy and (Augustinian) theology into one unified whole. The university curriculum institutionalized at this time could not accommodate such a novel and inclusive vision. Theology went its own way, eventually becoming marginalized in the university. Philosophy became the dominant area of study in the liberal arts curriculum but, along with the solidification of separate compartmentalized disciplines, quickly degenerated into the

sterile exercise generally called scholasticism; it has never since regained any recognition as a master discipline in the universities of the
West. The present intellectual disorder that reigns in these institutions
is partly the result of a decadent and lost or meandering scholasticism. The 1960s students, in some confused but real way, sensed what
they were being fed: an abstract, disembodied, meaningless, and disordered potpourri, not just in this or that odd classroom but by the
institution qua institution.

Meanwhile, another movement was taking shape in America, sometimes connected with, sometimes rather independent from, the universities. An early institutional expression of this movement occurred at
Esalen, on the California coast, while one of the first written expressions, *The Teachings of Don Juan*, appeared while I was at UCLA. Carlos
Castaneda, the author, was a doctoral candidate, also at UCLA. There
was a great controversy among some of the anthropologists. Was the
book a record of empirical research, or a product of Castaneda's fertile
imagination? Within an amazingly short time, it didn't make much difference. The desiccation of academic intellectual life was enlivened by
a combination of searching activities, most of which were centered on
the self, *my*-self: explorations using drugs and sex, gurus and breathing, together with exciting new forms of popular music and instruc-
tions from a never-ending supply of soul or spirit, body or sense man-
uals. Huge new consumption and distraction industries were quickly
established for the "counterculture."

I believe it possible to trace this movement, sometimes called New
Age, to a way of reading that began in the fourteenth century, and
came to be called "spiritual reading." The heart was wrenched free
from the intellect in those centuries, and the two *separate* resulting
traditions—scholastic and spiritual—have reached a certain height of
absurdity in our time. Any serious university reform would have to
confront *this* historical record. It now seems to me that the exercise of
one's critical faculties must be anchored in the heart, in one's emotional life, and in one's physico-cultural-historical place. If this exercise
is to occur in a college or university, then reform is obviously necessary, a reform that directly deals with the pre-Cartesian person in a
pre-sociological society. The life of the mind and heart would have to
be united, and grounded, in a manner analogous to the way Sangamon
State expected the faculty to be incarnated in Central Illinois. The
pieces would have to be fitted together again; the historical break between head, heart, and place must be healed.

Even if academics could figure out some way to overcome the fragmentation of the disciplines, even if they could imagine a world bringing together the two cultures, of the sciences and the humanities, a more ancient, and more intractable task would await them: how to practice serious, critical study in an integral act of reading, exercising a kind of involvement in the page that would demand the commitment of all one's faculties, all one's person, all one's history . . . over all of one's life.

But none of us saw this at the time. Each person, from the members of the board to the president, faculty, and staff, worked to build what we thought was a new university, one meeting the needs of students and public life in Illinois. Since students were considered the direct subjects of concern, we wanted to assure that they received the best of possible experiences in the classroom. One aspect of this was the quality of teaching. We believed that students should have something to say about their instruction, have some control over the instructors themselves. So, a committee was set up to formulate and propose a method of faculty evaluation, and I became the chairman.

First we studied the evaluation systems in use at other institutions. From this, we decided to devise an evaluation instrument, some kind of questionnaire. The specific questions to be included entailed long discussions, since there were many opinions on what was desired or appreciated in an instructor. For example, was he sexist in his language or dealings with women? Did he or she give confusing assignments? Did he or she "put down" students? And so on, almost without end. We invited experts to our committee meetings to instruct us on the use of statistical tabulation and significance—for the answers to questionnaires would be analyzed statistically. We had to work out procedures for anonymity, so that no student could be punished for her or his opinion. We had long discussions *against* formulated questions and in favor of an open procedure—let the students evaluate faculty members in any words or sentences they preferred.

Finally, we settled on an instrument of about twenty questions, one of which was open-ended. But for the purposes of faculty retention (whether the person would be let go because of simply awful teaching), promotion and salary increase—all of which would be partly determined by teaching—we considered only two questions really important:

—Does the faculty member know his or her subject matter?
—Is the faculty member a good teacher?

The student was asked to respond—on all the other questions, too—on a scale from one to five.

The procedure was submitted to university governance for approval, and then to the administration for implementation. The results of the process, repeated each quarter (later, each semester), entered the faculty member's permanent personnel file. I hesitate to calculate the number of hours we met to come up with what, in retrospect, appeared a fairly straightforward method of allowing the students some voice in who their faculty were.

Over the years, I came to conclude that the system did not—as some had maintained it would—work like some kind of popularity contest. One could trust the students to answer the two crucial questions intelligently and fairly. Ultimately, they could tell if a faculty member did or did not know his or her stuff, and whether that person could or could not teach. Given the fact of an institutional setting of professionals, student evaluations, since they counted, contributed directly to the perfection of that structure.

One of the principal reasons justifying the existence of institutions is that they can work to support those practices that realize the goods specific to some virtue. Professionals are expected, by the very nature of their calling, to exercise some virtue, to seek some good—for example, health, justice, or wisdom. Further, in any democratic society, laypersons would have some kind of power over their professionals. But there are few if any areas in modern life where a layperson is given institutional power to judge a professional. Academics—superseded perhaps only by some clergy, monastic recluses, mental health "professionals," or persons in the various psyche callings—are potentially the most dangerous professionals in the society because those who are intelligent and sensitive can touch the very souls of their students. If they are also devilishly clever, they can twist those souls. In any case, they always have an effect on the minds and hearts of youth.

Therefore, I came to believe that the evaluation system we instituted genuinely aimed to achieve a good, one of many minor but necessary efforts that the society become more democratic. However, this was only one institutional-building exercise; there were also many others, each complicated and each in immediate need of implementation. Further, in addition to preparing rationales and programs of instruction—in lieu of conventional disciplinary departments—most of us carried a full teaching load. Generally, this meant three courses meeting a total of about twelve hours a week. Since we sought to carry out the ideas and mandates of the institution in our teaching, the courses required extra preparation. Graduate school did not prepare one for an experimental university! But everyone breathed the bracing air of an invigorating renewal; all were infused with a blithe spirit of quiet excitement: We were participating in a new creation, we glimpsed the possibilities of a new learning for our fellow citizens.

I found it thrilling to go into the classroom each day; on reflection, I also found it frightening. I never ceased being in awe before the freedom of professors within the loose frameworks of the institution. The faculty largely determined the substance of the curriculum. This obviously included course content—what was taught. But much more, too: the view of what constituted a good life, a good society; the nature of tradition and its meaning; what was true . . . and false. For I have never believed in the possibility—or advisability, if it were possible—of some kind of Weberian value-free study and teaching. Everyone is moved by his or her conception of the good in every human action undertaken, be that conception objectively vicious, banal, or noble. Although influenced by the institution and their intellectual peers, the faculty themselves, following their personal intuition of student and societal need, determined the content of the specific courses they offered. Further, they could choose almost any books for the students to read, and present nearly any point of view or opinion on these books. Since at that time there were no "spies" in the classroom to report on political correctness, nor was there an institutionally inspired compulsion to follow any of the prevailing ideological orthodoxies, the power of the faculty member was simply astounding. Where else in the society is this kind of freedom and autonomy permitted in one's chosen work? Fearsomely, freedom here serves power.

But many of our faculty and students, sharing in the general *Weltanschauung* of the society, came to the university with a primary preoccupation—themselves. They were familiar with the vocabulary and learned feelings of a modern self, resistant to natural social demands. That is, the idea of a natural law was strange, foreign to them; the humility to accept a wounded nature appeared almost offensive. The cool consumer outlook, with just a touch of skepticism, had begun to penetrate the Midwest. Among many, one could say that the self had become the modern substitute for the soul. Ultimately, one could find the validation of everything in the self. Implicit in the arguments of some was the belief that there are both good and bad forms of selfishness.

This became evident after the university was in operation for several years; some of the faculty began to organize a union. There seemed to be two reasons for such an appendage: This would give the faculty leverage or bargaining power with the administration in fights over academic and personnel policies, and a collective power to demand more material rewards, for example, increased health benefits. Those interested in pushing for a union organized wine and cheese or coffee hours to inform and proselytize faculty. I went because two questions bothered me: How will membership in this union improve my study or research? and, How will participation in this organization help my teaching? In the minds of the union promoters, however, these were not the proper questions to ask. I further alienated myself from them by stating publicly that I thought we were overpaid, in terms of the wage and salary structure in the society. The spiritual and material advantages already enjoyed by university faculty in the country made the demand for a faculty union embarrassingly anomalous.

It also seemed to me that, if one knew something of labor history in America, if one had some knowledge of persons such as Big Bill Haywood, the Haymarket martyrs, and Eugene V. Debs, then it was a grievously shameful act to organize university professors—one of the most pampered groups in America—into a union. The situation was especially poignant, since one of the genuine heroes in the struggle for worker justice was the late nineteenth-century governor of Illinois, John P. Altgeld. Acting directly counter to public opinion, and thereby destroying his own future in politics, he pardoned three men ignominiously imprisoned through the hysterical reaction to the Haymarket riot. I found the idea of a faculty union even more scandalous in light of the fact that the grave of Mother Jones, a fearless organizer of exploited workers, was only a few miles south of the university in a coal miners' cemetery in Mt. Carmel, Illinois. If any union enthusiast knew this fact, he or she never dared mention it; it was another inconvenient historical detail.

The self-interested union membership drive was especially painful for me, and sharply separated me from many of my fellow teachers. My grandfather, an immigrant from Poland at the beginning of the century, worked in a coal mine all his life. When he arrived in Illinois, the UMWA (United Mine Workers of America), although founded in 1890, was still struggling to exist. Collective bargaining rights were not won until 1933, federal coal mine safety and health standards not established until 1969! Miners were at the mercy of selfish and brutal mine owners with no sense of justice. I was astonished that this history was unknown to my colleagues, and sickened by the realization that those who did know showed no hesitation in identifying with a tradition in which so many had suffered for so long. I came to see that the community in which I lived was wounded, that I needed to stop and consider my neighbors from a different angle or place; I needed some distance from them. I began to suspect that I might not fit in their "community." I certainly no longer felt the naive enthusiasm of my first days at Sangamon State.

Painfully puzzling questions began to afflict me. The university, although perhaps still an honorable place to work, appeared unable to set itself apart from the surrounding society; the institution qua institution could not achieve the freedom to raise the critical voice America's people so desperately needed. How could I continue to live within an elite circle in the midst of an unjust society? How could I daily enjoy the perquisites of privilege while others exhausted themselves seeking the barest of necessities? How justify raising myself higher and higher above the confused majority? How participate in an institutional effort designed, basically, to maintain and extend the status quo? Further, I began to see more clearly that I must speak about the arrival and perfection, that is, the frightening hegemony, of a new society, the technological society. The questions raised by Marxism were now of secondary importance, if not largely meaningless. The liberal left were as wrong as Marx in their reading of history. American democratic pluralist theory was helpless before the new world imposed by what Jacques Ellul called *la technique*. Earlier, I had thought that public discussion should be centered on a prolegomenon to politics. Now I believed that the question was yet more fundamental: in light of the technological imperative, how do we discuss the very possibility of a *human* way of life on earth?

One Sunday after Mass, I asked the priest, a professor from a nearby seminary who was helping out at the parish that day, if he had an old breviary he could give me. I knew that the older breviaries, with the Latin Psalter of Saint Jerome, were no longer used. Years ago, I had studied that Latin, and for some unfathomable reason felt called to read the Psalms in that language, and in that translation. I needed to go back several thousand years in my tradition, looking for a place to stand. The Psalmist, waiting for me there, would understand my questions. Yes, the priest answered, he had a number of them, gathering dust, and I could certainly have one.

At that time, we lived just outside the city, and when I drove to the university each day I passed by a large lake. There were places where one could stop, park, and through the trees look out across the lake to a wooded area far on the other side. Each morning I would stop at one of these spots and read some Psalms from the Psalter. The word-images called out to their sources stretched before my eyes:

Rejoice, sky! Exult earth!
Let the sea and its riches sing.
May the fields and everything in them
leap with joy. (Ps. 96)

Perhaps it was a prayer.

The traditional way to read the Psalter was to pronounce the words with tongue and lips—a purely mental reading was not sufficient. The words should have an impact on both my soul and flesh; I should let them enter all of my existence. This was the way I tried to read on those mornings, taking in to myself the two books of Revelation, that of created nature and that of the inspired language. The order of Creation and the order of Grace slowly entered my world. The sublime poetry complemented the radiant landscape, and the evanescent synthesis worked on me.

One day the president of the university invited me to lunch. When I arrived, I saw that I was one of about fifteen persons served a very simple box lunch. There was a guest of honor, Dorothy Day, who was introduced as an old friend of the president. I had met her briefly when I visited a Catholic Worker house in New York City in the 1950s. After reading *The Catholic Worker* paper for some years, a friend and I stopped in one day to meet the legendary woman herself. She and the work of the Catholic Worker movement flitted in and out of my awareness now and then over the years, but I never let them stay to confront me, possibly to trouble me. I thought of them as interesting people, undoubtedly doing good work, but I never stopped to consider why, precisely, they should be interesting, nor what, exactly, was the nature of the good work. Looking back, I see that Dorothy Day's evangelical radicalism never touched me, never moved me. Because I sympathized with her ideas and admired her courage, I thought it was enough. Although we lived in two very different universes, the fact that I knew about her work deluded me into believing that I shared something of her life. Clearly, I had been a superficial reader for many years.

After that luncheon, I suffered a bit of indigestion. Suddenly, my pleasant job, our attractive home, a thoroughly "bourgeois" life, appeared like the furnishings inside a cage that imprisoned me. Trying to look out through the bars, I found that the apparently transparent spaces only reflected the objects behind me, all still inside the cage. What was on the outside? Dare I try to find out? Should I consider an escape?

I felt I needed to look more closely at Dorothy Day and what she was doing in America. How did she face the challenge of being an American, of living in *this* world? Rereading some of her writings, I slowly formed an idea of her place in the country, and in the Catholic Church. Although she was much influenced by Peter Maurin, a Frenchman by birth, and credited him with being the co-founder of the movement in the 1930s, it seemed to me that "the Worker" was thoroughly American . . . and evangelically Catholic. Being strict and unyielding pacifists, those who stuck with Dorothy Day did not support World War II. There were other pacifist groups in the country, but I knew of none who were also such thoroughgoing anarchists. For the Worker movement, anarchism meant a radical commitment to the other and to the immediate community, with a much lessened sense of obligation to or dependence on the State. But I never heard of the Catholic Worker movement seriously accused of being disloyal or unpatriotic. In fact, the more I looked at them, the more attractive their patriotism—their practice of this virtue—appeared. As Americans, they had found a splendid and apparently incorruptible way to confront the realities of our age. In the face of the growing power of the State, they chose anarchist nonsupport; in the face of mindless consumption, they chose poverty; in the face of technological abstractions, they chose to touch their neighbor; in the face of society's respectable affluence, they chose to stand with the disorderly and despised.

Peter Maurin stressed the importance of workers and scholars meeting to talk to one another. Before the term was invented, he advocated a real "free university," a democratic encounter, a place where those whose lives were dominated by manual labor would sit down with those who had dedicated themselves to study. From the way he spoke and wrote about this before his death, and the forms the ideal took in various Worker houses, I could see that it was a fruitful, embryonic idea that allowed many interpretations, depending on people, time, and place. This proposal, as with all Worker philosophy and programs, expressed a certain ideological simplicity; Maurin was determined to protect the movement from cant. Further, anyone was free to set up a house and call themselves participants in the Catholic Worker movement. From my limited experiences in Catholic Worker houses and knowing people active in the movement, I think I can see why they do not need any credential committees or watch-dog offices.

It seemed to me that there was—and is—a built-in guarantee that assures the faithfulness of potential followers of Dorothy Day. This is the daily practice, in their city houses, of directly serving, that is, personally touching, those wandering and lost on the streets, those who are the extreme misfits, who have decisively failed to meet the competitive criteria of contemporary respectable society. As has been pointed out by those who write for the *Catholic Worker* paper, it is not a movement that tries to uplift the bums and bag ladies; the Catholic Worker movement has no program to "reform" addicts of any kind. Catholic Worker volunteers do not live on the skid rows of America to achieve structural social change, or any kind of social change at all. As Jeff Dietrich, director of the Catholic Worker house in Los Angeles, wrote after being there twenty-five years,

> We are not here to cure the poor or to fix the poor or to mainstream the poor; we are not here to create programs, make converts, raise money, or build great buildings. We are here to enter into the pain of the poor, to expose the wounds that make the suffering of the poor inevitable. We are here to submit to that radical surgery which will take away our hearts of stone and exchange them for hearts of flesh. Anything less than this is pious self-aggrandizement or pompous professionalism.
>
> Our collective experience of this century demonstrates so clearly that the "little way" of Dorothy Day and Peter Maurin is not some outdated, pious, pie-in-the-sky theology, but it is rather the only means of achieving our end—a more human world. The instruments of power, whether political, military, or bureaucratic, can achieve only disaster, even though the world would wish us to believe otherwise.

And as Dorothy Day answered Robert Coles when he asked her about affecting or moving the society:

> Shouldn't we be fighting the larger causes of civil rights and human rights and justice for the poor? Why, yes, of course, we should be everywhere, if it is morality in the abstract that we are talking about . . . for some of us anything else [than being here, preparing soup for the persons on the Bowery] is extravagant; it's unreal; it's not a life we want to live. There are plenty of others who want that life, living in corridors of power, influence, money, making big decisions that affect big numbers of

people. We don't have to follow those people, though; they have more would-be servants—slaves, I sometimes think—than they know what to do with. Isn't there just a small space in our world, our culture, for men and women who want to follow the lead . . . of the Lord? . . .

After thinking about Dorothy Day and her ragtag followers, I nevertheless continued to believe that institutions were necessary, and I still felt—though with some doubts—that institutions of higher learning were a good; I felt that I occupied a decent place in the society, that the university could perhaps serve as a light. I continued to find my meetings with students, in and outside the classroom, exciting and rewarding. But Dorothy Day's presence did not leave me in peace. Again, she flitted in and out of my awareness, but now she pricked, she nudged me; she became something of an annoyance. Indeed, she affected me as Daniel Berrigan had several years earlier. I found, ever more frequently, that I had to repeat to myself the arguments defending my way of life at the university, any university.

A book then fell into my hands that introduced me to a world really foreign to me—Helen and Scott Nearing's *Living the Good Life*. To this day I am uncertain why this book appealed so strongly to me, why it captivated me. Of course, I admired Nearing's courage; I liked the way he did things, for example, the way he gathered rocks to build his house and the way he put his hand tools away at night. Here was a man who did not cut corners, who seemed to make no compromises. He did indeed attempt to live a good life. But I knew people in the university who also strove to live a good life, who were most conscientious in their work. And I knew people in the Catholic Worker movement who, in addition, went further. They deprived themselves of precious goods like privacy and the personal freedom to arrange one's evenings or weekends. But Nearing's example appeared to show that one could—and to suggest that others perhaps should—actually live the republican virtues Jefferson thought necessary that we have a good nation. Nearing brought me back to face yet again the practical ways to be patriotic, to live as a loyal citizen, in *today's* America. Not all will be called to a life of study, and certainly not many will be called to live on skid row, but there is a sense in which all Americans could embrace the virtues of self-reliance, of accepting limits, of foregoing consumption, of actually producing something—actions that characterized Scott and Helen Nearing's lives. They had found a way to say no, to reject the false promises of labor-saving technology, to move outside the bubble of an affluent society built on the exploitation of the hungry, and to do this with style, with a luminous *joie de vivre*. As I contemplated the meager fruits of my amateurish gardening efforts, I wondered about the meaning of Nearing's book. Why had he come into my life at that moment? What was he trying to tell me?

Not long after this, my wife gave me a present of Wendell Berry's just published book, *The Unsettling of America*. I had heard Berry read his poetry during a spring literary festival at the university, and liked it. The university president's wife, an enthusiastic Berry fan, had earlier urged me to read his work. But I never looked at him seriously until I picked up *Unsettling*. That was exactly its powerful effect on me—unsettling. The book entered me as I had imagined occurred with readers during the early Middle Ages. Berry's view of contemporary America was the clearest analysis I had yet read. He saw how the major institutions of government, the universities, and private sector businesses had "conspired" to wreck the dream of Jefferson, had worked, finally, for the destruction of the country.

This book represented the kind of work, I felt, that should be coming out of the university. Its scholarship was sound, and he directly faced important questions about the country. Berry also presented a historical vision of America, at once moral and empirical. He was able to break through the "is-ought" conundrum that so confuses academics, whether their fields are philosophy or biology.

Berry helped me to see the centrality of agriculture in any thought about the possibility of a decent society today. His ideas on orthodoxy and marginal thinking opened up new perspectives I had not imagined. For example, he cited the Amish as a community of people who practice "an exemplary marginal agriculture."

> Nothing, I think, is more peculiarly characteristic of the agricultural orthodoxy—as of American society in general—than its inability to see the Amish for what they are. Oh, it *sees* them, all right. It sees them as quaint, picturesque, old-fashioned, backward, unprogressive, strange, extreme, different, perhaps slightly subversive. And that "sight" is perfect blindness. What is not seen is that the Amish are a community in the full sense of the word; they may well be the last surviving white community of any considerable size in this country. And for this there are reasons. It is especially the reasons that we do not want to

see, for these reasons invalidate most of the assumptions and ambitions by which we proudly characterize ourselves as "modern."

One paragraph in particular stuck in my memory. Writing about remedies for the situation of contemporary Americans, he noted that

having exploited "relativism" until, as a people, we have no deeply believed reasons for doing anything, we must now ask ourselves if there is not, after all, an absolute good by which we must measure ourselves and for which we must work. That absolute good, I think, is health—not in the merely hygienic sense of personal health, but the health, the wholeness, finally the holiness, of Creation, of which our personal health is only a share.

I knew that, in coming to Sangamon State, I had chosen a fringe institution on the very edge of academic respectability. But I also believed that living and working in a borderline place was of some importance. Now I found Berry insisting that

the marginal possibility, the marginal place, and the marginal humanity that I have been describing are reinforced by a marginal way of thinking—until now a sort of counter-theme in our history, so far always subordinate to the theme of exploitation, but unbroken and still alive. This is the theme of settlement, of kindness to the ground, of nurture.

Perhaps the ideas of marginality and agriculture, as Berry presented them, were of supreme significance, not only for the nation, but for me. . . .

One innovation in curricular offerings at the university was the public affairs colloquium (PAC). This was a course in which the faculty member selected some public problem for study. Students had to take one of these courses to graduate. I offered different PACs over the years, but eventually developed one that I repeated: a critical examination of industrial/technological society. Among the books I used at various times were Robert Heilbroner's *The Human Prospect*, E. F. Schumacher's *Small Is Beautiful*, Ivan Illich's *Tools for Conviviality*, Jacques Ellul's *The Technological Society*, Eldridge Cleaver's *Soul On Ice*, and Simone Weil's *The Need for Roots*. In such a course, one directly confronts questions of the public good. But such questions demand that one get beyond the self, transcend the culture of narcissism. Further, one would come to feel the importance of acting as a public person. But in an age of individualism, people are not easily moved to be publicly spirited. Moreover, teachers who are greatly exercised over more employment benefits necessarily appear to be rather self-seeking; they have difficulty standing up as exemplary embodiments of their own teaching.

My experience with the students was also frustrating. At first, I thought their youth constituted a hindrance to grasping the seriousness and immediacy of the issues such authors presented. But then I came to believe that the students were anesthetized, bamboozled, blinded by the glitter, really distracted by the amusements; that they were, finally, addicted to the images and promises, the idols and fetishes the hucksters provided. On the other hand, the generally older part-time students already employed had also fatally succumbed, just as their younger classroom companions, to the debilitating and destructive allurements offered both to winners and losers in the consumption game. In addition, the older students were so deeply entangled in the daily business of surviving—paying bills—or getting ahead—making career moves—that their capacity to relate personally and directly to the arguments of Illich or Ellul was almost nonexistent. And I could find no way to make these arguments come alive. Nor could I bring into high relief those occasions in which the students had confusedly experienced the grotesqueries and horrors of the technological milieu.

Generally, I could not find a solid, experiential basis matching these authors' critical claims. This was especially the case with Simone Weil. The importance I placed on her ideas seemed to be in inverse proportion to student interest in them. This young woman had gone to Germany in 1932 to see fascism for herself, to work in a factory in 1934 to know that world firsthand, to Spain in 1936 to participate in the war, to grape vineyards in 1941 to submit her body and soul to the fatigue of farm labor. Her writings directly and forcefully expressed the anguish of her experiences in each of these places. After her death in 1943, these writings became known, and were hailed on both sides of the Atlantic as works of genius.

The feeling that I inhabited a world more and more estranged from and foreign to the students and faculty grew in me. My daily "time out" while I recited the Psalms in Latin and attempted to read the beauty of the world as it revealed itself in the early morning light across the lake; my reflections on the fire of consuming love that drove Dorothy Day into sharing the daily hardships of modern society's failures; the simple attraction of the life that Scott and Helen Nearing made for themselves; the irrefutable logic of Wendell Berry's vision for an America faithful to both its origins and the challenges of the contemporary world—all this worked on me, gave me no rest. In addition, a series of frustrations in the overall collective life of the university led me to rethink my loyalty to this or perhaps any modern institution. Seemingly endless discussions of academic minutiae in committee meetings revealed a kind of small-mindedness that finally wore me down; there was no energy left to tackle important questions crying to be addressed. Continual jockeying for power within the small and relatively insignificant world of the university—the institution belittled by the very motivations animating such fights—seemed to me jejune and silly. If there had been a clash over issues of some historical sense—for example, a struggle arising from an insight like Nietzsche's in the nineteenth century, moving him to cry out, "No genuinely radical living for truth is possible in a university," or a controversy over a fundamental characterization of American society like that provoked by C. Wright Mills after World War II (*The Power Elite*), then I could respect the protagonists since they would ennoble the place with a fight of this nature.

A kind of pattern appeared to be forming. The original vision of founding an institution—with roots reaching down into the critical intellectual tradition of the West—in the social and political life of Central Illinois was being lost. In its stead, people who thought academic nit-picking and ideological position-taking were important, who were in the forefront of attempts to play childish power games with the administration, who were leaders in the indecent efforts to establish a faculty union were, in fact, giving a very different character to the place. Instead of becoming incarnated in the people and communities of the region, the university increasingly became more remote, absorbed in constructing an enclave of self-interest. There were, of course, faculty and administrators who fought against the ideologues and gamesmen, who defended the priority of sound scholarship and open public debate on the important issues facing the students and people of the nation. But they seemed to be more and more marginal to the main thrust of the institution. The students and public, I felt, were being shortchanged. But, in one sense, this situation did not really affect me. I was free to continue challenging students, and to participate in the affairs of the community.

Slowly, however, I came to formulate some insights: I enjoyed the freedom to give direction to my life; I could not assume that the cultural production of so-called meanings provided by today's institutions express the truth; I had to set out on a possibly lonely road to make sense of my life, to consciously construct a meaning for it; I could do this through a narrative structure. From my experience and study, I came to see that the pacifist and anarchist position of the Catholic Worker must be accepted—I could no longer live with an employment that supported the government with tax money. The vision coming out of Schumacher, Illich, Ellul and others was an apt response to the industrial/technological Leviathan and its supporting economy—I needed to move out of this economy and discard its high-tech toys. The witness of Berry and the Nearings specifically outlined another way of life, a mode of living that related directly to the disorders of today's political and economic systems. I began to think of subsistence farming, of directing the story of my life in a different direction.

According to the AAUP (American Association of University Professors) practice and the policy adopted by the university, a faculty member, after seven years' employment, had to be given tenure or dismissed. Reflections on my life situation became more acute as the moment for my tenure decision approached. Then, when I actually received tenure, I immediately knew it was time to get out, to move on. Meditating on the Psalms by the lake, I asked myself, "How can I continue to participate in the pollution and destruction of Creation?" Considering the rejects and victims of modern society, How can I remain in a position with high pay and prestige, secure for life? Thinking about the final words of Simone Weil's *The Need for Roots* . . .

> . . . all other human activities, command over men, technical planning, art, science, philosophy and so on, are all inferior to physical labour in spiritual significance.
>
> It is not difficult to define the place that physical labour should occupy in a well-ordered social life. It should be its spiritual core.

I decided that I needed to find out what she was talking about. It was disingenuous to tell students to read her, to ask them to seriously consider her arguments if I myself, in my own life, was so far removed from them, from her personal example. This young woman—she died when she was only thirty-four—one of the truly inspiring intellectuals of our age, understood how to live: one needed to exercise both the mind and the body, but in a manner fitting the historical moment in which one lives. After many discussions with Mary throughout the weeks prior to the tenure decision, talks that ended with her enthusiastic agreement, I notified the university that I was taking an indefinite leave of absence—another privilege of academics!

3

Life at the Margins

There are a number of crucial truths, usually ignored,
about what we have for so long thought of as nigger
work: it is necessary; no society can exist without some
form of it; at times it has been done beautifully, as in
Japan and in Tuscany, and occasionally even in America;
a man who is incapable of it is less than a man, not likely
to survive hardships that in the history of the human
race are fairly normal; before it encountered the racist
mentality the men who did such work and did it well
considered themselves dignified by it.

Wendell Berry

E leven years after beginning a Ph.D. program at
UCLA, eight years after abandoning America,
seven years after trying on an academic career, I set out on a journey
to an exotic place, the backwoods of America. But as a trained academic, I first did some research. Studying conventional socioeconomic
indicators, I looked for a region of the country that was described as
economically poor and "underdeveloped," from which people were
emigrating, which boasted of no large cities, a place that, apparently,
contained few social, economic, or cultural advantages—according to
the opinion of enlightened moderns. Such a benighted locale, I reasoned, would be the ideal place to live well. For although I had lost my
taste for many conventional comforts, still I sought the enjoyment of
beauty.

I had come to believe that the predominant industrial/technological
mode of production, together with its sophisticated marketing strate-
gies, not only determined the shape and direction of the society but,

providing everything from jets to health care to culture, imprisoned me in an ever more narrow padded corridor leading to nowhere I would ever choose to go. I decided to walk out. The glamorous institutional conveniences appeared ugly, mean, destructive of friendship, family, community, and nation—blights on both the land and its people. I had thought long about the story of Odysseus's return to Ithaca. In a ravished country, he found his father, Laertes, the old king, shabbily dressed, but taking excellent care of his vineyard and orchard, a fitting work in a land that had "fallen into the hands of wicked people" (*Iliad*, Book XXIV). The image of Laertes' action provided a powerful suggestion of where to go, what to do, in a land largely fallen into the clutches of greedy money moguls and their puppet experts. For me, the strong smell of sulfur became more pronounced, more frightening, precisely in those spectacular achievements of the society that appeared most sophisticated, most audacious, in a Sisyphean race to an ever-receding technological paradise. Formerly, moral sensibilities had only to confront the perversion of natural beauty. Today's moral sense, however, was often blunted by the sheer ingenuity of high-tech design.

When the semester was over, we sold the house, and I withdrew what I had paid into the university retirement fund. Cutting off any support from insurance schemes, we piled our belongings into a rented truck and headed for a forty-acre square of wooded, hilly land we had purchased just north of where the Ohio and Mississippi Rivers meet, in Southern Illinois. There we set up a small, used circus tent and a summer house, four walls of screens with a plastic roof. I dug a hole for a privy, erected an outdoor shower, and the four of us started work building a house and growing food.

We had chosen this particular tract after looking at various parcels of land in the area. At this place we discovered, about a mile in each direction from the acreage, a family with children the same age as ours. This was important, since we had decided to take the kids out of school and let them learn on the homestead. Hence, to have other children their age within walking distance was a distinct advantage. We talked with the respective parents and were delighted to learn that, although they were very different from us in so many ways, they immediately inspired great respect. We were impressed by the ways they viewed themselves and their children, their land, and the cosmos. They obviously saw themselves as people of *this place*, happy in the thought that their children also might choose to remain within this "limited" horizon. Then, driving away from the home of one of the families in the late afternoon, we looked out across the fields and saw six deer walking slowly across the setting sun. The beauty of the scene confirmed our opinion about this as a place to settle, to see our children grow. We immediately contacted the real estate agent, and bought the land.

Why, suddenly, do the security of a pleasant, well-paying job, a lovely home that looked out through a forest to the river, friendly social and intellectual intercourse with a few good colleagues, various educational opportunities for the children, all come to seem very lesser goods, benefits, yes, but something that can be discarded? I don't know. But I can relate some experiences that stopped me, which made me question and think. For example, one day I was able to observe our son at his gym class—in an exclusive private school that made a great to-do about how all the elements of the educational process there were intelligently and sensitively adapted to the child, and not the other way around. Shocked by what I saw, I nearly wept when I realized that Ben was standing alone to one side, completely ignored by the teachers who, like many teachers in school systems, concentrated all their attention on those children who could already perform the approved exercise sequences well. Because he had been born with metatarsus rarus—a slight curvature in the bones of his feet—he was not quite as agile as the other children.

At the school, I noticed that our daughter not only excelled in those activities that teachers encourage, but also strove fiercely to out-do her fellow pupils, to be the star achiever. Such behavior was thought right and proper by the school professionals. It became painfully obvious that school, for very different reasons with each child, was not a good place for them to be. Mary not only understood my objections to school but, based on her work as a teacher at various levels in the system, supplied more extensive and pointed evidence for why school was a bad idea for our kids. Our respective experiences led to the same conclusion.

I came to see that in this setting—modern urban living where each of us was continually submitted to someone's professional judgment or caring service, to attractive distractions or cultural "musts"—the children were being offered up to institutions and authorities for whom I had less and less respect. As parents, we were cooperating with the civil and cultural managers in submitting the children to the currently approved series of treatments and therapies, curricula and indoctrination, toys and entertainments, which form the modern historic creation of upper income bourgeois childhood. To sentence our kids to a training regime for a life of endless consumption and inevitably boring diversions, backed up by economic necessity and ideological mystification, appeared to be a deliberate act of cruelty.

Enjoying the comfortable and privileged life of an academic in a society that assaulted me continually with its ever more outlandish idiocies, I felt the need to look toward another world, to seek a very different notion of how to order my days and challenge my mind, to free my imagination and pleasure my senses. Reaching back into Western history, I came to the sixth-century ideal of Benedict, often expressed by the phrase, *orare et laborare*. Looking beneath the surface glamour of malls and movies, and coldly regarding the prevalence of darkness and disorder in mainstream culture, both popular and "high," I thought that this might be the moment to seek a modern understanding of living in the synthesis of contemplation and work. I might be facing precisely the historic opportunity where I'm supposed to question the ethereal ideal of the "intellectual life," and to find out if there is an intimate and rich connection between doing the necessary labor of living and enjoying the leisure of spiritual adventure.

Supported by large numbers of slaves and the domestic work of women, some Greeks, like Plato and Aristotle, developed the curious idea that the perfection of man [*sic*] consists in the contemplation of truth. In the heads of less clear thinkers, such a notion led to a deleterious break between body and soul in the individual, and between low and high culture in the society. I came to suspect that the long experience of slavery, the strict dichotomization into body and soul, and the anxiety-ridden striving for high culture, together with the sustained search for labor-saving tools, contributed greatly to making a wasteland of the world and freaks out of men and women. It might be the moment for me to seek a contemporary path in a way of life long ago indicated and sometimes beautifully realized.

Whatever the reasons, the journey had begun, taking us away from being held hostage, mortgaged to modern institutions, into the unknown and unused practice of an old virtue that, in the Middle Ages, was known as that kind of prudence called "economics." To practice economy was to live well in one's household actions—*conversatio domestica* it was called. But as a modern person, I had to overcome a state of nescience. A virtuous person would know how to construct shelter, how to cultivate the earth. One has only to look at any traditional society to see abundant evidence of this. I, however, was a successful employee, well integrated into a very different kind of economy, the market one, built on scarcity. I knew almost nothing about the basics of living well, that is, with a certain measure of freedom and autonomy, genuinely risking failure.

Reflecting on my ignorance, I was deeply disturbed that I knew so little about activities in which men and women have been engaged for thousands of years, activities permitting one to inhabit the earth and flourish in the enjoyment of its gifts directly and immediately. For example, to see that tomato plants were properly pruned and tied up; to know that one could turn over the soil only when it reached a certain dryness in the spring. I had seen people speak to and touch suspicious cows and nervous horses—but I had very little personal experience with plants, dirt, and farm animals.

Soon I was pleasantly startled by what the removal of my ignorance bequeathed me. Each day my awkward actions of learning led me more deeply into a primordial and wonderful experience, that of the world of the senses. No photo or packaged view, no abstract text or programmed image filtered the world to me. As almost never before in my adult life, my entire body became the immediate sensorium of everything surrounding me. This meant that I slowly became familiar with a place and its creatures, I came to know the seasons, I came to feel at home in a specific soil. Both by direct experience and reflectively, I pleasantly walked into a new and heretofore unknown universe, a richly sensual place. Much of the time, it was impossible to separate immediacy from reflection; experience took on a new character.

The ignorance was something of an advantage, since it opened the way to strong incentives for its removal. If we wanted to eat, we had to become knowledgeable about a bewildering variety of factors and conditions. We were forced to make huge learning strides in really important matters, and rapidly. We soon saw that the necessary familiarity entailed the recognition of infinite subtleties and nuances in combinations of temperature, moisture, soil character, kind of plant, and the timing of seeding or transplanting. I, at least, readily understood that my remaining years were insufficient to master the basic art of growing food, much less to reach the leisure and pleasure of graceful country living. But the excitement of each day's clumsy advances was all-absorbing; I was continually amazed at what I *could* accomplish.

The very impossibility of perfection led to one of the most memorable and enjoyable aspects of life in that "remote" area. Before leaving the university, we once stopped by the president's home for coffee with him and his wife. They were good friends, and we wanted to tell them of our dream. He was aghast. "But you can't take your children to such a place!" He seemed to be thoroughly imbued with the illusion—common, perhaps, among those who fancy themselves cosmopolitan, who believe in something called high culture—that the children would become narrow, "provincial," seriously deprived among rural people. After living in this area, I reflected on that earlier conversation. The people he had in mind—without ever having met one—were now the very ones whom I had come to know fairly well, on whom I had to depend continually if I wanted to survive in this place! Who were these people who, indeed, differed markedly from us?

I had to know my neighbors, which meant that I had to learn how to become sensibly aware of them, somewhat as I was learning how to sense the soil. I knew, even before I met them, that we would be like foreigners to one another. Except for one family down the road, all the neighbors had been there for several generations; their sensibilities and speech only roughly matched ours; their religious beliefs and practices were thoroughly strange to us, sometimes even bizarre; their ways of speaking and laughing were new, often puzzling. One day, we were discussing with one of the women of the church what we would bring to a potluck supper. My wife explicitly pointed out that I would be preparing the dish. But the woman never looked at me and continued to address only my wife. In that society, the husband did not cook the dish for potluck suppers!

Since I was the outsider trespassing on their native ground, I knew that I had to exercise the greatest circumspection. This meant, first of all, learning what was important to my neighbors. I soon found out: family, church and hard work. I tried always to exercise caution and restraint in expressing opinions. This was difficult, of course, since I was so full of them! But I knew that the primary task was to listen, to attempt to enter the sensible and imaginative universe of their lives, their beliefs, their myths, their illusions. The preaching and singing in the country churches I found especially strange and perplexing, fascinating and foreign. Whenever possible, I went to the "gospel sings" when a visiting group of musicians came to one of the local churches. Their enthusiastic performances both enlarged and bewildered my sense of sacred music. But this dramatic expression of a people's religiosity was sometimes troubling and disquieting, too. From extremely infrequent and momentary exposures to television, I recognized that the musicians and, especially, the female singers, had picked up gestures and tones, a certain provocative, sexy manner, all of which grated, turning the mysterious message of the Gospel into a bastardized exhibition . . . or so it seemed to me.

Listening to my neighbors, I heard "small talk" continually transformed in ordinary conversation. Seemingly mundane matters opened up more important questions: how to live off this land, how to rear our children in this place. Looking back years later, I remember that I never came away from one of my neighbors without having been enriched. Comments about the weather, for example, were not empty and polite exchanges, but important facts and interpretations about what mattered, that is, about the immediate experience of the *matter* on which one's livelihood depended: for example, this temperature meant that that vegetable would be damaged by morning. One did not just relate the latest escapade of one's children but, rather, discuss the ways in which the next generation was being prepared to incarnate itself in this place. How important is it for my child to own his own horse? One did not gossip about other neighbors so much as tell the stories that made up the living history of this community, the tales contributing to the collective memory of this people, all those of the immediate area: so-and-so still had the first nickel he ever earned. I wondered . . . How many are there, like my friend the president of the university, who live in that hermetic ignorance of the learned? in the untroubled insularity of the educated? On the other hand, however, it may be that my neighbors were not especially gifted people at all. Rather, my ears, in this new mode of moving and listening, had been opened to heretofore unheard frequencies.

Although I have heard and read many imaginative and sensitive commentaries on art and literature, what is generally thought to be the high expression of a culture, one remark above all has stuck in my memory over the years, a simple, rooted statement of a neighboring farmer. In this new life, I had to learn the proper times and places for talk and listening. One man, whose conversation I especially treasured, could always be found at home on Sunday, after he had been to church, for he would not work on that day. So I often stopped there on Sunday. I shall never forget one afternoon in late spring. I got up to leave, and he accompanied me to my old pickup. As I started to get in, I noticed that his head turned and he slowly surveyed the surrounding countryside. From the hill on which he built his house, one could see far into the distance. The rolling countryside was now green with the new year's freshness, the red bud trees just finishing their blooming, the dogwood beginning to flower. Quietly, in his accustomed tone and manner, he said modestly, naturally, "It's all so beautiful." Far from the world of the salon and esoteric discourse, I met a man whose esthetic sensibility grew out of and reflected "everyday" perception, a man who spoke openly, candidly, without any affectation; a man whose voice rang true because he spoke out of the place where he and his family belonged—out of his native land.

Slowly, over the years, I became familiar with many of the stories of this place, with the continuous oral tradition that held the history of these people, which expressed the beliefs of this neighborhood and the surrounding community. By listening carefully, and asking prudently, I found that I could learn how to cultivate my land and how to live among this people. As I had suspected, the stories contained the collective historical experiences, the wisdom of the place, but I was completely unprepared for the color of their humor. Often I was surprised at the way in which an ordinary event of the day brought to mind an old story that expressed the living memory of people laughing at their own folly. Having been exposed to the necessarily grim and grotesque world of so much modern humor—literary, artistic, political, professional—I had little experience of a people artlessly laughing at themselves, unaffectedly rejoicing in the incongruities of their own major and minor embarrassments. For example, the behavior of a friend in the neighborhood was well-known—and smiled at. He always raised a few head of cattle, and he would feed one more carefully for his own family consumption. But he named the animal and went out to greet it each day. When the time came to take it to the slaughterhouse, he could not bring himself to do it! He asked me to borrow a cattle rack for my pickup and transport the beast to be killed and butchered. Once the creature arrived in neatly labeled packages, he could enjoy his steak in peace.

Eventually I came to see that much of the intercourse between me and my neighbors was an infinitely rich exchange, a mutual giving of gifts. These actions occurred frequently, in many different forms, colored by the variegated atmosphere of the time and place. To think about a number or an accounting would be patently ridiculous. For this was not a world of math and measure; the universal serpent of envy appeared restrained. I had come among a people whose lives were not always ruled by the "law" of scarcity. I was surprised by the time they gave one another, whether to talk or to help with work. They freely shared information on services, markets, opportunities. But they were not dull or stupid. As I came to know them better, I saw that there were subtle, delicate, but firm judgments made: For this kind of help, you would call one neighbor, but not that other. And then I saw further that these kinds of action—a continual sharing and giving— were an essential aspect of the very possibility of their lives in this place. In certain aspects, many of these families approached a kind of subsistence agriculture. They would not be able to live without helping one another, without sharing and giving outside the formal economy. Indeed, because of the personal and communitary character of the actions, they could have no price. For example, a neighbor mowed and baled the fescue from my ten-acre pasture each year (other than a rototiller, I possessed no farm machinery), and then we shared the hay. With this kind of behavior, repeated in all kinds of actions throughout every year, neighbors came to know one another intimately and to be bound together in this community.

When I became more proficient in working my land, I joined the local Farmers' Market Association, a democratically-run organization of thirty family growers and craftspeople. Each Saturday morning, from April to November, we loaded up the work of our hands and presented our goods to the people of a neighboring town, a city of about twenty thousand persons. Here I saw growers, in direct competition with one another—selling the same produce—helping one another, expressing obvious affection for one another. I saw people acting in ways that market economics would rule out. Not everyone, of course, and not with the same generous spirit. But "non-economic" behavior always shone out; you had only to open your eyes to see it. The glowing atmosphere of those Saturday mornings was one of a pleasant agricultural fair. Since we sold only those products that we ourselves grew or made, we could speak knowledgeably about them to potential customers. Selling fresh herbs unfamiliar to some Southern Illinoisans, I could speak about the flavors they would give to different dishes. Some people, for example, did not know of the great difference in taste between curled and flat parsley. But some also knew *too* much. One day a man demanded to know the ratio of roosters to hens in my flock of chickens before he would buy my eggs! It was a world far removed from the methods and possibilities of a supermarket chain. I shall never forget the range and resonance of feelings—winter poring over seed catalogs, spring preparation and planting, summer weeding, followed by the joys of harvest . . . celebrating the work of my own hands. I could then proudly display my produce for the city folk for I had some part in the growing of these beautiful things. One day, as I put some especially delicate and fresh lettuce in a bag, I heard the customer say, "You handle that with real love."

From seeing my neighbors so closely, and reflecting on my experience with them, I was led to another stage, completely unforeseen, in my journey. As an adolescent, I had indulged in long musings on the question of a self, my self. After several years in college, I settled the matter with a "final" decision: I had a "religious vocation." For about fifteen years, I embraced and faithfully followed the life of a Dominican friar. But then the self came to appear incomplete without marriage, and this state became the setting for further explorations. Historically, where do I fit? Spiritually, how do I stand? Socially, what do I do?—all modern questions, reflecting the muddles of our time. Many contemporary texts legitimate and stress the importance of the questions, together with prescribing ways, ranging from the prosaic to the fantastic, to answer them. But I always doubted whether these recent expressions belonged to the tradition that I knew from the ancient Greek admonition, "know thyself," and its stark elaboration in the Gospels. Then, as I became more familiar with the intricate patterns of my newly-adopted rural neighborhood, moved more freely in the established pathways, participated more deeply in the local rituals, I found that my earlier questions sounded more and more eccentric, off-key. Of course, there was some meaning to the questions, but the mode and context of their emergence, together with their form, became more and more unreal *to me*; they were no longer *my* questions.

I had indeed come to move in a new place, and to be *in* that place. This experience radically changed or dissolved all the old questioning. With a feeling of being refreshed, lightened, I found that my center was the daily living. And this was built around connections—to the fields and household, to family, friends, and neighbors. Indeed, reality came to consist in the actions and feelings that established and nourished these bonds. Once I recognized them, I immediately saw their rightness, their definitiveness. They were something like Aristotle's first principles, *per se nota* (directly known). To define myself by my relation to these others appeared as a brute cosmic given, something independent and outside of rational proof or disproof. I shall never forget seeing the complete incomprehension between two men who once met at my house. One, a friend from the city visiting me, the other, a local farmer. My friend, serious, fully believing in the question's importance, asked the farmer, "But how do you know what to do each day when you get out of bed?" The farmer, totally bewildered, had no idea what to answer. To him, of course, the question appeared unintelligible . . . or stupid. Living within the experience of generations of farmers, he simply did what his father and forefathers did. He had only to look around himself, take in all the signs, and act out of the accumulated wisdom of centuries; he possessed the habits (virtues) of farming. The only real question is moral, not pragmatic. Do I have the strength and courage to be faithful to the tradition? Recognizing my duties to my parents, my household, my land, do I practice what the Romans called *pietas*? Such obligations come from the very heart of things, they are natural, or religious. My articulation of them, however, is only an indistinct shadow. This kind of truth can only be known in fleshly, particular experience, not through incomplete and distorting language.

I understood that the establishment of these bonds through touching—one's soil, the other—took on a transcendental character precisely to the extent that it was real; that it was cosmically legitimated by its specifically sensual nature. One could not hear farther than earshot; one could not see beyond the horizon; one could not help others without physically reaching them. And it is just this very materiality that unites me to the unfathomable mystery of the other. Limits permit limitlessness.

Thus the conventional questions concerning a modern self could not arise. Voicing some purely personal goal, seeking to realize some individual ambition, could not be imagined. Rather, the modest, repetitive actions of daily necessity became all-important, the specific attentions and acts that attached me to this place and its creatures. That meant the people of this place, my family, friends, neighbors, livestock, wildlife, and everything growing in the soil. Through all these, I would be taken beyond myself, know great joy and peace, the peace of awe-filled gratitude. But I am still a fallible and lame creature. The character of this experience will only be in proportion to the purity of my single-mindedness and generosity.

Our neighborhood was not some idyllic and isolated lost paradise. Other outsiders knew it well and had arrived here long before us. Representatives of a distant and foreign government had systematically taken control of the children's education. Bureaucrats told farmers how to practice farming! "Entertainers" tried to capture, shrink and distort the peoples' imagination and humor. The universities and corporations provided the expertise and machinery to facilitate these marauding incursions. The goal was brutal and crude: to integrate the lands and lives of these people into the national and international economy through the acceptance of an industrial mode of production and living. The "virtues" of rationalization, specialization and economies of scale were ceaselessly preached as a new faith, a collection of promises offered by those who always "know better." The appeal, too, was raw and vicious: It spoke to people's greed and envy. Some did not understand that the new ways were genuinely new, that their adoption would mean a wrenching break from the past. Some succumbed, loosening or breaking the ties that bound them to a noble way of life, to the sacredness of a place. Many of these then failed; market economics, as practiced in industrial agriculture today, forced them out, destroyed their rootedness in a historical community.

Looking back now, it is possible to see the invasion of this lovely landscape, together with all the other rural landscapes of the world, as the principal theater of a war, a war against subsistence, against a way of life where people stand on their soil and reach out to one another. Some dare to assert that the campaign was necessary, good even. The American farmer is said to be one of the most efficient producers in the world. Political, scientific and commercial programs, all replete with violence, designed to transform a farmer into an industrial worker, have largely succeeded. The data are there to prove it. But if one looks, not at the graphs and charts of the profiteers (business and academic), but at the land and people affected, one sees the costs: the ugliness, the emptiness, the sadness. An unbiased story reveals the cruel imposition of industrial efficiency and economic competitiveness, together with the all-important fact that it was a war, with both winners and losers.

It is a fashion today among academic historians to study and write about those "at the bottom," those left out, especially if they existed long ago. But, to the best of my knowledge, almost all the studies describing clearly and truthfully this modern despoliation of a land and its people emanate not from the computerized offices of academic careerists, but from the pens of those who have chosen to remain in the countryside. If you want to hear the whole story, you must go to them; some speak with a true eloquence born of heartbreaking experience.

There was a large state university, with a department of agriculture, within twenty miles of our parcel of land. But the academics from this department did not come out to listen to, to study, to tell the tragedy of our neighbors. For example, one man living near us used to have a small herd of dairy cows. Then one day the government decreed that, to sell his milk, he had to install a lot of expensive "scientific" equipment to ensure that he not poison his family and customers. Up to that day, no one had ever fallen ill from his cows. But laws are universalistic, reaching across a nation, and one of them is the law of probabilities. Our neighbor could never afford to buy such machinery. So he was forced to sell his cows and seek a job in town in order to stay on his farm, working it in the evenings and weekends. Of course, there are grand-sounding words to justify such violence, such as "progress" and "public health." Imbued with their ideological mystique, bureaucrats devise rules and programs that destroy the vital connections between one person and another, the basis of human trust. Innumerable such links between our neighbor and his customers were lost forever. A further distance was imposed, moving people from a community of mutual trust toward uneasy and constantly revised truces between conflicting and contentious rights.

If one searches, one can find isolated voices pointing out that the primary victims in these vicious rituals of superstitious belief—legislation or bureaucratic decrees make unpleasant and evil events impossible—are farmers, both in America and in other countries, especially those of the South. But, as individuals, they are only part of the story. Indeed, as I learned from experience, it is not exact to call them individuals at all. They are—or were—members of living histories, of beautiful communities with a remembered past. And to see what was destroyed one must travel to where they lived, to the battlefields.

Within a radius of about ten miles from our piece of land, nineteen cemeteries were scattered. Some were isolated far back in the forest, some were in the midst of a pasture or cornfield. In the last century, there had been a small country church and community of people around each one. Now there is the silence of the forest and fields, interrupted only by the singing of birds. No buildings remain, no people live nearby, no one has been buried in them for years. A man who has attempted to make an inventory of all the old county cemeteries told me that the records showed many more. But they have been destroyed, perhaps by vandals, perhaps by farmers. He personally knew of one that had been turned into a pig lot. The Union County dead are undisturbed, up to now, only in those nineteen remaining tracts. Nothing is left of the people and their small communities except the names of these cemeteries and the mute tombstones. But many of these are of soft sandstone, and the peoples' names will not be visible much longer.

Looking out over some of my neighbors' fields, I saw what the foreign experts, the modern carpetbaggers, have largely accomplished. Their cruel war against a mode of living based on traditional memory and neighborly faithfulness has resulted in making mainstream American farming an extractive industry, mining both the land and its people, leaving behind a wasted landscape. This exploitative aggression destroys living places, including the soil itself. At times, it appears to be a kind of mindless strip mining. Where some soil remains, rural America is now structured and organized according to the centralized logic of a colonial economy: Raw materials—food and fiber—are shipped out, and manufactured goods and services are shipped in.

Where the autonomous variety found in more traditional subsistence, neighborhood and community no longer exist, standardized packages of food, education, health, and entertainment must be imported. Historically, all colonial centers have exacted the same kind of bargain: the periphery is kept in debt, while the metropolis invests in consumption and speculation. I saw neighbors, one after another, forced to take a job in town in order to pay their debts and remain on their farms.

Today the planners and policy makers, with their academic backers, arrive spreading yet another plague around the country. Farmers are told that they must adjust to a new mode of existence: They and their land are valuable resources for something called "sustainable economic growth or development." Nature is no longer the living mother in whom their communities subsist, no longer the bountiful limit and measure of possibility. But their work will still be calculated in terms of something called the Gross Domestic Product (always spelled in capitals!). When a society is so intensely economized or monitized, individuals, formerly known and cared for in the sensual embrace of their local community, now become interchangeable parts of a system rationally managed by some very foreign expert, in terms of the currently fashionable abstraction, the planet. Here, one can begin to speak about a kind of conspiracy. For all talk of sustainability is, at bottom, a rationale to protect the economy first. Listening to the stories of the old-timers, and looking around me, I saw that as the national economy—with its school, health, insurance, banking and entertainment systems—flourishes in a region, people and places disappear, local economies die, the landscape becomes lonely and barren. When we first started looking for land to buy in this part of the country, we had to pass up some wonderful possibilities that were wildly beautiful and amazingly cheap. There were many long miles between the few remaining houses in these severely depopulated areas. Since the children were not going to school, they would have no companions they could reach on foot.

As I saw the many-faceted encroachment of the economy on the lives of my neighbors and their community, my heart was filled with sadness. After years of such close association with them, sharing in their hopes and disappointments, their joys and their sorrows, I felt a great affection for them. From many signs, I saw that we had come to love one another. I would always be the outsider—I was not born there—but this did not prevent them from taking me into their hearts. Thinking about this I came to understand that a great affection, a sensual love, is necessary that there be the practice of agriculture. This feeling and sentiment, a deep attachment to a way of life, emanate directly from one's familiarity with a place, its inhabitants, all its domestic and wild attributes. Such familiarity takes time—usually, generations. I had only hit upon its necessity when I first came here because of my very ignorance.

Rural space, if untouched, is always beautiful, always wondrous. When populated with a rooted people whose principal bond to their land is one of affection, such space can still shine with a marvelous radiance. But when affection is absent, dishevelment inevitably comes to reign. Then one sees the disaster of dead and decayed rural space. This is quite different from modern, undifferentiated space, that found in most institutions, like airports and supermarkets. This kind of architectural space has the totally sterile smell of technological death. Rural space, once it has been touched by human presence, needs the fruitful warmth of a community's affection or it deteriorates like any unloved creature.

In this somber mood, I attempted to ask the question: How can someone reject an economic and industrial mode of production in farming? And this immediately led to another question: What is agriculture anyway? The only sure way to answer this, I thought, was to look at those farmers who have resisted colonization. It should appear obvious, I think, that land is not there to be exploited by outsiders, nor are farmers working the land in order to make distant cities rich—in spite of the fact that such a situation obtains in much of the world today. What have others, through millennia, done before us?

My initial insight, when I first came to this place, seemed to lead me toward the answer. Familiarity, which I recognized as a first and necessary step to become a farmer, appeared to be the key source for the continual practice of agriculture. Without an intimate knowledge of one's land—which means its soil and its people—one could not hope to be a farmer for very long.

Taking into consideration what occurs in the rural areas of today's world, is it possible to specify the element or means leading to familiarity? From my observation and experience, I think it is. Familiarity will be more intimate and true as one increases the amount of hand labor and decreases machine or hired labor.

Two historical threads also lead to this conclusion. The introduction of the tractor, the removal of the farmer's feet from a soil, constituted a historical break with a definite before and after. A person's relation to a soil was thereby radically altered. The farmer was put in a place that, over the years, removed him further each generation from the customary familiarity he had enjoyed—with his soil and with his community. This loss of carnal touch permitted and led to other losses: The loss of a sense of living within certain rhythms—of the seasons, of one's neighbors, of one's own body, of the cosmos; in sum, loss of a sense of creatureliness, of living within strict limits.

The other thread is a fault that runs through Western history: the idea of servile labor. After classical Greece, people in the West who attempted to understand the human situation generally believed in a kind of hierarchy: the work of the mind was above the work of the body. A major aspect of the genius of Saint Benedict was his devastatingly sharp and profound vision; his idea for healing this fault is caught in the Latin expression, *orare et laborare*. The work of the spirit might be named first in the formula, but the two actions were to be coordinate, one complementing the other, one incomplete without the other. As the history of monasticism sadly shows, the West was not ready to accept such a radical idea. With very few exceptions, from Benedict's time to our own, the monasteries and convents have continually reverted to the Greek fallacy: the "pure" intellectual life is higher, nobler. Now, perhaps, as the West experiences unprecedented kinds of bewilderment and perversion in the use of both one's hands and one's head, the moment has arrived to reexamine the anthropological error, thereby opening the way to heal America's, and the world's "hidden wound."

The flight from hand labor, the exaltation of "white collar" work, the addiction to urban "closeness," the mania for devising so-called labor saving machines, have obviously, I would argue, reached a dead end. A neighbor told me one day, "As a boy, I worked with horses. Today, I am as mechanized and computerized as I can get. I cover a lot more ground than I did then, but I'm probably more tired, too, at the end of the day." On that occasion, he did not mention how much he is in debt. After that conversation, he was forced to sell some of his land and to take a full-time job in a distant town in order to pay his debts and stay on his remaining land, a farm that has been in the family for over a hundred years—in America, a long time. . . .

Simone Weil, out of a deeply rooted experience of her own country, France, in the midst of World War II, wrote:

> The unhappy peoples of the European continent are in need of greatness even more than of bread, and there are only two sorts of greatness: true greatness, which is of a spiritual order, and the old, old lie of world conquest. . . .

> The contemporary form of true greatness lies in a civilization founded upon the spirituality of work. . . .
>
> But one can only lay hold of such a conception in fear and trembling. How can we touch it without soiling it, turning it into a lie? Our age is so poisoned by lies that it converts everything it touches into a lie. And we are of our age. . . .
>
> [Physical labor] is an answer to the uneasy feelings of all people at the present time. Everybody is busy repeating, in slightly different terms, that what we suffer from is a lack of balance, due to a purely material development of technical science. This lack of balance can only be remedied by a spiritual development in the same sphere, that is, in the sphere of work.

My experience modestly, but exactly, certainly, confirmed what Simone Weil wrote in 1943. She wrote before nuclear insanity was publicly revealed, before technology *cum* consumption polluted the entire planet, before the fraud of virtual reality, before international financial speculators affected *everyone* who in some way is plugged into the economy. My experience, then, nicely filled out a detail of Weil's position. Nature, the other, in short, reality, can only be respected through familiarity. Familiarity, as the condition *sine qua non* of an agriculture, only grows out of hand labor. Further, agriculture may be the primordial place, a prime exemplar, to teach us the character and necessity of hand labor.

Formerly, such work was recognized as both necessary and good—good because necessary. I learned that this labor genuinely *counts*, not just to know and cultivate the land well, but to be a neighbor. Often someone needed, not another machine, but a helping hand. "Can I give you a hand?" spoken to my neighbors, opened the way to a genuine intimacy with them, together with the customs and lore of the place. I believe that we were warmly welcomed into that community precisely because we often came forward "to lend a hand." Once, a neighbor's five thousand tomato plants had to be set out, by hand, that day. One Sunday morning, while returning from the village church, I noticed some unusual activity at a farm down the road from my place. This man's cow had slipped in the mud, fallen into the creek while calving, and could not get out by herself. Together, we were able to save the cow. On another day, I noticed an approaching storm and knew that my neighbor in the other direction was making hay. With my help, we were able to get the hay in the barn before the rain hit. I would need many pages to relate all such incidents, especially the times neighbors came to rescue us from our ignorance or folly. Through them all we came to know and be known, and so able to participate in the work of that place, the human work of that community.

All these connections that the practice of agriculture entailed, binding me to a land, a family, friends and neighbors, taught me how to insert myself in the temporal world. While living in the industrial economy, I found myself continually pushed toward possession: *my* house, *my* time, *my* career, *my* children. And so I lived in frustration; confident and sure possession is impossible. But relations in an agricultural community are of a very different character. First, everything moves in cycles: the seasons of the year, of plants, of animals and people. All ends in death, yet birth is ever-recurring. This is especially evident if one is not trapped in monoculture, but cultivates a variety of crops and cares for different animals. In daily contact with the wonders and mysteries of the natural world, one simply cannot imagine the kind of control that possession demands. To live off a land, from animals, with people, requires a delicate balance of work and care, in accord with natural rhythms, but fully aware that I am not in control, that I am only a creature. In these kinds of actions, great intimacy can be enjoyed, but I end up recognizing my dependence, humbled before the workings of the universe. In short, agriculture can teach one how *to be* in this world, how to be fully and joyfully alive to this moment and, simultaneously, peacefully resigned to the fact that my death lies just beyond.

Those for whom I came to have the greatest respect in that community were the most conservative persons. In spite of my liberal academic training, I was able to recognize the truth and beauty of their lives. Much of their time was dedicated to a two-fold activity: conserving the land and conserving the stories. And both efforts require much time! They were patient and careful farmers, always seeking to replenish the soil they obviously loved. They were also solicitous for the community's memory, making the effort to inform their children well, not with the latest "news," but with the stories of this place.

These actions of conservation constitute the very source of what is usually called culture: they make possible graceful human living in a place over time. Culture, then, is not to be divided into high and low, but into its plural incarnations. The soil and the stories of each place are different. Thus, to understand culture, one must come to see its specificity, its "narrow" local character, its sensuality. Anything beyond immediate sense experience and a community's memory of particular people and events is an abstraction, cannot be a people's culture. To know and experience this limited, "small" world is to be alive in the way given to men and women who are still in the realm of time.

Finally, I came to see that small-scale subsistence farming opens one to an awareness of the *genius loci*. Each place has its protective spirit. One does not have to travel to Tibet or other so-called exotic regions to experience the unique power and beauty of a place. The poets have spoken truthfully: To know a place is to be captured by its spirit-demon and hence to live there in awe and reverence, in humility and gratitude.

4

The Last Farms in America

He told them another parable: "The kingdom of heaven is like a mustard seed, which a man took and planted in his field. Though it is the smallest of all your seeds, yet when it grows, it is the largest of garden plants and becomes a tree, so that the birds of the air come and perch in its branches."

Matthew 13:31–32

I had just buried my father. Now, on the five-hour drive home, I felt attacked by conflicting images and thoughts. On either side of the highway, fields stretched out to the horizon, containing some of the most fertile soil on the planet. Today, I would see about 250,000 acres of crops. They were up, the corn about two-feet high already. Now and then I could look down the perfect rows, a marvel of straight lines, uniform distances between rows, and no weeds. Was this really the work of flesh and blood farmers? Or the imposition of some gigantic green stamping machine? Field after field: corn and soy beans, soy beans and corn. The monotony was only rarely broken by a patch of wheat or oats, or a lonely pasture with some cattle. If I searched carefully, I could sometimes discern a kitchen garden next to the infrequent roadside farmhouses. This was not a land where one is greeted early by cocks crowing and then, like echoes returning from an endless space, hearing soft answering shrieks from the neighbors'. An eerily silent landscape, except when the huge tractors are crisscrossing the fields.

The myriad thoughts and images kept me alert throughout the tire-somely prosaic drive. I sometimes think that sky-diving and bungee-jumping are direct responses to the dullness and boredom of modern means that move us across or over the earth. The passing fields, re-peating themselves, reminded me that my father had wanted to buy a farm. But just then, at that very moment, an unexpected memory shock shook me; I realized that his wish was lifelong . . . and never fulfilled. Is that somehow connected to the fact that I left my urban job at the age of fifty and moved to the country, to put my hand to "farm-ing"? . . . But what is the relationship between scientifically engineered seed producing military parade ground precision and farming? . . . Re-cently, a neighbor complained bitterly that his crops, doing very well this year, will not bring in enough to cover his operating costs. . . . But the rows look so clean, the bugs obviously all dead. . . . Some claim that this mode of using the soil, now predominant throughout Amer-ica, is destroying the physical basis for an agriculture faster than any known historical despoliation of a people's habitat. . . . The life-giving sun, how long will it patiently wait? . . . I notice numerous accounts in the media about something called a crisis in the economy of agricul-ture, and panic fear about the possible disappearance of the family farm. . . . Yet I know farm families. . . . Are they just barely hanging on? . . . To what folly have I devoted myself?

Disquieting thoughts, confusing images. But still, there is a soil out there, beyond the highway ditches. And I knew, from my own experi-ence of now living directly on a soil, that it could strongly impress my sensibilities, my spirit, as it has affected others, too. I immediately thought of the poet Gerard Manley Hopkins. After reading his poem, "The Windhover," one could never forget the power of the soil image at its end, in juxtaposition with falling embers, expressing the experi-ence of beauty possible for the human spirit who *sees* a soil.

> No wonder of it: shéer plód makes plough down sillion
> Shine, and blue-bleak embers, ah my dear,
> Fall, gall themselves, and gash gold-vermilion.

The bright green growths obediently and bravely proclaimed the flow-ering of yet another annual cycle in the living mystery of nature, a movement that, in human terms, could go on forever. What *was* I see-ing about me? A deceptive chimera? An earth-shattering struggle be-tween organic nature and industrial chemicals? Perhaps the produc-tion system's product I saw on each side of me had already lock-stepped too far in its robotic march into a world of unnatural monstrosities; now it was too late to lose sleep over the coming plague of the bioge-netic engineers.

Then, suddenly, an idea seemed very clear to me: in these quarter of a million acres I had not seen a single farm! Rather, I saw a mechanized and chemicalized landscape, the industrialization of what used to be the human activity of agriculture. The modern mania for control and profit had transformed a ten-thousand-year-old way of living into nu-merous discrete commercial and technological actions that, knowl-edgeable persons point out, lead inevitably to the utter impoverish-ment of whatever soil and people still remain in the countryside.

How do I understand, and then articulate, what occurs? It would seem, ultimately, to require a cosmic moral sense. But a moral sense directly implies either virtuous or vicious action. Today, however, some speak seriously about the "end of virtue" in the West. Others point out that contemporary philosophers have great difficulty con-structing a rational ethics. Traditional concepts, beliefs, and practices seem hopelessly muddled. Whether I look at the academy or at public and private behavior among the populace, I find a bitter sort of con-tentiousness, an eagerness to point the finger . . . there, at that one. Moralism abounds, but moral vision and courage are much more diffi-cult to find. Perhaps the often-cited insight of Yeats,

> Things fall apart; the centre cannot hold;
> Mere anarchy is loosed upon the world[,]

fits even better today than when he wrote. I suspect that those who indulge in nostalgic sadness are partly right: much of what I feared and respected, honored, and rejected when I was young seems lost; there remain only scattered and unconnected remnants; what was formerly judged wisdom is now patent anachronism.

Further, as some have noted, one can also speak about the "death of nature" in the West. Traditional peoples not only reverenced their nat-ural surroundings as being alive but also supplicated the spirits who dwelt there. I would guess that few people today—except for those generally regarded as being marginal—pay careful heed to the spirit or gods who dwell in each place. And yet I have always felt that if a person reads Plato's *Phaedrus*, he or she could not fail to be moved to belief after reflecting on the prayer of Socrates at the end of the dia-logue, a petition offered up to "Beloved Pan, and all ye other gods who haunt this place."

Surely there are some connections here: the world of philosophy stumbling to construct a rational argument making sense of the practice of virtue; the idea found in both popular and "serious" thought questioning the position that looks at the earth as unfeeling matter, merely a place for the unlimited realization of men's "dreams of reason"; the neat rows of sterile green stalks, parading as plants, on each side of the highway. Although many today seek to break themselves up into even more separate pieces, and although one hears much talk about the disintegration of society or culture, continuities often reveal surprising strengths. How to recognize true breaks? I suspect, for example, that there is a historical moment when farming ceases to be a way of living and becomes just another industrial occupation. The break can occur in the life of a person or of a nation. The historical periodization of this transformation is the task of a nation's intellectuals. Now it seems evident to me that my father's dream, rooted in the experiences of his peasant ancestors in Europe, was indeed foreign, not to America, but to modern ways of working and living on the land.

That night, far from the highway, alone in the quiet of my remote home, I thought again about the media reports. From what I had read, they were unanimous: there is a farm crisis in America. But what if these writers have seen nothing of what is out there? What if contemporary cultural filters have effectively blinded them? What if there are no farms left in America? . . . except for those few that are treated as folkloric curiosities or sentimental throw-backs, picturesque settings for a Disney film. What if the subject of the well-intentioned urban literati is not a farm at all, but only another industrial enterprise? I now feel that the reports, like so much in the media, serve more to provide employment to their producers than to speak the complex truth about worrisome political policies.

The stories always cite specific farmers who are in "economic" trouble; those who are found to be doing well are presented as *economic* successes. It seems that, ultimately, the bottom line is not only relevant, but the all-important and all-inclusive factor. The writers further accept certain features as givens: the modern economy, with its predominant emphasis on profitability, thereby optimizing efficiency and rationality, is never questioned; all farm work is to be organized in terms of a market—however distant, uncertain or even non-existent; the farmer has to imagine himself a modern businessman producing and selling a commodity; this man, although often a de facto employee, is idealized as a rational manager. The fields I had passed faithfully reflected these historically freakish assumptions. Careful reading of the stories revealed that distant and alien experts—from government, land-grant universities, large corporations, and financial institutions—defined agriculture in terms of textbook abstractions, engineering problems, technological novelties, and political policy, domestic and foreign. From under all the rational, scientific rhetoric of these calm and clear-sighted analysts, the slimy passion of the huckster oozed out—a subtle, but proselytizing appeal to the farmer's greed. If he only acted according to their ideas and prescriptions, he would become rich; otherwise, inevitable failure, for which he would have only himself to blame.

So much for mainstream public information and comment. Now, how get around this? How learn if there is any truth in these experts? To do this, I needed to reach a place that would give me another language, even an entirely different world. Farming has not always been what I had seen from my car window. That is a very recent Western invention. World literature reveals a far broader, also more complex, panorama. From Genesis, for example, I see that a man and woman's relationship to the soil is fraught with mystery. The religiocultural practices of all peoples, up to the quite recent innovation of scientific farming, richly manifest the various ways different societies have sought to live in this mystery. In drawings of rural life made during the European Middle Ages, I was surprised by the frequency with which the artist portrayed farmers' dances and wedding celebrations. Among the Greeks, Romans, early Europeans, American Indians—to cite only a few possible sources—I came across evidence which indicated that for people in these very different places and times, living from the soil opened one to experience a world that lay far beyond the depths of the human heart. But my initial thoughts and questions were occasioned by specific sensual experiences, not by reflections on books I had read. I now lived in a rural area, among farmers. Why not look at them in the light of my unease?

Most of my neighbors' houses sit close to the road, which can be concrete, "black top" or, like mine, gravel and dirt. Each house is surrounded by a yard. When I first came to live here, I was mildly scandalized noticing that most farm families carefully mowed and trimmed these yards each Saturday, apparently like people I had known in the suburbs! Later I learned that their action flowed from a lifetime of belief and behavior quite foreign to urban experience. For example, every aspect of one small farm down the road a few miles from my place appeared almost obsessively neat. Not only was the grass cut weekly, but one could see no evidence of anything in need of repair, anything out of place, any kind of trash. All outbuildings and fences stood ready for a military white-glove inspection. There was not one item of worn-out and discarded equipment anywhere. The couple who lived there were now quite old. When they started farming, it was only a weekend possibility. They had little money, and they had to remain in town where the husband was employed as a mechanic. But they worked and saved and eventually moved to their small parcel of land as full-time farmers.

I came to know them, visited them, listened to their stories. Slowly, I was able to understand how radically out-of-date these people are today, how embarrassingly out of place they would appear at a modern farm show. The neatness of their yard and farm evidenced a kind of life that, I recognized, was filled with a rare and courageous imagination. For example, I was especially impressed by their large and handsome barn. It seemed to be—and was—much better built than the house. The house was already there when they bought the place; they had continually repaired and fixed it up. But this man had designed and built the barn himself. He first cut down the trees in the nearby forest—his land was hilly and partly forested—hauled the logs out with horses, devised a system of chains and pulleys to lift them to the saw platform, and then cut them into boards . . . himself, alone. The design and workmanship were outstanding. But I only saw these remarkable qualities very superficially; I needed to learn more about the lives behind them to understand what I was seeing.

Shortly after passing this farm, one comes to another barn, a new, much larger one, a modern pole barn, whose sides and roof are thin sheets of steel. The farmer living here selected the size barn he wanted out of a catalog. He placed his order, and the materials—posts, trusses, and sheet steel—arrived on a truck, along with a crew of two men who set it up, ready to use, in a couple of days; one has only to send a check. The two structures look quite different. One is clearly "hand made," the other a product of machines; one reveals the individual character of a person, the other appears what it is: another product of coordinated information systems and suppliers—treated posts from one state, sheet steel from another, cement and sand for setting the posts from yet another, all brought together and delivered as a package to be assembled on the appointed day by workers you would never see again. Looking into the lives of the respective owners, two altogether different pictures are revealed. When I sit down at the kitchen table of one man, I can look forward to an account of modest, yet solid accomplishment; the brightness of his eyes reveals the peacefulness of his spirit. With the other friend, I learn of grander projects, but also about the intricacies of farm debt structure. His eyes often show worry; behind them, creditors loom.

When I opened the equipment shed of the older man, I found it full of "ancient" tools and machinery; these things had been used for many years. But every piece was also perfectly maintained; no rust, all moving parts were coated with grease or oil. Another neighbor told me that the old man took his tractor apart each winter and overhauled it himself. And all his machinery received such care. He had no need for new equipment, no need to abuse his land or increase his acreage in order to earn more, no need to become a businessman. As I came to know him and his wife better, I found that the graceful beauty of their farm was a true reflection of the awful beauty of their lives, lives devoted to hard work, family, and neighborhood church. Their inner integrity always shone out directly from their faces: their eyes reached out to you in a friendly embrace, their features glowed with warmth, their mouths automatically, naturally expressed a smile whenever I met them. It was so refreshing to see old people whose mouths have not settled down into that sad, bitter shape one sees so often. The hardness of my neighbors' lives was transformed into a brightness of deep cheer.

If I looked beyond the large and carefully mowed yard on another farm, I also began to see the outlines of a unique and rare life. The fence along the road, enclosing a very long field, was made with truly formidable posts. A close examination showed what I suspected: they were double-length railroad ties, timbers I could lift only one end at a time. This farmer's son told me that his father had hauled these here many years ago, by himself, on a wagon pulled by horses, from the railroad about ten miles away. Of course, he dug all the fence post holes with a hand augur. When I help farmers build fence today, I find that they invariably use a power-driven augur attached to the back of their tractor when setting wooden posts; and these factory-made posts are generally purchased new. When I picked up free discarded—but still good—railroad ties along the tracks, I faced no competition. I only had to drag them some distance, through weeds and brush, to reach my pickup. I suppose others judged this too much labor; or unthinkingly believed that one must buy everything for landscaping and terracing.

When my neighbor of the recycled fence posts died, his body was taken to a funeral home in the nearby town. It was summer, I was working in my fields, so I went in to pay my respects at the end of the day. When I arrived, I found a slowly moving line of people running out of the distant funeral home and down the sidewalk to the street. I greeted the funeral director whom I knew, "Well, John, it looks as if everyone else did what I did; they worked all day and just now came to town." "No," he answered, "it's been like this all day." I found it hard to believe. This is a sparsely populated area. Where did all the people come from? And how would they know he died? There is no local daily newspaper, only a weekly. Later, I learned that news of the community is broadcast daily on a radio station in the area; everyone listens. The older women also regularly call one another on the phone, maintaining an extensive neighborhood electronic grapevine. The effectiveness of this talking and listening was evident in the numbers of people I saw there at the wake. But picking up pieces of their comments and conversations, I got some sense of *why* they had come. Each had been strongly touched by this man at some time in their lives. The beauty I saw in his fence-making also shined out in many other actions throughout a life lived in this community. He was truly *known* by these people. But the body's appearance in the casket made me catch my breath. His habitual dress gave a distinctive stamp and flavor to his character. In the years I knew him, I never saw him wear anything but overalls, even to church every Sunday. Finally, in the casket, I saw him outfitted in a suit and tie!

This man, along with others I came to know here, seemed to have a unique sense of time and history. For example, he had a large collection of arrowheads and other Indian artifacts. When he farmed with horses, he had the time to look down, to spot these last remains of a lost people come to light as he worked the soil, and to pick them up. His curiosity led him to carefully record where he had found each item. Wanting to learn more about his discoveries, he studied the way Indians hunted and moved in this part of the country. Then, reflecting on the inferences he made from his own experience and observation, he found himself in disagreement with the learned academic historians he had read. Using his own imaginative powers of historical reconstruction, he mounted and labeled all his finds on several large boards and prepared a wonderfully humorous lecture that he would freely give to any group or person asking. But I never heard that anyone from the nearby state university ever came to speak with him about his research, nor to invite him to talk to the students there. His erudition, based principally on perceptive experience and time-ignoring reflection, will only be kept alive in the memory of his family and the people of his immediate community. Academic learning in the "local" institution will remain isolated by its own blinders and prejudices.

After his death, I occasionally dropped in at his home to visit his widow. Sometimes I met the grandchildren there, helping her to keep that huge yard neatly mowed. But she did most of the work herself, maintaining extensive flower and vegetable gardens, and a small flock of chickens. One Saturday, I joked about the yard not really needing to be mowed. I do not remember her exact words in answer. But they were such as to indicate that this action, so widespread among the people of the neighborhood, was a kind of ritual, a symbolic act of cleansing, of preparation for the Sunday service in the local country church, a weekly ceremony of central importance in their lives. I had traveled a great distance from suburban lawn-mowers whose Saturday work meant nothing more significant than bodily weariness, to be relieved by the Sunday labor of reading *The New York Times*!

The distinct character of these peoples' lives, however, cannot be ascribed to something so categorical as clock-time. But one can begin here to enter the space in which they live and move. Several of my neighbors, for example, heat their homes with wood in the winter. Cutting enough wood for heating—and, as I have found, for both heating and cooking—takes some time. If one is cutting green wood, at least a year and a half of waiting for it to dry out before it can be burned. Another farmer I know waited until 1946 before buying his first tractor, although most farmers in America had replaced their horses with tractors years earlier. He still farms with this same piece of machinery, more than forty years later. In his equipment barn, too, I found everything old and worn, but in perfect repair. As another neighbor remarked one day, "If you take care of it and keep it well oiled and greased, some of this old stuff will last forever."

The only man I personally knew who farmed with horses until his death was my maternal grandfather. One of my sharpest childhood memories—I must have been seven or eight—is of the day we went to his farm for threshing the wheat crop. My father took a day off from his job to drive one of the teams, hauling the shocks from the field to the huge, puffing threshing machine. Neighboring farmers had also come with their teams to help. After being threshed, the clean grain had to be transported to a local elevator—by team and wagon. The entire operation had to be completed in one day, since the threshing machine was rented for that day alone, and my grandfather had no storage capacity for the wheat on his farm.

When Grandpa died, Grandma sold the equipment and livestock at an auction. All the living children were daughters, and no one among them was able to continue the farming operation. An important moment for the entire family then occurred, the conclusion of a lifetime of good work on the land, and we children were allowed to skip school to participate in the sad solemnity. A farm auction is one of the richest and most dramatic events in rural America, and the direct and interested participants, I suspect, never forget the emotional impact of the experience. Everyone carries forever vivid and unforgettable memories of that day. Mine remain clear and sharp, over fifty years later: I saw my grandmother cry—as I remember this, it was the first time I had witnessed an adult's tears. And, second, the beautiful team of horses. The auctioneer's assistant led them out of the barn. I distinctly remember hearing several men comment on their strength and excellent condition. They also added, ruefully, that the team would not bring much. Progressive farmers in that part of the country—Central Illinois—were already (by 1939) hooked on the machine myth. Very few—only the most "backward" or sentimental—still worked horses. For most, farming as "a way of life" had ended. These peoples' children would never experience the excitement and neighborly celebration of a day working together in the hot sun, helping one another to bring in a crop. Rather, if they remain on the land at all, their descendants find themselves alone, in the cab of their tractors or corn pickers, late at night, trying to finish a field with the headlights.

Among the memorable images of the more old-fashioned farmers still remaining in our area, one especially continues shining vividly, its sharp outline indelibly engraved in my memory. Late one afternoon I had stopped to see a neighbor now become friend and, shortly after I arrived, he said he had to go down to the barn for a few minutes. Usually, I would have stayed at the house and talked with his wife, a lively conversationalist. But, on impulse, I accompanied him to the barn. He was a man of few words, and I had to ask him what he was doing. It was early spring, and he had a number of new calves. Because it was also cold and windy that day, he had kept the calves in the shelter of the barn while letting the cows out to pasture. By the time we arrived, both the cows and their calves were making a loud and mournful racket with their bawling. My friend had divided the ten or more calves into two groups, each in a separate part of the barn. The impatient cows, massed at the wide barn gate, milled about without ceasing to voice their lament. When he opened the gate, the mothers—to me, huge, frightening, dangerous—rushed together toward their offspring. Standing directly in front of them as they came toward him, my friend had to identify quickly each charging cow and direct her to the proper side of the barn to be reunited with her crying calf. He had only an instant to accomplish this, with frantic animals crowding each other and moving as fast as they could in the general direction of the calves. Calmly standing before this massive onslaught of beef on the hoof, speaking gently and touching them only with his hands, he guided each cow in the right direction. I have seen elaborate acrobatic acts and classical ballet, but I have never been moved so powerfully by the perception of danger and gracefulness joined as on that afternoon. I had heard from other neighbors that this man treated his livestock with exceptional care and gentleness, but I never imagined a scene of such perilous beauty.

Similar actions are repeated each day, in remote nooks, in hidden landscapes, all over the world—the practices of traditional arts and crafts. Once, in Spain, my train stopped for what seemed a long time because workmen were laying the bed for a new super-fast train alongside our track. I looked out the window and saw an older man in his vegetable field. With a slight shock, I realized that I knew exactly what he was doing; I remembered that I, too, had experienced that posture. He was bent double, using a short-handled hoe to weed. He moved slowly and deliberately through the field . . . never straightening up. From my comfortable seat, I wondered: Dare I say that that is beauty? . . . for such it appeared to me. Usually, no outsider or observer is there to see, to record, to report on, the awesome grace of skilled workers. That day with my friend, therefore, is singularly dear to me; I was greatly blessed that spring afternoon.

After these and other such experiences of an unknown, a more veiled America, I came to see that there are farmers quite unlike those usually seen in the media, those who are the subject of high level public discussion, those who are the beneficiaries of the university hired guns. My friends are marginal and modest. They tend to question the assumptions surrounding a belief in economic scarcity. They try to live with a certain independence, that is, they struggle to be free from knowledge capitalists, salesmen, and money lenders. They suspect that chemicals and high-tech "solutions" carry hidden costs, and can seriously interfere with their delicate relationship to land and livestock. They sense that their life as members of a comely community might be jeopardized by a large cash flow—people are still subject to envy and greed. In terms of what generally holds in America today, these people are quite backward—in their perception of "needs" requiring cash.

They have small farms that they work intensively with only that minimum of machinery that, after long consideration, appears to be really necessary to buy. As someone told me about one of them, "If the equipment manufacturers depended on him, they would have gone out of business long ago." Almost all their tools are old and worn, but in excellent condition. Now and then I found an ingenious tool that they themselves had designed and made. None of them practices monoculture; great diversification characterizes their farms. They raise small quantities of various crops, some for home consumption, some for sale. One farmer still picks his corn by hand. He grows enough to feed some calves he raises for market. I always got fresh milk from a friend who kept a cow that gave more milk than his family could themselves consume. Another friend gave me freshly killed venison and wild goose in season. He was an enthusiastic hunter and would kill more than his family needed. "I would crawl on my belly two miles to get a goose," he once told me, laughing. The geese feed in the open fields and it is difficult to approach close enough to get a shot at them.

Jefferson believed that "the small landholders are the most precious part of a state." After my experiences, I agree with him. Some contemporary revisionists, influenced more by certain moralistic rather than moral issues, are critical of Jefferson today, but I wonder whether they have any close knowledge of the world he envisioned: the independent farmer, living close to subsistence—which means as far away from the cash market as possible—living and working in close cooperation with his neighbors. Propaganda from the USDA and the academy is received critically by these people. They have learned to distrust the institution-based expert with his degrees, the deracinated professional who is equally "at home" in Brazil or Missouri. They are the cautious, careful, conservative people you can trust and depend on. Their word alone is always good.

After coming to know the different farmers in my area, I now see that one can speak of two Weberian ideal types. Generally, a farmer will tend toward one or the other with a certain coherence and consistency. People can live off the land, while dwelling in one of two very different worlds: one that is slower, particularistic, smaller, more sensual; or one that is faster, universalistic, larger, more abstract. The difference is clearly seen in a conversation between an older neighbor and myself. I had decided that it was time to get chickens. Having read books about these creatures, I knew that there were different breeds, each with its own characteristics. So I went to this man, spoke of the different types of fowl, and asked him, "What kind of chickens should I get?" In the instant after asking, I saw from his eyes that it was the wrong question; it didn't make any sense to him. I had trained myself to watch peoples' eyes when I asked my sometimes foolish questions, so I was more or less prepared for his reaction. I immediately asked another, "What kind of chickens do you have?" His eyes sparkled and he smiled, "New Hampshire Reds." "Why do you have that kind?" "Because those are what my father had." I decided to forget the books with their definitions and attributes, and listen to my neighbor's experience. I started with New Hampshire Reds. In subsequent years, caring for a small flock of these chickens, I never regretted my decision. Indeed, I came to have a great affection for these particular chickens.

Farmers like this neighbor are immersed in the world of sensible experience, of living historical memory, of a genuine tradition. They instinctively look to the past, recognizing that there is a certain wisdom there; people have learned from their mistakes and have passed on this knowing. Partly because they also depend so much on direct sense knowledge, rather than on instruments and experts, these farmers are acutely aware of the conditions of their land and livestock, their families and community.

They are not usually in debt, an extremely rare situation among American farmers today. One explained to me how he formerly got started each year. He had a field—five acres, I think it was—of asparagus. This was the first plant up in the spring. He harvested the tender spears himself, and shipped the crop to St. Louis each day (at that time, a daily train stopped at a nearby town, picking up various crops from these farmers). This was called "the seed crop" because its sale covered the cost of seed and other expenses at the beginning of the new growing year. Many farmers today get a bank loan each spring . . . and start the year in debt.

The other kind of farming looks to the abstract (non-existent) world of the future. Someone imbued with this outlook believes in research, especially if carried out under laboratory conditions. He readily defers to experts. He generally buys the latest equipment; in addition to its other advantages, it is advertised as "labor-saving." One does not have to do things like repeatedly cutting a field of asparagus, bent over for many hours in stoop labor each morning. However, these farmers are usually heavily in debt and must work long hours, day and night, to pay for all the labor-saving machinery and chemicals.

From reading, and work with my more traditional neighbors, I found that two qualities predominate in their farm work: awe before the wonder, the mystery of growing things, and a cooperation *with* nature.

One easily notices these traits in their speech, sees them in the ways these people treat animals and fields. But among other farmers, I could see a very different stance: attempts to achieve an engineer's control over crops and livestock, a rational plan motivated principally, pointed toward exclusively, by a thirst for profit . . . formerly stigmatized as a moral failing: greed. This is the world served by modern science and technology, ruthlessly imposed on rural America. Its apologists claim that only this system can feed the country. They propagate their new faith in bright packages; the salesmen are clever professionals, devilishly persuasive. So, country people face a peculiarly attractive array of bizarre temptations.

In addition, cultural sensibilities, whose historic origins can be traced at least to classical Greece, are skewed and contorted into one stereotype. Nearly all Americans carry within themselves a collection of derogatory and scurrilous images. Rural, distinguished from urban areas, are regarded as the land of the hayseed, the hick. Popular humor and the media are almost universally unrelieved in their portrayal of the more traditional farmer as the comically stupid country bumpkin. Farmers are tempted to escape this perverse and cruel defamation through the adoption of technologically sophisticated methods of production. They must then try to manipulate the wondrously complex processes of living organisms as if they were isolated and inert chemicals in a controlled laboratory—for their own self-respect. The name for this: scientific farming—inevitably, a contradictory, suicidal hoax. The methods of modern science are too simplistic, too artificial, too dependent on laboratory control to be applied to an art so complex, so respectful of nature's laws and vagaries, so important for the exciting drama of a community life. The scientific project is guided by the principles of business management for profit—necessarily a formula for the destruction of the land, its people, its local communities and, ultimately, the very nation itself, its body and soul.

In earlier ages, some who were both greedy and lazy were able to become rich off the land through the ownership of slaves. Up to the middle of the eighteenth century, slaves and serfs appeared to belong to the natural order of society. One hundred years later, landowners in the United States and Russia were forced to give up these forms of compulsory labor. In the meantime, however, various kinds of wage slavery were devised, with the result that a relative few continued to get rich from the labor of many others. Except for a few sectors—notably, much vegetable and fruit culture—American agriculture did not imitate the industrialists by establishing a form of wage slavery on the land. Instead, chemicals, machines and scientific management were designed to replace human labor—and they did. The farm population of the United States dropped dramatically in this century. One of the most massive movements of people in history occurred . . . some claim, peacefully. Today, only a minuscule proportion of the population works directly on the land—hardly enough for the Census Bureau to count them! But can one still speak of a farm? A farmer? In most instances, I strongly doubt it—at least, in any traditional understanding of the concept. In this instance, truth is found in tradition rather than in innovation.

In America, the very glut of agricultural commodities suggests that few farms remain. One can now detail some of the costs of the kind of production that results in these surpluses. Such costs lead to a clear conclusion: A farmer would not do to his soil, his livestock, his family, himself, what has been done through the industrialized exploitation of our commons. The soil, together with its living creatures, makes up a commons. No one can appropriate this to himself; nor can one abuse it. But, throughout much of America, this common wealth has come to be the possession of ever fewer people. As the expropriation processes proceeded, this rich heritage became progressively more remote from the lives of urban Americans. They "knew" it only from their car windows or TV screens. The measure of contemporary blindness can be gauged by the lack of outcry against the alienation of land, against the destruction of the soil's tilth, against the torture of animals in confinement structures and feedlots. Perhaps the proper term for this blindness is morbidity; the people suffer from moral obtuseness.

The sterile appearance itself of fields filled with chemically produced crops, the conversion of land into a pseudo-factory for ever greater yields, would raise questions and doubts for a farmer. He knows that great violence is required that fields be forced to take on such a "clean" look. He also knows that the fields and forests of nature never move toward impoverishment. A good farmer's do not, either. What kind of work produced what I saw along the highway? That I hear late at night when a tractor is kept going, no matter the hour? Industrial man has to work long hours, pay dearly for chemicals, fuel, and equipment, in order to deplete and finally destroy his land and himself. Farming, however, requires a much lighter touch, a more subtle approach, something akin to my friend's soft voice and gentle handling of his cattle. It demands an especially nuanced intelligence, imagination, a strong moral character, humility.

There is a queer illusion abroad among some politicians and commentators. When I hear their opinion, I am tempted to react with impatient contempt. They state apodictically that the brightest and most ambitious people abandon the drudgery and boredom [sic!] of rural life for the opportunities and excitement of the city. The truth, I suggest, is not so simplistic. What would urban people do if all the packaged entertainment—theaters, shopping centers, museums, sports events, art galleries, music, and an assortment of clubs and spectacles—were to close? Yes, the city does provide many forms of passive distraction, many varieties of therapies, many kinds of drugs. But the land offers the possibility for experiences like the one I enjoyed that afternoon in my neighbor's barn. I had learned to make time to drop in on the conservatives and old-timers, men and women, when I could. The stories they told evoked a world now largely disappeared, a world that, from my limited experience, appears wonderfully attractive and appealing, a world from which, perhaps, one could still wrest the remnants.

Among these more traditional farmers, I never met one who showed any indication of being bored. Indeed, I saw that they constantly confronted combinations of weather, land, crops and animals that required all the intelligence one possessed, an imagination rich enough to sense the possibilities, a virtue strong enough to do what one knew from a living tradition to be right, a rigorous self-control over the fears and passions that tempt all to fall into ambition and greed, illusion and self-indulgence.

In the media, farmers are often conceptualized and divided up in a strange fashion. They are looked at in terms of something called success, then simplistically placed in one of the two obvious categories. All this is done according to strictly economic criteria; sadly, the kind that count most with so many. From observing the people who live in my area, I suspect that one can roughly dichotomize, but the division occurs differently. There are those who turn themselves into the pawns of outside experts, and those who resist. A cruel irony comes to light when one realizes that the bureaucrats from government, university, manufacturer, bank are, in a disastrously real sense, parasitical blood-suckers living off those who do the *work* of farming. Once farmers succumb to the blandishments of a modern economy, they must turn themselves into rapacious exploiters of land and livestock, their very selves, in order to support this multitudinous throng of middlemen, many of whom constitute a horde of unscrupulous freeloaders. An idyllic garden of delight imagined by some urban sentimentalists has been, for many, a macabre dance of death.

But, as I look around, I see some vital signs of life—a few nonmodern, more traditional farmers remain. Curiously, these people seldom appear in the media; their stories are largely or completely unknown. Or, if a feature is done on one, he is noted as a rare exception, perhaps as a genial eccentric, generally as folklore from some distant past. For example, reports on the Amish do not present theirs as a way of life to be reflected on today by every American who has asked the question: Is there something beyond traffic, employment, career, the urban scene? Is some radically different kind of life possible today? Few point out that these quiet, modest, hard-working, "unambitious" people may be America's outstanding collective example of family farms gracefully thriving in quiet rural communities. One must be careful, however, not to idealize, not to falsify, these flesh and blood people . . . they are still human.

The day to day experience of these families who, for many in America, are hopelessly backward and narrow, incarnate certain truths about the realization of the good, the experience of beauty on this earth that far transcend the visible surface reality of their lives. Their very marginality makes possible the practice of a living wisdom from which all the nation could drink. In fact, modern society, in its ridiculous gaucheries and pathetic debaucheries, stands in desperate need of seeing and somehow touching certain experiences that are the common daily round of some landed families. This need goes much deeper than the issues of soil erosion, poisonous chemicals, bio-engineering, overcapitalization and specialization, and Jefferson's dream of a democratic polity in this country.

Among the principal images of the Western tradition are the metaphors enlivening and enriching the imaginations of my neighbors, the myths shaping their moral character, contained in certain stories or jokes. These speak of a vine and its branches, of a mother hen and her chicks, of a mustard seed that grows into a tree, of leaven in bread dough, of seed that remains sterile unless it falls into the ground and dies. One hears of a shepherd who searches for a lost sheep. . . . But these figures, when first proposed to portray a way of living, were based on the immediate and daily experiences of the hearers; they were *lived* metaphors, not literary, allusive abstractions. As I have learned, there are still people, two thousand years later, for whom these images are vitally alive, whose lives are informed by the truth of the stories partly because of the resonances felt and repeated each day. These are not mythical legends merely recounted in the Book. Rather, the tales are acted out in the daily events that give substance and character to their lives.

Metaphors can be powerful, and a good deal has been written about the ruling metaphors of an age. But no one seriously includes any of the above among them today, except sometimes in the ironic ridicule heaped on so-called religious fanatics by secular liberals. I would argue that the beauty and goodness of my neighbors' lives—individually, and as members of families and communities—illustrates the truth of these ancient parables. Further, their way of working and living reveals to them, and strengthens in them, the wisdom of the truth in the myths. Should everyone, then, seek to become a traditional farmer? No, neither personal vocation nor societal possibility permit such a drastic simplification. Among every group of people and in every sector of society there is always the possibility of truth and honor. But the history of the West and reflection on the activity itself suggest that farmers and farming possess a certain fundamental or primary character among the forms of settled living on the earth. We have stories in our tradition pointing to events in this way of life that reveal transcendent truths. Therefore, the humorless mechanization and destructive practices that characterize so much of American agriculture today call for a clear rebuttal: people need not live such a diminished and mean existence. Our Western history teaches a different way; another, earthy wisdom exists . . . and it is accessible, not in any esoteric gnosis, but in some quite common experiences of a traditional farm.

Within the Church there is a tradition that a community of faith could not exist without some enclaves of silence and prayer, sometimes found in monasteries and convents. There is an even more ancient Hebrew tradition that God refrains from destroying a wicked society for the sake of a few just men. In a gross, material sense, no society can exist unless someone works to grow food. There is now enough evidence to show that too many people have been forced off their farms, too much poison has been dumped on the land, too many have no knowledge of the historical activity of farming. But where there is a will to make a new beginning in America, individually or collectively, inspiring examples for emulation and imitation still exist . . . out there . . . some rather hidden, some disappearing, some only in the memory of the old folks.

5

From Science to Poetry

What is all this talk about radioactivity in the milk and wheat of the middle west? My feeling is that we should be like the three children in the fiery furnace, singing canticles to the Lord. If we take up any deadly thing it shall not hurt us.

Dorothy Day

Rachel Carson's *Silent Spring* changed my perception of the world. To judge from the recent number and intensity of public events, warnings of crises by experts, media reports, political fights over policy proposals, others' perceptions, too, have been changed. All this interest and activity centers on the ecological problem, sometimes expressed as "saving the planet." But that's a rather large, unwieldy project, quite beyond my understanding. So, after many days of thinking about how the so-called crisis touches me, I came to believe that my neighbor had inadvertently showed me the way. He was a farmer in the hill country of Southern Illinois, a man living in a marginal—some would say, backward—area of the country. We were standing between his barn and the house, looking out over the surrounding hills, partly covered by forest, and he asked, "What will I leave my children?"

In an immediate, material sense, he referred to the soil on his farm, the extremely thin soil of those hills. This kind of land, because heavy, sudden downpours—called "gullywashers"—are a regular occurrence, is especially susceptible to the inevitable erosion resulting from conventional row-crop farming. Yet there are some farmers in the area who seem not to notice such soil loss, just as there are many urban Americans who continually travel from one office to another, from one house or apartment to another, from one city to another, with no thought or feeling for place, for the possible loss of place. Being in one's proper place is surely as important as soil remaining in its field.

Meanwhile, some clergy, politicians, students, scientists and "ordinary" citizens have commited themselves with enthusiasm and zeal to the work of rescuing the planet. I, too, have been moved by the warnings, and the many fine examples of dedicated action. But the reports themselves, and the analyses, also have left me feeling uneasy. I wondered whether I've learned anything that "makes sense." Puzzling over this, I reflected on the remark of my neighbor, together with other experiences of the last few years among the people of this rural community. Listening attentively to friends and neighbors here, I noticed that their perspective and perceptions were quite different from what generally reverberates through the world of modern communications.

Almost every new public report or demand for action is based upon a scientific analysis of nature. The serious sectors of the ecological movement rely on science, that is, on one historically contingent view of "what is" and how one should think about it. Science is not neutral or "objective," as people are not neutral or objective. To think otherwise is to lose oneself in delusion. Every scientific proposition, insofar as it really says something, implies a stance, a moral position. To deny this is to acknowledge the poverty of one's imagination. In other periods and societies, different views are found, many having little or nothing in common with modern Western science. And some voices today argue for views that, they claim, are more inclusive than that of conventional science. But it was the example of my neighbors' lives that finally led me to think that I should try to find a way to stand outside the scientific worldview rather than to attempt to distinguish between good and bad, relevant and irrelevant science. In fact, I came to believe strongly that science itself is an important and integral part of the ugly morass in which the world finds itself; that is, science has contributed hugely to the deteriorated earth. Further, it has been a scientific perspective that has hindered me from seeing the connections that made this devastation inevitable, and then has prevented me from acting wisely.

Most contemporary actions to save the planet flow from science, that is, the actions are rationalized in terms of a prior scientific finding and analysis. This means that when I look at what is "out there," I must imagine a complex array of interrelated, interlocking systems. Such a view can establish an empirical connection between my action of turning on an electric light and—if he should ever come to exist— my great-, great-, great-, great-grandchild getting zapped by leaking radioactive waste (originally produced by the atomic energy plant that supplies electricity to my house). Or the connection between my enjoyment of a banana and a rise in the incidence of cancer among the children of a certain village in Costa Rica. My bug-free banana is an industrial product whose existence required the use of certain chemicals in a plantation next to the village. These chemicals are not harmless.

A few centuries ago, before the development of modern science, people only *believed* in connections—they had no scientific proof of them. For example, between the configuration of stars at the moment of my birth and subsequent events in my life. Or a peculiar quality in an old woman's eye when she looked at you, and your later misfortune. Significantly, there was also a certain congruence between belief and behavior since people acted in accord with these beliefs. It is not a tautology to state that the beliefs were truly beliefs. Today, paradoxically, it appears that almost no one accepts the scientifically established connections, and fewer act on them. For example, scientific studies themselves, carried out with accepted, rigorous methodology, establish that conventional scientific agriculture does not work; it degrades the soil, water, and living creatures affected by it. But the near-universal reaction is to introduce new and more advanced scientific treatments; no basic change is considered. Although science helped mightily to advance the destruction of the common habitat, it is powerless to effect a rescue. The situation is vaguely similar to what occurred in the communist countries of Eastern Europe in the 1980s. Neither the official authorities nor the common followers believed in the ideology any longer; it had lost all power to motivate action.

It is in this context that I see a tendency today for the scientific view to coalesce around the position that systems are "designed" to support or maintain something called life. And life is assumed to possess some supreme value. For the sake of life, then, expert prescription can impose universal, that is, system-wide remedies if science finds them necessary. Against this new, ever more inclusive rational and scientific model of the way things are, there is no possibility for public debate. The experts lay down their directives as orthodox dogma for a secular salvation. How argue against life? Who knows enough to dispute expert opinion? Such a situation gives new power both to the ideology—as a means of social control—and to the ideologues (the scientists)—that they might continue to enjoy their accustomed perquisites.

To the extent that people acquiesce in the imposition of a scientific systems view of reality, to that extent a democratic society becomes impossible. Expert scientific opinion is contemptuous of lay efforts to control one's life and that of one's community. Witness the enlightened frenzy over creationism. According to the scientists, people should not be allowed the freedom to protect their children from what they regard as error; they are too stupid. Further, if reality is a set of scientifically derived systems, then system maintenance is primary; there is no free space for messy democratic movements. At the moment, scientific leadership in the country attempts to push public policy in this antidemocratic direction. One can see, on the horizon, the possibility of a peculiar kind of totalitarianism, with technocratic elites in control. Of course, America is already far advanced along this road. But I must lower my eyes, and look at what lies before me. I want to see how, from the perspective of the daily rounds of my farm chores, I can confront these issues, for all knowledge begins with the particular.

In the historic record, one can read of the changes, including flip-flops, among those who have pretended to know "how things are." Further, the fact that at least three very different concepts, no one of which is clearly understood, are convoluted in today's systems model does not inspire much confidence. First, the very nature of science itself is disputed as never before in history. Second, "life" is a strange, rather bastardly concept, derived partly from religion and partly from biology. Third, although the word "survival" is generally preferred, the intent is to secure a secular salvation. The meaning of this, too, is unclear. "The survival of life through science," if examined coldly, is at best confusing because of the problematical character of its three substantive concepts.

Quite independently from the dictates of science, many public-spirited citizens now agree: the earth's inhabitants must begin to think about self-limitation, restraint, conservation, all under the umbrella concept of sustainability. There is no agreement, however, on who should seek less, nor on the question, "less of what?" . . . with one possible exception: commentators living comfortably in the North, looking southward, generally speak about too many people . . . there. But the affluent of both North and South—the chief culprits in the eco-catastrophe scenario—show few if any signs of a disposition to cut back, to seek a much more modest mode of living. Hence, some concerned public figures, their eyes turned toward the possibility of a future on this planet, now suggest that the sacred be invoked—sometimes conceptualized as God—as a transcendent imperative to impose moral brakes on insatiable appetites and maniacal ambitions.

The more careful of such proposals do not, *prima facie*, naively suggest an up-dated version of a state church, something that grew out of the Edict of Milan. The European experience, however, is a terrible warning. In 313, Christianity was tolerated in the Roman Empire, but not yet made the official religion. Then, within a few years, Constantinian legislation gave powers of jurisdiction to bishops; they could hear cases, and their verdicts were fully recognized by the civil authority. As Simone Weil points out so bluntly, the brutal authoritarianism of the Romans then infected the Church. The modern version of totalitarianism finds its origin in these years. In the succeeding centuries, the Church has repeatedly legitimated or quietly tolerated the imposition of every kind of cruel and arbitrary regime. This history lies in wait for the unwary reformer. One does not have to believe in the immanence of "The Second Coming" to shudder in fright when reading the last lines of Yeats's powerful poem:

> somewhere in the sands of the desert
> A shape with lion body and the head of a man,
> A gaze blank and pitiless as the sun,
> Is moving its slow thighs, while all about it
> Reel shadows of the indignant desert birds.
> The darkness drops again; but now I know
> That twenty centuries of stony sleep
> Were vexed to nightmare by a rocking cradle,
> And what rough beast, its hour come round at last,
> Slouches towards Bethlehem to be born?

In the fourth century, the basic groundwork was laid for men of the West to use religion for secular ends and secular power for religious ends. In either case, there was a corruption of faith, and the destruction of the social conditions necessary for a community of faith. The "pure and undefiled religion" advocated by the Apostle James (Jas. 1:27) became more and more rare. Further, one would never end counting up the victims of regimes invoking religion, explicitly or implicitly, to justify their horrors.

The story must be faced. The historical costs, for both religion and society, have been great. Repeatedly, in diverse ways, from that time until today, people professing faith in the Christian God have fallen into the awful sin of using God. In men's hands, the cross has supported the sword to conquer and destroy enemies at home and foreigners abroad. God has been invoked to "purify" the cultures of numerous pagan peoples. Divine "truth" has been invoked as demanding that society demonize sociopolitical movements—most recently, modern communism—thereby encouraging and justifying some of the worst human torture ever recorded. Vast care and service systems, begun under religious inspiration, have turned into monster machines that destroy the dignity of individuals, the bonds of family, the generosity of friendship, the initiatives of community. Who has not agonized seeing a parent, friend, or neighbor fall into the cold and unfeeling embrace of a professional care institution? These peculiarly modern cruelties find their origins in a religious impulse, in a desire "to serve" God.

Although the latest and seemingly benevolent version of these perverse projects is proposed by high-minded persons who make no claim to be "doing God's will," the Western experience stands there—to remind and caution us. I have heard of an appeal to the beliefs common to the principal world religions. From these it is hoped that an ethic can be constructed, a universally valid philosophy to save the planet. I fear that all such efforts will end as an ideology in the hands of those who have greatest access to the international media—the cosmopolitan concerned intellectuals . . . and from there to some political authority, to be imposed on all the rest of us . . . all for our own good, of course.

Further, the invocation of the sacred means that God becomes necessary that secular man and woman survive at all, that there continue to be a history. God becomes the supremely useful hypothesis. One acts "as if God exists," grotesquely contradicting the famous phrase of Dietrich Bonhoeffer, "Etsi Deus non daretur." For a traditional person, such a position is patently blasphemous. For a modern, it should be recognized as dangerous. I am amazed at the rapidity with which some highly trained leading lights of faith communities rashly join the enthusiasts proclaiming "theologies" of the ecosystem. Have these people never studied theology? Or read history? Have they never examined the history of scientific thought? Do they know nothing of the sociology of scientific concepts and theories? The history of both theological and scientific thought amply demonstrates that really new ideas and schemes were never accepted without long and bitter battles. Some of the more challenging conceptions derived from the social construction of scientific paradigms lead me to exercise great caution; in the present moment of intellectual ferment and confusion, skepticism may be not only prudent, but wise. Some call this the age of mass cynicism, with the blasé cynic the really typical person. I wonder . . . seeing this extraordinary naïveté.

I fully agree with the judgment of the farmer/poet Wendell Berry when he says that we live in the midst of "the most destructive and, hence, the most stupid period of the history of our species." But his opinion is not based on the latest scientific report, as found in either the professional journals or the local newpaper. Rather, it comes from the sensibility and intelligence of a poet who is thoroughly familiar with and works a very particular patch of soil. Because of his many years' experience restoring and cultivating the worn soil of his small farm, he has the authority to speak, not about the earth but about the dirt under his feet. And he clearly understands and states that one cannot act "to save the planet." To speak plainly, such an intention is simply presumptuous. Traditionally, presumption has been understood as a belief in my power to do something that in fact I cannot do. One forms this belief out of vanity; thus, presumption is a sin altogether typical of our time.

But the voices of which I am so critical come from worried citizens, good people, desperately seeking ways to pull back the social juggernaut from the abyss . . . before it is too late. A few years ago, the doomsday clock of an atomic "accident" superstitiously suggested the limits of human capacity to live with the terror of threats in an utterly mad stockpiling for universal cataclysm. Now the threats increase: the explosion of visual prurience, massive self-drugging for every mood in all sectors of society, impending ecological apocalypse, the reification of morbid fears and anxieties through the media, the enclosure of the world in the coercive bonds of techno-marketing, an ever-encroaching pointlessness, meaninglessness, and absurdity. How defend oneself? Honest spirits strain to find an answer. But I strongly feel that many of their voices, almost all those that I hear in the mainstream, sound a false note, that they invite us to venture further into even greater folly.

I would like to suggest another path, much more restricted, much more modest, a path first pointed out to me by my neighbors, those marginal farmers. First, though, to clear the air . . . I can have no interest in the planet—I cannot see, feel, smell, hear, or taste it. And my internal senses have no experience of it; it does not reach my heart. I do not know humankind, or the people of the world—rather only my children, family, friends, neighbors, and acquaintances. I have no capacity whatever to see the future; it simply does not exist. So, every thought or proposal based on these presuppositions, on these recent technological creations—a planet imagined from space photos; "populations" produced by the statistics of social science; a fantasy projected by a computer program—all these I must regard with extreme critical skepticism.

Further, looking around myself, I find two competing modes of thinking and imagining. One might be called mystical, the other is apparently rational. Although recent history contains ample cautions against both the Yogi and the Commissar, the poverty of the modern imagination conspires to restrict the possibilities.

A "mystical" way of perceiving, as practiced today, for example, by some New Age folk, makes me suspicious. I don't trust it. I fear that these efforts are seldom more than therapeutic adaptations to "what is," or esoteric means of individual escape, mostly for the affluent. They will not lead me to face, and look into, the mess of which I am inextricably a part. They will not lead me to change my life radically. When such moves also look to the East—popular, it seems, for many the past few years—I am even more distrustful. The wisdom of the East is of the East. Is the Westerner prepared to strip himself or herself of a body, mind, spirit, set of habits—of imagining and acting—for another, really foreign? Or is such a thorough transformation possible in one lifetime?

The "rational" arguments, insofar as I understand them, necessarily entail a utilitarian calculus based upon the latest scientific findings. For example, if scientific research showed no "harmful" results from some new kind of Paraquat, I could use it to control weeds in my fields. If the experts could find no "measurable" pollution of the atmosphere—what in India would be called the fifth element, Akash—I could in good conscience let myself be moved about the earth by modern transport vehicles. Or if the government reports that there are no dangers to "health," I could tranquilly eat the products sold in supermarkets. Although utilitarian arguments can be extended and refined to take into account some of the more obvious externalities, there is no rational way to ensure that all such effects have been accounted for. But there are, I feel, better grounds for not depending on herbicides, for not using transport, for avoiding the market system.

Reflecting on my neighbor's comment about soil and his children, on the conversations and lives of other neighbors, on my own experiences in a rural community, I find a world markedly different from the one I have known, and can observe, in the institutions that seek to organize and monopolize power, wealth, the life of the imagination and intellect, "culture" today. In the major institutions I see a consistent and sustained effort to make and maintain three kinds of segregation or isolation: I am severed from flesh, place, and poetry. These three kinds of separation, I believe, contribute decisively to what can be termed "the modern mess."

Inspired by some of my neighbors, I tried to live, as much as possible, as an all-round drop-out. This means that I was able to practice, in an up-to-date way, a way that fits today's temptations, an ancient discipline: to guard one's senses. When we built our house in Union County, we installed no electricity. So, for some years, I freed myself from mechanical, chemical, and electronic images. In order not to pollute my vision, I restricted my eyes to real things only, to the things around me within the actual range of my sight. I dwelt in a place and manner that my hearing, smell, taste, and feeling would be affected only by what are known as natural phenomena, the things of nature, together with the people and their artifacts within my reach. I heard only the voice or the musical instrument of the person in front of me. I tasted—almost exclusively—what came directly from my labor or that of my neighbors. I enjoyed the pleasure and pain of my own body free from the interventions of modern medicine or recreation.

I found it good, exceedingly good, to restrict myself to what was within reach, to the possibilities of genuine sense pleasure, to a wantonly sensual life. Reflecting on the time before I came to live in a rural backwoods, I concluded that the rich reality that had become commonplace for me may be largely unknown because not experienced by many today. That is, the more one is confined to specifically modern modes of perception and movement, the more that person is effectively removed from the world of direct sense experience. This latter is still the world of my neighbor, the farmer. In spite of being shown, being told, being made to feel, being moved around, he is still able somehow *to see* his children, *to feel* the soil beneath his feet, *to hear* the wild birds sing. He modestly accepts that his knowledge and range of action extend only this far, no farther. He feels no responsibility for the world, much less for the planet.

Following the example of my neighbors, I have come to treasure my senses, and all the range and subtlety of feelings to which they introduce me. I am surprised, then, by how much I now feel upset by artificial images, mechanical and electronic noise, chemical tastes and smells. I am annoyingly distracted by someone walking up the aisle past my place in the country church, exuding a pervasive odor of some perfume or lotion. Although I would wish never to sacrifice the pleasure of meeting with my friends after Mass for conversation and a cup of coffee, I fantasize about how to introduce something other than the industrial donuts.

I suspect that to enjoy this quietly exciting and ever-changing contact with reality, one needs to seek some kind of marginality from the mainstream: physical places in which to drop out, psychical realms in which to dwell apart, spiritual disciplines through which to reach and practice a healthy detachment. Perhaps one should look into vocations to foolishness, to being an odd ball, to living queerly.

And there is place. What does it mean today to live in a place? To be closely, lovingly in touch with a place? For years, I tried to settle, to be in some way rooted, in one place, on a piece of land in an isolated and quiet area. If I listened carefully, I could hear in the distance the school bus and the mailman pass each day when their vehicles hit the loose planks on the bridge over the creek. Some days, no other vehicle traveled the gravel road—with only one good lane in the middle—that ran past my land. No other outside sounds reached me. I wanted to find out, to experience, what it is *to be* in a place, to be confined to very narrow boundaries, to come to know intimately the soil beneath my feet, the grasses, weeds, volunteers and trees, the wildlife of these forty acres. I wanted to walk only in the place where I was, to be only in the place where I was.

During this time of continual surprises, worlds of unsuspected complexity and richness revealed themselves to me. The longer I lived there, the more I learned the stories, the memories of that place, the more I came to know a local, a rooted people. And although I shall always remain an outsider, I experienced something of the possibility of being part of a living tradition, of belonging to a historical community. I shall never forget the day I met and talked with a woman in a nearby village. She had been a teacher in a small country school and took it on herself to search for and gather together all the materials she could find, so that one could study the history of the place. She organized these in a corner of the tiny public library for all to see and study, to share her enthusiasm. When she spoke I heard, not the "cultured" voice of a voracious consumer of antiquities, but the modest and generous spirit of one who embodied in herself the dreams and disappointments, the hopes and sorrows, of a people, her people, a small but historically vast community reaching into the past. Because she was so deeply and joyfully immersed in the life of this tiny town, she was able to speak eloquently and candidly of the ephemeral and earthy, the work-filled but celebratory presence of a people in a place. A graphic indication of a disembodied status in abstract systems can be guaged by the distance that separates one from a lively participation in some such community.

Distinctively modern institutions are not organized around place. They are designed to foster mobility, more intensely in their higher reaches. One is expected to develop loyalty to a profession, to some expert technocratic or administrative skill, to friends in high places, or just to money. My friends in Union County, by the very fact of having remained there in that one place for more than three generations, a rural place with no great "future," were judged by conventional criteria to be failures, backward. But from seeing these neighbors, and reflecting on my own experience among them, I concluded that if there is to be a world, it will be populated by people rooted to a place.

Finally, the removal from poetry. I can only conclude that the institutions that claim to be the guardians and teachers of the West's poetic tradition have failed. Rather than giving people poetry, they have taken it away. I assume that, for literate persons, a daily speaking and hearing of poetry is necessary that there be a certain wholeness in their lives. Plato believed that poetry both instructs and delights. In a well-ordered community, teachers should take care that the young are exposed to or taught good poetry, since, in some way, this experience contributes to virtue. Whether this occurs, and how, has been in dispute from Plato's time until today. I was thinking about these matters when, driving from my father's house to the farm, I turned on the car radio to keep from falling asleep. The station was broadcasting Country and Western music. Unfamiliar with the genre, I listened to the lyrics and melodies. The principal themes were remarkably similar, from song to song: the love between two people, the joy in its promise, and the deep sorrow in its failure. People listen to these very same themes, day after day. Why? Part of the reason, I am convinced, is that these uncomfortable truths are spoken to them in poetry, the songs voice their most intimate feelings, their common experience, *as poetry*. I suspect that professional literary critics seldom listen to this music for the pleasure of its poetic quality and, indeed, would probably deny that this is poetry at all. But these *littérateurs* are integral parts of the very institutions that have failed to inculcate a love of poetry, to foster the daily enjoyment of poetry. A genuine attachment to poetry is prevented by the schools. In how many homes is there a book of favorite poems that are regularly shared aloud, because this practice started with the reading of poetry in school?

I often attended special events at one of the two local "fundamentalist" churches near my farm, the churches of almost all my neighbors. One Sunday afternoon there was a Homecoming celebration in one of them and I was there. As part of the program, several persons each sang a solo, a hymn. Then one woman, the gatherer of neighborhood news, arose and recited a poem she had written for the occasion. I suppose most academics, except for specialists in folklore, would condescendingly regard this as an expression of "popular" culture. But her sentiments and candidness, her pleasure in the action and her lack of embarrassment or self-consciousnes, were wonderful to witness. Poetry was obviously an important part of her life, and was appreciated by the farmfolk present. What a difference between the ingenuous response of these people and the more usual affectation at poetry readings by "serious" poets!

And what of all those somewhere in between? It appears that the major presence of poetry in society is in the lyrics of popular music. Here I am reminded of sugar-coated pills given to children. Have people been made afraid to take their poetry straight? Further, much popular music appears to contain built-in dynamics driving it toward ear-splitting volumes and outrageous spectacles, all dependent on the most sophisticated technology. Is this a case of technology using poetry, or poetry using technology? Is the poetry lost in the process?

Traditionally, poetry has taken many forms. But this, its most widespread and popular expression today, appears designed to remove the person from the experience of the word. The technology separates me from the poetry somewhat as a photo separates me from my child. After seeing the photo, can I still see my child? After hearing technological sound, can one ever hear poetry again?

I have almost no experience hearing recordings. One day a friend took me to a state of the art book and audio store, complete with gourmet coffee lounge. We went into the audio room and he put earphones on my head. I heard a strange singing. Taking off the earphones, I asked him, What was that? That's a CD recording, he answered. But that was not a human voice, I protested—it was too perfect, too real, too . . . engineered! Can other people still remember the first time they heard a CD?

I have the impression that plain poetry in our society is found in the required exercises one endures in school, perhaps in a passing interest when one first falls in love, but is otherwise confined to the esoteric preserve of specifically literary people and their gatherings. In oral societies, poetry is unaffectedly enjoyed by the people as a regular expression of community life. In literate societies, its absence is one of the most ominous signs of spiritual darkness. Therefore, the presence of poetry in popular music is a sign of hope. The inclusion of poetry in that country church's Sunday afternoon program bore witness, perhaps, to the fact that this was more an oral than a literate society. These people were, indeed, fundamentalists; they were certainly grounded in some of the essential basics.

Each time I pick up one of my favorite poets, or read a cherished poem in an anthology, I do so with a mixture of sadness, for I suspect that not many Americans join me in this regular activity. Yet the tradition is so rich, so glorious! And its enjoyment lies totally outside the modern experience of scarcity; the only limits to my pleasure are my own deficiencies in the appreciation of truth and beauty.

Poetry teaches, not like a pedagogue or a preacher, but by placing before me the eternal dramas of human passion, the perennial themes of human meaning, ever new and fresh images of power and terror, beauty and order. I see myself in the truth of its language; I am invited to reflect on the truth of myself. In some sense, poetry is as Plato maintained: "beautiful poems are not human, or the work of man, but divine and the work of God . . . poets are only the interpreters of the Gods by whom they are severally possessed." One still speaks of poetic inspiration. The truth of this fire is revealed in the distances it crosses.

Once, alone at my farm, I suffered a personal tragedy for which, I felt, there existed no earthly remedy. The pain and confusion were too great to bear. Descending deeper and deeper into despair, the relief of a quick and final exit waved tantalizingly before me. In this disordered state, like a sleepwalker, I was literally moved to the poetry section of my bookshelves and took down an old copy of Gerard Manley Hopkins's *Complete Poems*, a gift from a dear friend, many years earlier. I instinctively and directly opened the book to the familiar lines of the six untitled "terrible" sonnets. Reciting these poems aloud, over and over, I was forcefully reminded that he, too, knew pain . . .

> I am gall, I am heartburn. God's most deep decree
> Bitter would have me taste: my taste was me;
> Bones built in me, flesh filled, blood brimmed the curse.
>
> Selfyeast of spirit a dull dough sours. I see
> The lost are like this, and their scourge to be
> As I am mine, their sweating selves; but worse.

I saw that his pain was much greater than mine . . .

> That night, that year
> Of now done darkness I wretch lay wrestling with (my God!)
> my God.

I clearly understood that he was carried to regions of suffering that made the sorrows of the Country and Western songs—though no doubt genuine—sound distinctly minor . . .

> O the mind, mind has mountains; cliffs of fall
> Frightful, sheer, no-man-fathomed. Hold them cheap
> May who ne'er hung there. Nor does long our small
> Durance deal with that steep or deep. Here! creep,
> Wretch, under a comfort serves in a whirlwind: all
> Life does end and each day dies with sleep.

In the perspective of my body and the sensual experience of a place, of learning what a place is and how "to be" there, a privileged approach can be found in our poetic heritage. For example, a rich collection of poetic expression was first formulated at the time of the origins of the Western experience, and is found in the Semitic book of Psalms. For many, they are more than poems. For persons of faith throughout the world, they constitute one's daily prayer, a speaking or crying out to God, continually recited for several thousand years. But I can also look at them as an example of poetry, as a sensual vision available to us Westerners, as the ancient wisdom of a people who stand at the beginning of our world.

The poet is quite clear about his own origins: I was conceived in sin. And although this sin is found in my flesh, it reaches further, it affects every aspect of my being. It can induce blindness, end in selfishness; it can make me mean, sour, poison friendship. But this is only a part of the whole. I learn that I am placed just below the angels, that some men and women have been rightly crowned with glory and honor (Ps. 8).

The Psalmist's voice reaches to the limits of his imagination, beyond the sensible universe. He celebrates the ancient belief in the contingency of the natural world; the universe is held in the hand of God:

> Everything which pleased the Lord, he did—
> in the sky, on the earth, in the sea, in the depths.
> He moves the clouds great distances,
> And his lightning illumines the rain. (Ps. 135)

If one is quiet, she hears the thunder speaking; if one looks, he sees that the heavens are beautiful. And the poet reminds us that this takes place with the waters raising their voices in chorus (Ps. 93). In wondrous amazement, he asks:

> Oh mountains, why do you exult like wild goats?
> Oh hills, why do you play like lambs in a flock? (Ps. 114)

> Because the earth has been visited, blessed, it is drunkenly rich, overflowing with marvels. (Ps. 65)

During the last few years, as I spoke these verses each day, images of what men and women have done, and continue to do to the land intruded . . . distracting, grating, disturbing: the transportation networks creating ugly scars across lovely landscapes, the communications systems polluting the purity of the atmosphere, the great urban centers spewing out mountains of garbage, scientific wonders violating the order of nature. The poetry celebrates beauty, the modern projects create squalor.

Regarding the world of nature, the poet repeats one of his principal themes:

> Let the heavens rejoice, let the earth exult;
> The sea and all its creatures join in.
> The fields and all growing things in them are jubilant. (Ps. 96)

This poet, as with so many in the tradition of English poetry, *our* tradition, sees, and helps us to open our eyes, and our lives, to beauty, to the loveliness of the world around us. The devotees of high culture rightly recognize the hideousness of such artificial deceptions as the various Disney-like reconstructions, at least in North America, if not yet in Europe.

The earth has been made unsightly in those places where men and women have attempted to dominate it, to remake it according to the dreams of their disordered passions and ambitions. These projects of defilement are carried out through society's most respected accomplishments: advanced institutional forms of making, serving/caring and communicating. But three realms of being and acting invite those who have doubts, who have lost faith in the current notion of progress. Inspired by a kind of crazy courage, one could venture there, beyond the sidewalks, the safety nets, the packagers of consumable distractions. One can seek to live purely in one's senses, to live a sensual life; one can attempt to stand in a place, to be rooted in a soil; one can share the vision of poets, daily sharpening one's intuitions. Overcoming habits of self-indulgence, one opens the possibility to know the joys and friendships of a more modest and graceful living. But just as sense experience is different in time and place and person, so is the character of soil and poetry. These are the tasks, then: to listen to one another, assisting one another to return to our senses, each to find his or her soil, each to discover and enjoy the power of those poetic images that echo in each person's sensibilities. Setting out on these journeys would indeed constitute a new beginning, the possibility of genuine patriotism, a loyalty to the other and to the nation.

The Greeks publicly celebrated regular festivals that were designed to remind people of virtue, and to assist their renewal and return. Poetry figured prominently in these rites. Today, many people are shrouded in a kind of existentialist agony, alone, isolated, left to seek their own way . . . and there is no return to a lost innocence; there is no road back to a fantasy Arcadia. But there are paths to truth and goodness; there are experiences of purity, of quiet, of lyrical beauty open to all who seek them. These can lead to the sharp, prophetic judgments and the limit-setting actions so much needed today. I don't have to depend on current scientific ideology, to make my move, to organize my life.

6

Word Roots

We are obviously subject to something we do not understand—why else would we be making so many mistakes? What the old believers in the Chain of Being have to say to us is that if we conceive ourselves as the subjects of God, whose law is in part the law of nature, then there is some hope that we can right ourselves and behave with decency within the community of creatures. We will be spared the clumsiness, waste, and grave danger of trying to make up our own rules.

Wendell Berry

Some years ago, especially in the 1970s, people started using the term, "post-industrial society." But I was skeptical. Trying to specify the actual meaning, I concluded that there was none, that the words signified only another pop-category, supposedly revealing some social reality. I felt that nothing essential in the established industrial installations would be abandoned, and that the "post" pointed to no precise namable denotation. Steel production would not drop, worldwide industrial agriculture would not diminish, while new forms of administration and control, of communication and commerce, would be solidly based on an industrial foundation.

As part of the discussions of the time, certain promises were implicit in wild predictions about "knowledge explosions," "information revolutions," and "communications breakthroughs." A new age of enlightenment was subtly intimated, or even confidently predicted. In spite of my doubts I was interested because, in those years, I was engaged in the effort to understand the relationship between word and place. Employed in a university, much of my work was with words. In this work, two recurring experiences helped me to formulate certain questions. At times I would come across words that moved me deeply, and I wondered: How do I keep these words? How do I remember them habitually? How do I make them a permanent part of my awareness, of myself? How do I become *them*?

Second, I often found myself reading words that made no sense. Why do I read this stuff? I asked myself. If I live in time, are there then strict criteria to apply to words? Do I have time only for certain words, not for others? Which are those words? Also important, Are there new kinds of infection that result from the deluge of information? Will all the junk words sicken me?

These questions led me to ask about place, my place. To be an academic in America is to live a life of privilege, enjoying personal freedoms and comforts greater than those of any "upper" class in history. An argument immediately presented itself: Given my education and my daily use of logic, dialectics, and rhetoric, I was moved in a certain direction. Logically, some things were certain: truth, goodness, and beauty are to be sought, their opposites rejected. But, dialectically, there are uncertainties: This specific action is only probably better than that one. Rhetorically, I was inclined to argue toward acting on what I knew or strongly suspected to be true: The gifts I had received from my parents and society were not given to be merely ornaments, or for my personal enrichment, but to be used in some common enterprise, that I might participate in the common good. Cicero's ideal to unite philosophy, the search for truth, to rhetoric, persuasion to make truth effective, seemed the only way to live.

But the public emphasis on information and communication did not include the question that more and more troubled me: Where is my *place*? Where does my personal history, with its peculiar gifts and talents, intersect with my society's history, with its contortions and dilemmas? Further, how can the daily stuff of my life, words, lead to this place? Light was thrown on the difficulties obscuring and inhibiting responses to these questions when I saw certain aspects of the historical situation in which I found myself. Something peculiar is happening today in the area of knowledge transmittal, but it is not what is being heralded and celebrated as a new and exciting age of communication. Advertising agencies might name a device a "personal computer." That does not mean that this machine has anything to do with what is traditionally known as the person, except perhaps its distortion. At this

moment, when an expansive and renewed democratic era is being proclaimed, one of the oldest forms of hearing the other—reading—may
be disappearing. The social movement involved is analogous to what
happened in farming. As farmers are rarely seen in America today, so it
may soon be the case with readers, too. The relationship between a
person and visual letters is shifting radically.

While working in the university, I was nevertheless still subject to
the power of words; the fact that they were my job did not kill my love
for them. With amazing frequency, they disturbingly affected me. Reflection on those moments inclines me to believe that certain ancient
and contemporary texts acted on me, caught me up in their *Weltan-
schauungen*. From these glimpses of other places, I was moved to
move. I recognized that I was in the wrong place, that I had to drop yet
another circle of friends and familiar routines, and continue my journey, my search. A respected university professor was not my proper
person. This was not the appropriate mode of life for me to be the
American I should be, to be the citizen the stars had destined for me.

In my rural isolation, genuine excitement was a daily occurrence—
through meetings with my friends and neighbors, the tiring but
endlessly fascinating work of the farm, the visits to the library of the
nearby state university, but also through the hours of reading and reflection. With no modern media imposing a daily distraction, I was free
to think. After abandoning the job of reading as an integral part of a
profession, I found the distance and leisure to probe the questions:
What is an incarnate, fleshly reader today? What is the moral imperative of literacy qua literacy?—for those who still profess some belief in
literacy.

To see and understand what is happening, one must look at the
history of reading in the West. For, like other human activities, this too
has changed over time. For a thousand years, there was an exercise
that can be called "monastic reading." As the adjective indicates, it
was practiced in monasteries during the late classical period and the
early Middle Ages. But this mode of reading originated even earlier, in
ancient Jewish ways of bodily consuming script. One read aloud, and
moved or swayed one's body rhythmically with the reading. The men
and women of the monasteries and convents adopted these customs
and some of the same texts, adding the Greek scriptures, preserved or
recovered classical texts, together with the accumulating Christian
glossae and commentaries. They read aloud, when alone or in common, and developed precise bodily movements to accompany the
reading.

This sensual, physical activity was directed toward the heart, one's inner senses, the very shape of one's soul. Throughout the first thousand years of the present era, literate persons, in the majority, men, worked out a way of reading oriented toward a way of living, believing that the reading itself would directly shape living. This was the most consistent and comprehensive, and also the lengthiest attempt in Western history to form the moral person through the act of repeatedly reading a text. In addition to the daily exercises of reading, a cloistered person's life included other complex social and religious influences, all designed to mold character that one would become free to love one's neighbor and open oneself to God's consuming fire. Reading was but one, albeit important, activity leading to the hoped-for transformation of one's very person.

Since one of the principal interests of readers in this period was the formation of the soul, great attention was paid to the texts and all the circumstances involved in reading. Some writers today dismiss the idea that one can look to the encounter with literature or art as contributing to or detracting from moral character. Art is not a therapeutic instrument, they claim. But the exercise of monastic reading had little or nothing to do with the psychologizing perspective of much contemporary comment, and was decidedly not an instrumental activity. One did not *use* reading to become "holy," as some might use meditation today to achieve inner peace. Wittgenstein understood the matter well. In the *Notebooks*, he wrote, "The work of art is the object seen *sub specie aeternitatis*; and the good life of the world is seen *sub specie aeternitatis*. This is the connection between art and ethics."

A terrible revelation of the power of truth in art, moral truth, came to light from the dark files of totalitarian USSR. Those gifted to craft words were arrested, tortured, imprisoned in the Gulag, and killed . . . because they dared to write the truth. For them, the necessity of art was the necessity of being a moral witness. Their jailers systematically tried to erase the future in order to control the present, knowing that, in the words of Osip Mandelstam, "Poetry is power." But the power of this poetry depended on its truth, which did not reside "in the individual poet, but in his tradition, in his fidelity to something larger than himself and more deeply rooted in the Russian past than Soviet power." Such people— Boris Pasternak, Aleksandr Solzhenitsyn, Nadezhda Mandelstam, Eugenia Ginsburg, Anna Akhmatova, and others— could not participate in building a future constructed on lies. Their words and their deaths are a living witness to truth, reminding every person who picks up a pen that writing evokes fright, the awesome realization that by my action I place myself in their tradition.

The monastic texts were carefully chosen, intricately and colorfully illuminated by the monk-artists, and respectfully preserved. Those that remain are among the most precious treasures of art museums. For the medieval readers, the words constituted one of the foundational sources of their beliefs, their sense and understanding of the real. One worked daily, through a lifetime of repeatedly reading the same texts—in a carnal or bodily mode, namely, aloud—to enter the texts themselves and thus be remade by them. For example, among some groups, the one hundred and fifty Psalms of David were chanted antiphonally every week. Participating in these exercises, people set out on a way, a path, an exploration into self and cosmos, a journey toward transcendent truth since, for them, there was a unity to creation, including their lives as fallen creatures. Their reading carried them from creatures to Creator.

They carefully organized various disciplines to direct word toward Word, believing that this way led to the conformation of one's life to Life. For example, their practices were ordered to form habits, to the acquisition of the moral and intellectual virtues, according to the tradition they found in Greek and Roman philosophy, and Hebrew Wisdom literature. This mode of reading placed them solidly in a tradition, a place in which they could grow. The awesome intellectual accomplishment of Aquinas in the late thirteenth century is an outstanding example of the vigor and creativity nurtured in this kind of life. The genius of Aquinas did not have to dissipate itself in epistemological ground clearing, tasks that confronted Descartes and Wittgenstein, for example. For the readers of our first millennium, words carried a transcendental power; words raised these people to the hope that they would be present when all "the creation itself will be liberated from its bondage to decay and brought into the glorious freedom of the children of God" (Rom. 8:21).

I do not remember ever hearing about this kind of reading in my education in various schools, colleges, and universities. I wonder whether anything like it exists at all today. The most "advanced" approaches to texts currently discussed in the universities would seem to have nothing in common with the monastic reader. The questions raised about the study of literature do not usually ask about reading as a way into virtue. Rare or non-existent is the teacher who would assign students in a literary theory class the powerful and disturbing essay of Simone Weil, "Reflections on the Right Use of School Studies with a View to the Love of God." What would university students do after reading the last sentence? "Academic work is one of those fields containing a pearl so precious that it is worth while to sell all our possessions, keeping nothing for ourselves, in order to be able to acquire it."

There is an essentially important difference between the thought of Simone Weil and the instrumentalization of reading. One sees this, for example, in the attitude of some Christian fundamentalists who are rigorous in their moralistic scrutiny of books; I sometimes wonder whether books are more than instrumental objects for them. But even among persons for whom books are central in their lives, the activity of reading may not be clearly articulated; there appears little or no agreement on texts and their relationship to the human condition, that is, the specific human condition that they portray or reflect. One does not often hear the question: Which texts most wondrously relate the truth of creation and the drama of human action, noble and ignoble? Dostoyevsky worried greatly about how to portray a good man in literature, concluding, finally, that there were only two true examples, Jesus Christ and Don Quixote. Which illustrates an important aspect of the difficulty: one is God and the other is crazy. Where are the persons today who read hagiography for the very goodness (pleasure) of the activity? How many are the writers who agonize over Dostoyevsky's question? Where is the literature anthology that includes hagiographic writing? In history and religion departments, however, the lives of the saints—in direct proportion to their historical distance from us— serve as material for academic careers. The instrumentalization could hardly be more dreary. But the question of the relationship between good—or bad—character and reading is seldom raised in a substantive manner, particularly in departments of literature.

In silence and solitude, seated at my all-purpose kitchen table as the stars began to appear beyond the glass wall of the attached greenhouse, I struggled to understand how to get from ancient, forgotten readers to modern ex-students. I think a distant example illustrates the matter. In Czestochowa, Poland, there is an icon, brought there from Byzantium in the late Middle Ages. On any day, throughout the year, one can find the church crowded with people, not just during the day, but also throughout the night, keeping an hours-long vigil on their knees, their eyes raised to the icon. I have met persons who regularly return, as often as once a month, to engage in this all-night exercise in the silent darkness. What they experience must be something similar to what happened to the early monks. Those who kneel before the icon are not fixed on an image, as is generally the case with devotees of museums and elegant art books, or the owners of paintings. Nor do they adore either the image or the icon as cult object. Their eyes go into the image, through the icon, to the reality that lies beyond. If they give themselves to this exercise in faith and love, what lies beyond the icon touches them, speaks to them, transforming them into different persons. One can indirectly but immediately learn what occurs, by going to Czestochowa, and quietly observing and then speaking with the people there. Or, one can kneel before the image and be taken to another, previously unknown world. But, like the acquisition of virtue, the journey requires time and exercise. And, like all genuine joy, it also requires a pure faith and a self-denying love.

Assuming that something happens in reading, some people argue about various criteria for determining what books to give children. That may be the discussion's most distinguishing characteristic: disagreement. There is little understanding about what can happen to the child who reads. A vague wishful feeling runs through the literate sectors of the population: Children should be exposed to "good" books and these will have some "good" effect on their lives and character. But to be realistic, one must admit that many would be happily satisfied if youngsters left school still reading . . . anything at all!

Some, such as George Steiner, suggest that reflection on Jewish historical experience over the past three millennia leads to further insights on the nature and end of reading. Jews have learned a transcendentally important truth from these several thousand years of study, wandering, forced removals, hopes, persecutions and joys: Their homeland, their soil, never has been and never will be a geographical piece of real estate; they can only find their home, their ground, in a text, in the Book. So . . . some argue.

The historical experience of Christians has been quite different, especially in Europe. As noted in Chapter 5, the Edict of Milan tolerated the Christian religion in the Empire. From this toe hold, various princes and churchmen, sometimes amicably, sometimes fiercely, conspired to create what is called Christendom, what some would call a Christian society and culture. Many would argue that this has now ended; the world is supposedly post-Christian, "post" denoting nothing more specific than in "post-industrial."

But there is another argument to be drawn out of this history for the Christian believer, just as out of their history for the Jew. Christians often fought against foes—pagans or fellow believers—to establish kingdoms on earth, lasting cities for men, according to their beliefs as Christians. Some would argue that these were, in fact, Cities of Man, always "worldly," at times turning into cruel nightmares; and, of course, the wars were always bloody. It seems possible to see a certain lesson in this history: The cumulative record establishes that such efforts cannot finally succeed, that the combination of "divine" sanction and men's secular ambitions always ends being deadly, in different ways, for both victor and victim.

The act of reading, then, can be examined in terms of a dichotomous possibility: the action can be either instrumental or substantive. As an instrumental act, in Jewish and Christian history, it has usefully contributed to the creation of a City of Man. Such a city, however, is ruled more by people's passions than by any inspiration from a religious source. As a substantive act, the record is not so clear. One can cite admirable and attractive figures, among both Jews and Christians, whose lives were transformed in large part through participation in the tradition of this kind of reading. Sometimes this transformation resulted in an institution that organized such reading for its members. But the institutional forms always deteriorated into empty formalism, if not worse. Every few years or generations another individual, solidly formed by entry into the textual source, had to arise to reform the institution, or found a new one. This is the history of conventual foundations for men and women in Europe, the history of monasticism.

One can learn from consulting this history of Christian religious foundations—monasteries and convents, orders and congregations— in the West. Many of these were founded according to the Rule of Saint Augustine, the Rule of Saint Benedict, or some other rule influenced by one of these. No foundation has remained free from corruption. The followers of Saint Francis tried to abandon his ideals even before he was dead! All attempts to organize a voluntary community life according to apostolic ideals, that is, a way of life attempting to imitate the examples of Jesus Christ and the Apostles, show a similar history of vigor and growth, then corruption and decline, sometimes followed by reform, over and over. These institutional forms are all meant to be, in their founders' intention, not worldly cities, but communities of men or women with their eyes fixed firmly on the heavenly Jerusalem. Although all of them took on fewer or more worldly characteristics over the centuries, their original founding documents were drawn up in a way to guard against such transgressions.

For the person who remains "in the world," and yet strives to live a life in search of truth, the picture has been even less clear. The monk or nun always has a Rule and/or set of detailed statutes for reference: their original way of life is clearly outlined for them, in accord with their beliefs of what is true, what false, in their daily efforts to enter the Kingdom of Heaven. Laypersons living within the same world of belief could, of course, pick up Scripture itself for their guidance. But the texts found there dramatically highlight the possible confusion. With respect to the construction of cities in this world, one would find these texts:

> Do not store up for yourselves treasures on earth, where moth and rust destroy, and where thieves break in and steal. But store up for yourselves treasures in heaven. (Mt. 6:19–20)

> Consider how the lilies grow. They do not labor or spin. Yet I tell you, not even Solomon in all his splendor was dressed like one of these. If that is how God clothes the grass of the field, which is here today, and tomorrow is thrown into the fire, how much more will he clothe you, O you of little faith! (Lk. 12:27–28)

Such texts strongly question worldly ambitions, whether these be aimed at building an empire or a comfortable future for one's children. Further, the texts suggest that the believer in Christ is more homeless than any Jew—if one may speak in this somewhat extravagant manner. Is the soil or place of Christians, then, also the Book? I believe the monastic reader would say yes. The primary land of the believer is the Word; all words in fact—or should—lead to the Word.

At first, this would seem to claim far too much. When one looks at writing relating words to Word, one sees that there is indeed a huge literature, but it is highly specialized, the domain of professional experts. Of course, there are many popularizations and much scholarly instruction offered to help one read the specialists. But is this what it means for a believer to find a place on which to stand? Further, the experience of words themselves is called into question today by the power and pervasiveness of screens, both silent and noisy. One might argue that words, as they have been known traditionally, are scarcely or not at all present today—for most persons, hunkered down before either a computer or a TV set. The realm of readers is being narrowed daily.

One can go to the original myth of our civilization in order to search for orientation. There, in the Book of Genesis, one reads that what is sensed, what matters, is Creation. This is the foundational truth of the story—all begins with a *created* world. Next, this Creation has a definite character—it is, simply, good. "And God saw all that he had made, and found it very good" (Gen. 1:31). But things did not remain this way. Adam and Eve's act of disobedience altered the world. After their sin, "the ground is under a curse." Through work, one can manage to live from it, but it will also produce "thorns and thistles," and Adam is told, "Thou shalt earn thy bread with the sweat of thy brow" (Gen. 3:17–19).

Before the Fall, there was a necessary unity between word and Word. "In the beginning was the Word, and the Word was with God . . . [and through him] all things were made" (Jn. 1:1–3). Adam was privileged to participate in the making. The Lord brought the created beasts and fowl "unto Adam to see what he would call them: and whatsoever Adam called every living creature, that was the name thereof" (Gen. 2:19). When Adam spoke, he spoke the truth, he spoke with power, he stated *what is*; he could not lie.

After the Fall, all speech becomes enigmatic; the simple truth can never be assumed. After the murder of Abel, the Lord asks Cain, " 'Where is Abel thy brother?' And he said, 'I know not: Am I my brother's keeper?' " (Gen. 4:9). From this statement until today, words have been used to deceive, to say what *is not*. The task is to return to the speech of *what is*, to speak the truth, to go from word to Word. But how?

Within the Western tradition one can find evidence of disciplines developed to remove obstacles to speaking and hearing the truth. These are designed to purify and guard the senses, outer and inner, and moderate the passions, through a lifetime of effort. With repeatedly self-imposed, willingly-undertaken exercises, one can hope to acquire a limpid, uncluttered mode of seeing and hearing and speaking that is habitual. This means that one is alert to the truth, even in the most trying and difficult circumstances; one has acquired strength of moral character. Monastic reading is the culmination of the most systematic and sustained effort to experience truth in this way, to *enter* the truth.

Given the problematical character of reading today, what can I learn from the historical experience of monastic reading? I asked myself this question in terms of my interest in place, my place in the world, as a reader. It seems obvious that one of the first issues is that of judgment: What shall I read? For the reader in the Middle Ages, the criteria were clearer and opinion more settled than today. But I believe that our very history can help us greatly. In every historical period, there is some kind of canon, some agreement on certain "classics" of that people. These works reveal the sometime painful, sometime heroic efforts of fallible creatures struggling to express the truth, to live the truth. These are the works that, after reading them, one says, "Ah, to take this in . . . to keep this forever . . . to make this a part of me . . . never to forget what I feel now . . . somehow to dwell here forever."

Some of the current polemics concerning the Western canon I regard as silly—the excretions of a very confused age. At the same time, one must recognize that genuine artists and sages can arise at any time, in any place; and great works can be written today. Part of the function of a canon is to help one develop those skills and sensibilities that enable one to make good judgments. My very grounding in the great works of the past enables me to recognize the great works of the present. This is true on the assumption that I view classics not as frozen idols or final statements but as valiant attempts to ask important questions, as witnesses to the perennial search for truths in word and being. All this is initially accessible, I would argue, when I pick up and read, for example, Teresa of Avila, Shakespeare, or Yeats. However, what I draw from these authors, and their texts' transforming power over me, is dependent on the discipline and depth I bring to them.

These texts, to the extent they are truly canonical, invite me to recover something of the sense and power of monastic reading. That is, their full flavor and richness can be enjoyed in an especially exciting way if read in this manner. They are written to be entered, and to enter me, to become a part of me. The moment I recognize what they are, what is their character, in that moment I seek to live in them and let them live in me. If I do not feel this strong inclination, then the text does not really belong to the canon, or I am not ready for it. I can remember a college teacher, years ago, warning us about the texts of Saint John of the Cross. He believed they were important parts of the canon of theological writings, but one had to be prepared before reading them . . . they were not just another theological work. They could burn with the fire that inflamed their author's heart. Such an experience could be dangerous; it was not to be invited lightly.

I pick up these texts with hope, set them down with gratitude. I have entered a privileged realm, a region of grace and light; I return blessed; I am edified, enriched. From these experiences, fortified by each subsequent reading, I come to a clear conclusion: I have only a finite time to read. Yet there are so many texts in my own canon, not to mention the canons of other societies, other peoples. And all such texts are such as to demand repeated readings. So I am encouraged not to waste my time on secondary texts, and to shun junk writing altogether.

A possible ideal, then, is to attempt some kind of recovery of monastic reading, and to practice this facing great texts. But to state the goal is to begin to see the difficulties. I seem to be surrounded with polluting visualizations and false images, pseudo-texts and corrupting texts, a plethora of distractions parading as words—not to speak of the infinitely varied concoctions and pleasures offered to relieve modern boredom, the peculiar acedia of our age. In any large city of the North, one has only to pick up the "city magazine"—which lists all the events, activities and entertainments of that day, week or month—to see the attractive but ultimately enervating temptations continually offered me.

But if I can practice a discipline of detachment, withdrawing myself from the world of distractions, and then immerse myself in a world where I find difficult questions and discomforting ideas, striking images and quiet courage, I might learn something about place. I might conclude that my earlier efforts to seek a place, to stand on a soil, were too superficially literal. There are dimensions of place of which I was not aware. The search can begin by reaching for the words spoken by Adam. I know, however, from all my various struggles and failures, that I live in a fallen state; I am a true inheritor of Adam's sin. Therefore, any discipline of withdrawal from the glittering and addictive drugs of perpetual consumption, and dedication to a very new and unfamiliar mode of reading will require a strenuous daily effort, indeed, a lifetime of dogged toil. But, in a very real sense, to begin the effort is already to have reached the goal. Thus, in my journey, I've found the best place so far. At the moment, I see no better place than the austerity of this farm. Its isolation and regular routines of hard labor perfect the process of purification—that I might be free to read.

The statutes governing the lives of monks and nuns prescribe in detail what they are to do when not engaged in reading. But if I am not a monk or nun, and if I am not devoting my talents to building up some "permanent" kingdom on earth, how determine my activities when not reading? And what of those persons who have little ability or inclination for reading? Here I find it instructive to look at recent American history. There I see an example that is fascinating, yet ambiguous: the Shakers, founded in eighteenth-century England. Under the leadership of Mother Ann Lee, eight members of the religious group emigrated to America in 1774. During the nineteenth century, they grew to number around six thousand faithful living in communities they founded and constructed in the northeastern and midwestern United States. Their essential beliefs were three: All of sensible reality is God's

Creation; all of it is good, indeed, beautiful; but we have no abiding home in this world.

Since they were people of profound faith, they zealously sought to live in the truth of their beliefs, with the result that their lives expressed this truth. I see a point of entry into this truth in their belief in the momentary Second Coming of Jesus Christ. Because this could happen today, they made the radical decision, as a community, to live as celibates, that is, there was no division among them as believers; they *all* lived celibate lives. Thus, if the community were to remain in existence, they had to recruit new members. At first, this occurred through the adoption of orphaned children and the conversion of adults. But then these sources of new members dried up and the community nearly died out in this century.

Their historical importance for America today does not derive from their existence as a nineteenth-century manifestation of religious enthusiasm, a phenomenon that affected various sectors of the country at that time. Other religious communities and movements that arose and flourished then also died out or considerably cooled off. But the Shakers are unique in what they understood—and effectively realized—in the expression of beauty.

For a long time I have puzzled over these people, suspecting that their lives speak to us in spite of the fact that they no longer exist. They lived in small agricultural communities and developed many community-scale craft industries; they were model farmers. In an economic sense, they flourished. Writers have noted the ingeniousness and quality of their many practical inventions. But I have been especially struck by something else: the beauty of everything they did and made. Visitors remarked on their courtesy and the amazing grace of their communal dances—from the "ecstasy" of which they got the name "Shakers." The layout of their farms and villages, the design and workmanship of their buildings, household furnishings and tools are characterized above all by beauty. The artifacts recovered from their communities are today preserved in museums; the physical remains of their houses and barns are guarded as artistic treasures. No place else in white America do I find such a clear example of authentically beautiful things produced, not by specialized artists, but by the community itself, for practical, everyday use. In their society, beauty was not disembedded; it was an integral aspect of daily living. For them, the creation of beauty in the world was a common enterprise for common use. True, as a society, they did not exist long enough for distinctions to develop between artists and other workers. But the seeds or possible sources for such differences, as also with the distinction between what is called high and low culture, were not present among them.

All beauty comes at a cost. And here, some point out: Yes, beauty pervaded many aspects of their lives, but they were religious fanatics, so much so that they willed their own non-existence; they are no more! Further, they are only one more of the various millenarian movements that sprang up in nineteenth-century America and that have almost disappeared.

I think it is this very result that, paradoxically, reveals the truth of their lives. Believing that they possessed no permanent home in the soil beneath their feet, and acting on this belief, they found the courage to take all the time necessary to make only good things. Their imaginations were freed to dream only beautiful patterns and images. Another, different beauty, but coming from the same sources, the same sort of beliefs, can be found in medieval illuminated manuscripts. The celibate monk artists lived even more circumscribed lives than the Shakers, but they also manifested greater liberty in their graphic expressions. One does not see the austere systematic order and quiet piety of Shaker books in monastic illuminated manuscripts. Rather, one sees the scribes' brightly colored images mingling with the letters of the text in a seemingly boundless sensual expanse of humor, spirited play and barely tamed vitality. The ape is seen everywhere, performing outlandish acrobatics across the page, inviting the reader to recognize an essential element at the core of human behavior, one's animal soul. No other art in history, some claim, expresses the human body, clothed and naked, with such abundant and varied imagery.

> The margins of books committed to a most disciplined spirituality were open to primitive impulses and feelings, and in a context of exquisite writing these miniatures, which are whimsical and often gross in idea, compete for the reader's attention. . . . They are a convincing evidence of the artist's liberty, his unconstrained possession of the space, which confounds the view of medieval art as a model of systematic order and piety.

All this from monks buried in monasteries in the Dark Ages!

This exuberance in the celebration of beauty, coming out of discipline and restraint, is also wonderfully evident in the poetry of Gerard Manley Hopkins, a poet who reached his maturity while living in the strict obedience of a faithful Jesuit, going where he was assigned, doing what he was told. In a representative example of his imagery, "Pied Beauty," he writes,

> Glory be to God for dappled things—
> For skies of couple-colour as a brinded cow;
> For rose-moles all in stipple upon trout that swim;
> Fresh-firecoal chestnut-falls; finches' wings;
> Landscape plotted and pieced-fold, fallow, and plough; . . .
>
> All things counter, original, spare, strange;
> Whatever is fickle, freckled (who knows how?)

These people—the Shakers, the monks, Hopkins—are able, out of lives that might appear to our contemporaries to be too constrained, too full of self-denial, too narrow in experience, altogether devoid—in conventional terms—of sensual delight, to reveal a path to beauty—*through sense experience*. It seems reasonable to hope that the disciplines of this place, a remote patch of land, will cleanse my senses to see, to know beauty, as these persons, whose lives merit such awe and respect. But the place promises even more: an ideal setting for reading. The daily and seasonal work, the isolation and quiet, not only purify my senses, they also free me; my lightness of being enables me to travel the obstacle-filled distance all the way to the great texts.

7

The Beauty of Saying No

In all those cultures, Greek, medieval or Renaissance,
where moral thinking and action is structured according
to some version of the scheme that I have called
classical, the chief means of moral education is the
telling of stories.

Alasdair MacIntyre

M y farm was so far from heavily traveled routes,
so deep in sparsely populated country, and
people were so addicted to "sexy" fantasies, of sitting in the driver's
seat, that no public transport could economically survive in that place.
Of course, this ensured my peace—no housing development or suburban mall would ever disturb the glorious tranquillity of my retreat. In
these circumstances, one gets to know the mailman pretty well. Since
the heavy planks on the bridge at the bottom of the hill were loose, I
always heard if he was early, late, or right on time. Checking the mail
box, then, was one of the major events of the day. I might be surprised
by a letter from a friend. The pleasure, of course, was always proportionate to the distance. One day I was particularly delighted to see the
stamps on the envelope—Eire. That meant a letter from a close friend
in Ireland; I'll call him Mark. His unusual bit of news was the report of
an ancient ritual that took place at his small cottage.

Mark had noticed a small bump on his back. Somewhere, on any given day, a similar experience is repeated by another, too, who knows what to do, immediately . . . that is, everyone living in those areas of the world strongly influenced by one of the principal modern projects knows to use science and technology to bring everything under control. Without any unnecessary delay, one goes to see the appropriate professional, a competent oncologist.

But Mark did not do this. Rather, he called together his friends, members of a small community, and they discussed the bump—what to do about it. After a calm, searching conversation, Mark decided to call the local priest and ask to be anointed. There is a specific ritual for this, and the family or community joins in the prayers at specified times during the ceremony. The priest came and anointed Mark with the *oleum infirmorum*, an oil specially blessed by the bishop each year on Holy Thursday, just before Easter. Mark and his friends believed that the effectiveness of this touching is dependent on the faith of the participants. "I tell you the truth, if you have faith as small as a mustard seed, you can say to this mountain, 'Move from here to there' and it will move. Nothing will be impossible for you" (Mt. 17:20–21). After some weeks, the bump disappeared.

At about the same time, another friend—I'll call him Peter—discovered a lump on his neck while shaving. He was on vacation in a foreign country and was scheduled to return home in a few days. So he decided to wait until then before acting. As soon as he arrived at his apartment, he called a colleague and friend who knew the medical personnel of the area. Indeed, beginning a few years earlier, she began direct contact with them after having been diagnosed with breast cancer and having a subsequent mastectomy.

After speaking with his friend, Peter contacted a respected oncologist who wanted to run tests immediately; time was all-important, he explained. Peter decided to take this step. Examining the test findings, the doctor strongly urged surgery—to be done two days later. It should be a relatively simple procedure, he explained, and would probably take care of the matter. Before following the physician's imperative recommendation, Peter first spoke with another close friend.

This person expressed strong reservations, a frankly skeptical attitude toward the contemplated procedure; he was not ready to accept the medical opinion so easily. In fact, he discussed the possibility of rejecting the diagnosis altogether, not just this test result and the concomitant professional judgment, but the very idea of a diagnosis. He talked about two radically different modes of life, one that emphasized the autonomy of the person, the other, the heteronomy demanded by advanced medical technology. Perhaps Peter was faced with the necessity of choosing one or the other. Perhaps these opposed paths, patently extreme and clear-cut, were nevertheless the most truthful statement of his dilemma. Perhaps he was given a rare grace, the opportunity to glimpse the final outline of his life, together with the power to shape his personal story into a purposeful order through one decisive action.

At this moment, Peter was blessed with genuine freedom: The choices lay before him, one presented by the concerned technical expert, the other suggested by his critical friend. He was still his own person, he could decide the direction, the very character of his life. After making this irrevocable step, he would not be able to go back. Setting out on one course, he would have to learn to live with his lump, as he now lived with ten fingers, or near-sightedness. As every person must—for him, perhaps earlier than for some others—he would have to learn the art of suffering. On the other course, he had only to submit himself to the best available medical knowledge and equipment, and . . . what? hope? relax? expect a cure? Peter faced, in a situation of heightened intensity and compressed time, what everyone faces—except that, for many, the reality of the choices is never so dramatically seen. They are often much more commonplace, or are lost in a pattern of living hardened by earlier choices made over many years. Further, there are endless distractions today, a profusion of beguiling chimeras, myriad insane delusions. Peter dimly recognized that he would have little control over tomorrow. As never before in his life, he would choose one faith over another: to rest in an ancient tradition surrounded by the love and support of friends, or to submit himself to the promises and marvels of modern medicine. Peter, a professional himself, a university professor, believed in the validity of science, in the competence of physicians. In one sense, he felt he had no choice. He had lived an orderly life. The decisions making that life evidenced a real consistency; they colored the character of the situation he faced. He decided to undergo the simple operation.

Since I could reach the hospital, I went to visit him the day after the surgery. But I couldn't find his room; they had no record of him in the building where he was supposed to be. Finally, I located the central administrative office in the sprawling complex and learned that he was in the urology building. I don't know much about physiology and anatomy, but I was certain that a lump on one's neck had nothing to do with urology. He was there, however, and explained to me that the operation was not exactly as the physician had predicted—not quite so simple. It turned out that he needed a second operation, immediately. They had to remove one of his testicles. After recovering from the two surgical interventions, he would have to undergo a series of chemotherapy treatments.

I could sense that he was somewhat dismayed by what had happened and by what was yet to come. Fear flickered in his eyes irregularly, independently of his more confident words' meaning. I had the impression that he was on the verge of teetering into a simultaneous schizophrenia, one part of him clinging to belief in the power of high-tech medicine, another part waiting for a dark, unknown terror ahead.

Shortly after the chemotherapy started, his thick black hair began to fall out. He shaved his head, wore a hat when he went out, and attempted to resume his accustomed life. I began to see that with only a few steps he was already stuck in a medical miasma that would progressively take on a heavy cumulative weight. I feared that he was caught in a malevolent quicksand. It would become ever more impossible to get out.

He, however, struggled to maintain his usual good cheer. He told me how impressed he was with the chief doctor—quite an intelligent and articulate fellow. He treated Peter like an equal; no condescension at all. He explained everything, holding back nothing. Peter felt he had a comprehensive view of his cancer and of the complexities of the necessary treatment. Over and over again, he emphasized the necessity of the procedures he had agreed to; he *understood* their necessity. Over the weeks, I sat with him many hours, listening . . . uncertain how to respond. But having seen that he was securely in the chambers of modern alchemy, I judged it best to confine myself mostly to listening. It was far too late to discuss candidly what I saw happening.

Two men, two stories. One had chosen to live outside, the other inside, the medical system. But there is more. Some years earlier, Mark had decided to live outside the employment system, the insurance system, the communications system, the entertainment system. Except for a tenuous connection to the monetary system—through picking up odd jobs now and then—he would seem to have almost no contact at all with the "normal" social systems. He also chose to live in an out-of-the-way place, one of the Aran Islands in the Atlantic, off the coast of Galway.

Mark believes that the place itself is important for him and for contemporary society, important for someone seeking to learn how to live in time. He once told me that, per square yard, there are more historically significant ruins on Aran than any other place in Ireland. Vig-

orous and exciting forms of community life, eventually affecting much
of Europe, once flourished on these three tiny islands, the largest of
which measures about eleven by six miles. He believes that people
today can find strength and direction through living in the place
where these ancient and mysterious flowerings once broke through
the crusts of self-interest and vanity. So he, together with the community of which he is a member, has chosen to leave his former home
and seek a precarious and near-subsistence living in that place.

Each of the three main Aran islands is an irregular rock, roughly
protruding above the surface of the ocean. Over the centuries, the
people have leveled the porous rock in many places, creating small,
roughly flat surfaces fenced in by stone walls. They brought up sea-
weed and sand from the ocean, composted them, and created a soil.
This soil is continually replenished with new compost. It is not deep,
and one sees almost no trees—only the brightly green grass, the stone
fences, an occasional stone cottage, and oddly-shaped, small rocky
mountains. Here and there, in the 14,000 patches of grass—average
size, just under one-half acre—cattle, sheep, goats, a donkey or horse.
The local people—now just under a thousand native-born—say that if
one extended the stone fences in a straight line across the Atlantic,
they would reach Boston. If one insists on a wooden literalness,
however, the fence would only reach about a thousand miles into the
ocean.

Life on the islands today is quite different from that evoked in John
Millington Synge's beautifully sensitive diary that he kept while living
here at the turn of the century; and from that described in Liam O'Flaherty's powerful stories begun a generation later; and from that presented in Robert Flaherty's stark, classic documentary, *Man of Aran*
(1934). But one can still climb the mountain, Dún Aengus on Inish-
more, and find, at the top, a perfectly flat rock surface, high above the
Atlantic, with the ocean crashing and swirling hundreds of feet below
under the sheer cliff. From archeological evidence, we know that people gathered up here thousands of years ago—but no one knows with
certitude why. Some believe this was a fortress; others, a place of worship. To me, the enigma is not so puzzling. One has only to stand there
in the resounding silences of the place, with the awful power of the
ocean pounding far below, with the ominous ever-metamorphosing
black clouds in all shades of gray scudding overhead—I have only
been there in winter—with the wind whipping the rain into one's face,
and then be startled by a warm and bright sun awakening one to a new
place, surely not in heaven, but only scantily still on earth, to know

why people would come here. I was compelled to keep silent, so as not to disturb the sacred space, to await the epiphany that breaks through in such pure wildness. No matter how many people ascend the mountain to stand there alone absorbed by the elements, the place will always remain a wilderness—if no tourist development destroys it. Except for a ring of stones piled all around the edge at the summit, there is no evidence of a human violation of the rock platform. In this setting, Mark finds the contemporaneity of his ancestors, here all notion of linear time collapses. Standing under the swiftly-moving sky, I felt I could understand something of the statement of an islander at the time Synge was here: "We send for the priest before the doctor if a man has a pain in his heart."

Peter inhabits a very different world. Time still runs in a line for him, it passes, yesterday was yesterday; the past is past. Knowing classical languages well, he finds a translation of *Winnie the Pooh* into Latin to be amusing, fun to read, a pleasant diversion of today's high culture. Peter holds a prestigious high profile job that entails regular international travel and contacts. He moves in this world, the world of sophisticated connections and glamorous cocktail parties. He is a leading member in several of the organizations and institutions to which he belongs. He actively participates in various civic programs. He lives very much inside the systems rejected by Mark. All these allegiances and activities strongly incline him to accept unquestioningly the various institutional forms that shape and support his life.

When Peter told me of the initial diagnosis, the day after he received it, I immediately thought of the good that could come of it: the shock appeared powerful enough to be unsettling, perhaps salutary. Finally, he would now be inclined to question many of the assumptions that imprisoned him. But I was wrong. The modern had too great a hold on him. His substance had become weak-souled, his rootedness shallow. He saw no brightly-lit space in the diagnosis, only a frightening dilemma. Whenever he returned to the hospital for more chemotherapy or radiation—the cancer had metastasized to other organs—I visited him. He always had the most detailed clinical report to give me. To my untutored ear, he sounded like a scholarly academic delivering an impressive lecture. What more was there to know? What other course of action could one reasonably follow? The cancer was an especially aggressive kind. One had to respond with equally aggressive counterattacks, using this great array of high-tech scientific medicine available today. But underneath all the learned therapeutic eloquence and ingenious antiseptic jargon, I discerned only the crude and now timeworn formula: cut it out, burn it out, poison it.

The respective development of the two stories—whether Peter ever recovers, whether Mark discovers another lump—is not so important. Whatever happens, each man will die. There is a long tradition in the West, to which many witnesses have strongly adhered, which holds that the crucial question is not when I die but how. One of the early persons I meet in this history is found in a tragic drama of fifth-century Greece, the young Antigone. The king, Creon, had forbidden the burial of her brother, with death prescribed for disobedience. In the king's judgment, Polyneices had forfeited any claim to an honorable burial because of his treasonous actions. Antigone believed that the virtue of piety required that she disobey, although the punishment for her act would be instant death. A young woman deeply in love with the king's son, betrothed to him, who also loved her passionately. She nevertheless acted. Her stated reason: there is nothing so awful as an ignoble death. That is, if she failed to act, her own death, whenever it might come, could never be a noble death, a good death.

The story Sophocles bequeaths us is instructive today, in spite of the fact that Antigone, as so many other steadfast figures in this tradition, seems to belong to a world very different from ours. She faced an apparently clear-cut choice: the good act was to bury her brother. She would then die well because she had lived well. To some today, it might seem that the principal virtue she then exercised was courage— she was not afraid to risk death. But her courage served her in terms of another virtue, piety. She clearly recognized the debt in justice she owed to her family, the nation, and the gods, a loyalty that could, on occasion, supersede obedience to the reigning authority. She was a faithful daughter and sister, a patriotic citizen and a pious child of God, that is, a person who acted out of the traditional sense of the virtue of piety.

The people of Thebes were of one mind in their moral judgment: Antigone had acted well, Creon badly. This very unanimity well illustrates the conundrum many face today: Agreement on the moral character of specific acts is rarely found in contemporary society. Further, I do not often hear that the primary consideration in any possible action is to ask oneself the question: What is the *virtuous* thing to do here? Or that it is necessary to act virtuously, no matter what the consequences. Do I think about the possibility that situations similar to Antigone's might arise today, too? Do I seek to reflect on my world in order to recognize such situations? And then pray for the strength to act with courage, as she acted?

There are huge empty spaces in both public and private life where, formerly, one found moral intelligence. I once noticed an especially sad example of this while working at the university. There suddenly appeared a campus-wide program, with much publicity, many meetings, discussions, lectures, audio-visual presentations, all kinds of leaflets and pamphlets, special library and book store displays, all referring to an action called "sex." That is, everything was designed to enable the students to protect their bodies from a malady called "disease" when engaged in genital contact with other persons. There was no mention of the larger drama in which such contact might occur, no suggestion that, for persons who professed to be literate, there are classic and powerful portrayals of the joy and pain to be found in the passionate love of one for another, such as the exciting and richly-textured story of Sigrid Undset's *Kristin Lavransdatter*, or that the philosophy and religious thought of the West contain subtle and nuanced comment to make sense of such tragedies as those that struck Romeo and Juliet, Othello and Desdemona. In short, I was appalled by the shallowness and ignorance of the proselytizing presentations, the falsity of the propaganda, the very idea of a campaign.

I was angered by the lies preached in this blitz of pop scientific pap. The students, considered by many of their elders to be altogether too hip, too sophisticated, appeared to me as innocent lambs being led to one of our peculiarly modern forms of slaughter: the stupid excision of traditional wisdom. They were being prepared for the narrow and parochial tunnel-vision of Peter's physicians, prepped for any quack's prescription.

Sitting quietly in my kitchen, reflecting on that cynical campaign, I came to think that my shock and disappointment resulted from the fact that I had not yet understood the university, as a modern institution. It now appears to me that the design and thrust of modern institutions is such as to prevent, insofar as such is possible, the practice of what has been known traditionally as virtue. The idea of protecting one's body from the other, in those actions that in former times were associated with love, is to deny the very possibility of virtue, of acting well . . . nobly . . . generously. It is to condemn one to selfishness and meanness. I came to recognize that the character of the campus program was not accidental or fortuitous; it was necessary; it came out of the institution as water comes out of a faucet. The young people were encouraged to act viciously, that is, to live a life of moral turpitude, because this is the very mode of living modern institutions are designed to initiate and foster.

To make a moral judgment is an intellectual act; it is to be able to recognize the difference between noble and ignoble, beauty and repulsiveness. All societies, as in the Greece of Sophocles, have worked out ways for their members to learn the distinction. These societies have also encouraged their members to act—out of a moral intelligence, that is, as virtuous men and women. The modern university is the one place in a secular society where a self-selected and trained group of people are paid to study, reflect on, and speak about the moral heritage of historical time. But this very activity, of its nature, is itself a moral enterprise—it can be done well or badly as a *human* act. Given the situation of contemporary society—emptiness, boredom, despair, mindless consumption, the various varieties of disorder and violence—the university is *the* most fitting institution to search for ways to act virtuously, that is, as an institution. But an ethics course offered by the philosophy department is probably little more than a palliative. Academic philosophy has become increasingly marginal to university life and public discourse. Further, with such a course listed in the catalog, all other faculty can relax and quietly continue to pursue their pet research interests in the belief that something is being done. Students will not set out on a lifetime of denying self and acting for the other by reading a textbook, listening to a lecture or participating in a "Socratic" dialogue.

In the past, there have been discussions, arguments, and wars over conflicting perceptions of the good. Today, pandemonium reigns, with occasional outbursts of strident position-taking, usually in a highly nonrational manner. In the meantime, I suspect that people have been bludgeoned into insensibility so that a general moral paralysis affects many.

For example, a particularly bizarre illustration nicely reveals the matter. I was offered a brief teaching job in Spain, a week or two of seminars and meetings with students. Coming down from my room on a Sunday morning, I noticed the day's newspaper on the counter, and the words over a photograph caught my attention. Translated: "He can be a father again," with the picture of a young man in a hospital bed, smiling. I picked up the paper and read the extended caption under the photo. This fellow, named and clearly identifiable in the picture, was celebrated as the first man in Asturias to have his vasectomy successfully—it was claimed—reversed!

My gut reaction was, "That's sick!"—a total obliteration of the traditional distinction between public and private. Yes, but what did I see there? I concluded that it was a contemporary expression of the grotesque, not in the rich and subtle meanings evoked by the figures in medieval manuscripts, but more in the sense of my children's remark about something that disgusts them, "Yu . . . uck!"

But this was the leading daily newspaper of the region, regarded as a thoroughly respectable journal. I then remembered that I have increasingly seen such public displays in both America and Europe. The young man and others involved in this pandering to voyeuristic curiosity have lost all sense of decency; they appear to have no notion of propriety, of modesty, of good and bad taste. Such parading of "private parts"—now an antiquated expression?—has occurred before, of course. And one can find worse historical examples. But what is new today is that few or none were outraged or nauseated that Sunday morning when they picked up their paper. That is, they didn't *feel* the incongruity of such shamelessness—(shame . . . another lost experience?).

The newspaper that published the picture and caption is part of a communications system or, in terms of mainstream news and information, *the* communications system—one could argue that there is only one today, worldwide. The university that promoted safe sex is part of the educational system—there is only one of these today, too. And so it goes with all the various services in modern society. Each one is organized in what is called a system. Indeed, the planning, production and marketing of all goods and services are carried out, insofar as possible, in systemic terms. This has come about, descriptively, through the wedding of rational control and the appropriate machines, principally computers.

More and more, the modern person—like my friend, Peter—lives in the institutions that make our kind of society possible. That is, they have little or no independent life apart from an institutional life. When they seek "to escape," they use the transportation industry to move them to a spot designed by the travel and tourist industries. This means that they live *in* systems. They never escape; they are never free.

The results, in terms of the possibilities for growth into a moral being, into what traditionally has been understood as a person, can be seen in a small electronic innovation. In the last few years, in Germany, a change has occurred in those buildings to which the public has regular access, whether it be a post office, bank, train station, or supermarket. The door is more and more frequently fitted with an almost invisible and seemingly innocent device: an electronic eye that opens and closes the door for you. I once had a teacher who insisted that the act of opening and closing a door was either virtuous or not. Virtuous, if one was respectful of the door itself, that is, if one did not jerk it open or slam it shut; it had a certain materiality that invited one's sensitive awareness, that allowed a good sense experience. One could appreciate and honor a well-made door, because one thereby honored both oneself and the doormaker, by the manner of opening and closing it. Further, one could look back, going out a door, to see if someone else followed; one could hold the door open for another; one could thank a stranger for opening the door. That is, something genuinely human and personal takes place at a door, the possible exchange of a smile and friendly word could accompany that simple act. Or, one could treat the door and the other viciously. In either direction, a *human* act. Often, this is no longer possible. And, I would argue, all modern institutions are organized in this way. As systems, they are designed to eliminate human acts, to deny the exercise of virtue, to prevent the growth of moral beauty in the society.

These designs are sometimes rationalized by saying that the goal is to cut out human error and increase convenience. True, people still make mistakes and some are lazy. And if someone in a wheelchair depends on a spontaneous helping gesture to get up the curb or down the stairs, he or she might have to wait, might be disappointed when another thoughtlessly (perhaps viciously) passes by. But ramps, electric eyes and all the variety of built-in safeguards and automatic activators in our institutions, which themselves are all-pervasive, remove countless possibilities for goodness, for the flowering of lovely actions.

The students at the university, the people at the newspaper office, the employees at Peter's hospital, to the extent they are inserted in a modern institution, to that degree cease to be free to act in a human fashion, lose the opportunity to experience goodness. The overall institutional effect is seen in the dramatic difference between two contrasting situations. For some years, I had to travel on trains in Germany. At first I marveled at the system. Everything is designed for convenience and comfort, schedules are clearly printed and posted in many places in the stations, the locations and times of trains plainly written out and announced. And, if all these helps were still not enough, information counters are staffed with knowledgeable bureaucrats. I do not remember ever needing to ask anyone—fellow traveler or official—for directions or information, and I was a foreigner, a stranger.

Some work with disciples and followers of Gandhi took me to India. While in the country, I had to travel by train several times. There were some signs and indications, but they were few, hard to find and usually subject to numerous changes and exceptions. But every time I needed help, someone was there to take excellent care of me, that is, another friendly passenger. I remember people helping me figure out schedules, guiding me to the right track, assuring me that I did not miss my train—it was only several hours late that day. One person even shared the simple breakfast he had brought with him—how good it tasted after an all-night train trip! Another bought me a cup of coffee when we stopped at a station. Once, a fellow passenger showed me where to find good drinking water on the platform when the train stops at a station on a hot day.

On a journey from the interior to Bombay, I grew increasingly nervous as I imagined the crowds of people and the probably complicated connection I would have to make to reach some friends in a distant suburb. I asked a passenger in my compartment if he could give me any general directions. "Don't worry, I'll take care of you," he assured me. When the train stopped, he accompanied me through the thick and noisy crowds, led me to the nearby station for local commuter trains, bought a ticket for me (!), and put me on the correct train, with careful directions about recognizing the station where I wanted to get off. I shall never forget these experiences, these people. Then, as I looked out the train window, I would sometimes see scenes that were truly foreign to a person coming from Germany: people living squashed together in sordid, makeshift shelters on the outskirts of every city. Then I realized that my repeated experiences in the trains and stations were equally foreign: the warmth, openness, friendliness and beauty found there are largely unknown in Germany; it has been institutionalized out of the people. They have been impoverished and diminished by efficient laundry systems. One must fight through years of administrative accumulation of impersonal institutional care and the now-ingrained cultural indifference to the other to reach out and give the stranger a hand.

The society's institutions, highly developed, are designed and operated in such a way that no one has to touch another, no one senses another, no one need ever reach out to another. From this, I can make an inference: To the extent that a society has perfected its institutional systems, to that extent beauty has been erased, wiped out; to that extent, the society is monstrous; to that extent, virtue is not to be found. Former people are on the way to becoming something other.

The memory of my friends, Mark and Peter, returned; their differences appeared clearer—and, important. I recalled that Mark, when he spoke about what he was doing, how he was living, the concepts and judgments came out of *him*. He was standing in a unique place, *his* place. On the contrary, Peter's language, when he spoke about his specific situation, came out of the mouths or books of experts. He was precariously perched on an institutional shelf and repeating what he had picked up. I wondered—am I seeing the birth of a new historical creature? If so, the reality was much more terrifying than the fantasies of science-fiction . . . because real.

The world of modern institutions, of interlocked systems, is every day being extended further and being perfected more. This means the annihilation of the moral beauty formerly shining out from lives illumined by the lifelong practice of justice, fortitude, temperance and prudence, the four traditional cardinal virtues. I have asked college students to name these virtues, described and honored in our tradition for over two thousand years, and they were unable to do so; they had never heard of them!

It seems necessary, then, to ask the question: Is a virtuous mode of living still possible? I am inclined to argue that the world of systems constitutes a kind of bottomless evil for, finally, it makes society be the kind of place where one is discouraged or prevented from reaching out to another, from loving another, whether that other be one's "intimate" or a complete stranger. In place of numberless opportunities to make goodness be and joy felt, there is only the scheduled delivery of programmed goods and services. Each time I have the opportunity or necessity to submit to these faceless public servants, I feel more confined, more restricted, more a prisoner. So much of that which supposedly establishes a high quality of life actually sickens me to death. A price must be paid for convenience, control, service, security, rights. And modern persons pay it—daily, hourly.

Now it is clear that as institutions *qua* institutions are perfected, no one is actually in control. Originally, much of the thrust and character of modern institutions came from the desire to establish control— over nature and over recalcitrant humans. But as control is perfected, no one stands behind it, no one is there. Modern institutions have made conspiracy theorists largely irrelevant. The contemporary situation, then, is one of overriding helplessness. Those persons today who speak about both the powerlessness and the reverse, empowerment, of certain groups in the society are perhaps missing the deeper engulfing poverty and weakness that affects all. This can be seen if one examines social, economic, political, or cultural reform efforts proposed today. These proposals, if enacted, will serve, first of all, to further legitimate and strengthen the existing institutional systems, along with the corresponding *Weltanschauung* that gives them meaning. The more rational and efficient the reform, the worse the result. That is, what has traditionally been celebrated and suffered as the conflict between good and evil is further eliminated, with the consequent emptying out of human experience.

In the past, one can see that the course of human affairs changed— through ideas, war-making, law-giving, social and religious movements, usually in some combination. But perhaps this time has ended; perhaps another threshold has been passed, dimly noted, especially by those who, on their own claim, are the persons dedicated to the practices of a critical intelligence. For is this not one of the principal claims of the university: to be the place where these persons are enabled to make their unique contribution to the common good?

The modern university finds its origins in the twelfth century. It was at that very time that the practice of monastic reading, as described in Chapter 6, ceased and a new approach to letters was developed, what is sometimes called "scholastic reading." In this kind of exercise, one could imagine an abstract text, independent of both the page and oneself. Very quickly, powerful thinkers such as Peter Lombard and Thomas Aquinas produced their great works, a very different kind of writing than that seen in the previous one thousand years. But the subsequent history of scholasticism, as a mode of reading, suggests that something was missing. Great subtlety was matched by great controversy between competing groups of thinkers, while overall a kind of creeping irrelevance became the common attribute of philosophical thought. In the West, commerce and science, colonial power and technology, came to dominate both the world and peoples' interests. Through these centuries, the idea of a moral intelligence came to be replaced by that of a critical intelligence as the governing concept in the academy. And universities are defended today on the ground that they are the unique host and nurturer of this ideal. This attitude, in its most extreme form, finds its ultimate end in the critique itself, not in an original text, nor in the person of the reader. Institutionally, such a practice takes place in the fragmented structure of academic specialization, where everyone vigorously competes for the available money and honors, thereby becoming more and more narrow, more deeply frozen. This was the world of Peter, whose humanistic patina could not protect him from the cold.

Thinkers in the academy were freed from the constraints of the ancient structure: the *artes liberales*, including only the *quadrivium* and the *trivium*; they were cut loose to pursue their respective interests. These included the construction of various new institutions as responses to modern human "needs." With the State as sponsor and a healthy economy as provider, a new era of well-being was promised by leftist ideology. People no longer had to depend on their neighbor, on the virtuous action of a friend or stranger. Social progress was automatic, just like the seeing-eye doors. Thinking about the results of such progress, both within and without the academy, those devoted to study face a pressing task today: How can one see? Has seeing largely departed the academy, to be exercised today instead in the pseudo-sight of technological devices like satellites, cameras, and those automatic doors, or in the penetrating, prophetic insights of independent spirits like Flannery O'Connor, Mark Rothko, or Simone Weil? But to be able *to know* what Antigone faces, to enter her world and have her world enter oneself, is to reach a kind of awareness, a kind of experiential knowing quite outside the parameters of a critical intelligence, as this is generally understood in the university today.

One also needs certain graces or gifts. Thinkers in the early Middle Ages were unanimous in recognizing that the perfection of knowledge only occurred through these gifts, which they attributed to the Third Person of the Trinity, the Holy Spirit. One of the Seven Gifts of the Holy Spirit they named "understanding." Through this grace, one knows, apprehending spiritual goods, subtly penetrating their intimate character. When one sees sensible reality, one sees *into* it. In a pure, piercing vision, one sees . . . what is there. All good poetry is filled with examples of this; it is common to say that a certain poet or artist is particularly gifted. That is precisely true. How else could he or she have seen, having access only to the same sense sensations available to all? When I read poetry, I immediately learn how much I have been missing, how much I do not see. Such a realization moves me to ask: May I seek to obtain the same gifts? Yes, but the tradition teaches that one must first undergo preliminary disciplines that, while necessary, may not be sufficient. For the gifts are mysterious, gratuitous—they are truly gifts.

According to Aquinas, the gift of understanding is opposed to blindness of mind and dullness of sense. He believed that these obstacles originate in the personal distortion resulting from inordinate or disordered sensual delights found in venereal and food/drink pleasures, respectively. That is, these pleasures, as human, can be enjoyed either virtuously or viciously. But today, one must add additional powerful distractions that are specific to our age. The traditional vices of *luxuria* and *gula*, although still vigorously present among us, do not nearly exhaust contemporary obstructions to seeing.

Historically, two kinds of experience contributed to the sharpening of one's vision: the very precariousness of existence and the various ascetical exercises practiced throughout one's lifetime in order to purify one's external and internal senses, the passions, one's mind and spirit. But today's religious and secular academics are among society's most protected and privileged persons. They are the very ones who most benefit from the securities, honors, and perquisites that the various social systems offer. Further, they often seem to be singularly unaware of the need for a *moral* askesis, that is, the lifetime practice of that complex of disciplines traditionally designed to affect and transform the various aspects of one's faculties or powers and being with a view toward reaching an unclouded vision, a crystalline insight, as a virtuous person. In this sense, one can recognize that the goods and services of modernity, the up-to-date, state-of-the-art institutions or systems are poisonous, sickening, making one blind; they are ersatz substitutes for virtue. In a strange irony of history, many of those things that the men and women of the labor movement ostensibly fought and died for over so many years must now be recognized as producing enervating obtuseness . . . worse, if one hopes to live by faith.

One day when I arrived at Peter's room in the hospital, I found the corridor cluttered with stacks of clothing-like articles and a sign on his door that read: Enter Only After Donning the Sterile Clothes. I put on the paper gown, cap, mask, shoes, and gloves . . . and knocked. Peter's voice invited me in. From all the treatments, he was in an extremely weakened condition, and the medical people were afraid he might pick up some bug—which would finish him off quickly!

Peter gave me the usual scientific up-date on the treatments and his reactions. He then started describing the next procedures that were to take place on the following days. As he spoke, an inner shudder racked my spirit. He no longer used the first person singular, only the first person plural. I realized that he had thoroughly changed, beyond anything I could have imagined. He had lost any capacity to view himself as a self, as a person independent of the system that had embraced him during the past year. The only subject of predication and action now was the complex of medical personnel, together with their belief system and technological tools. Peter, the person, was subsumed under, inside . . . but where? My friend had ceased to exist.

During the past year, before my eyes, I had watched the death of Peter. I had seen, in an extreme and exaggerated form, what a modern institution can do to a person. Step by inevitable step, always under the guise of care, motivated only by the desire to help, always acting out of the assurance of impeccable scientific credentials, the medical system inexorably replaced his person with an abstract hollowness parading as a we. The white-robed priesthood sacrificed him on the altar of knowledge, of progress, or perhaps only of hubris. Apparently, no one learned anything from this horror. The doctors and their scientific technological tools killed him before he could die. I would not have believed that such a monstrous murder could occur if I had not witnessed it myself, slowly taking place before my eyes . . . week after week. Now, Peter was no longer able to die.

I was deeply disturbed after leaving the hospital. In this state, I searched back through my reading and experiences to find some suggestion, an insight, a lead to understand what I had witnessed. Finally, I re-read Dostoyevsky's "The Grand Inquisitor," the prose poem related to Alyosha by his brother Ivan Karamazov. At first, the fit appeared frighteningly perfect . . . if I looked at the doctors' project as an unconscious secular vulgarization of the Inquisitor's acknowledged transcendental sophistication. But the more I reflected on the two situations, the more convinced I became that the Inquisitor and the doctors served the same master . . . the one definitively rejected by Christ in the desert. There remained one major difference, however: the doctors lacked the finely honed intelligence of the Grand Inquisitor; they were unaware of the full import of their employment.

Do Peter and Mark really exist? Yes. I have known them; I have been blessed by their friendship; they are important to me. But they are critical for others, also, not as individual persons, but as stories. Each has a story to tell, a story about the possibility and impossibility of freedom today. And as freedom is different for each of us—for example, all cannot accept or handle equal amounts of freedom—so each will interpret the stories differently. Each can learn something about his or her unique truth in the two stories. For me, it is a question of faith: in what, ultimately, do I place my faith?

An immediate objection arises: not everyone can cut himself or herself off from modern systems and flee to an island that has an especially rich cultural heritage. But this is to misunderstand the nature of story in human cultures; stories are not literal photos, not laboratory models. The objection is completely beside the point. What to think and do then? I assume that I cannot exercise control over, or change, the world of systems. It is there, apparently firmly in place, demanding acquiescence if not universal allegiance. I refuse, however, to accept my helplessness; I refuse to submit myself as a kind of powerless non-entity; I refuse to accept the world as it is today. I, too, want to experience the friendship of the saints, the sense pleasures and painful dramas celebrated by poets, the precariousness of creaturely existence.

The one action clearly open to me is to say, "NO." No, I will not go along quietly. No, I will not obey. I will not make myself compatible with the program. This may be a necessary absolute today to begin to live humanly and, to the degree possible, autonomously and virtuously. The decision must be clearly spoken, and spoken daily. To be real, it requires a regular reflection, a quiet time when I enter into myself to look out at what I have rejected, what I still accept and what I grudgingly put up with. Some believe that a good place to begin is with the contemporary notion of health. Recognizing that health today is an illusion, actually only survival in a technical system, I say, "No," no to the health system, no to the fantasies it fosters and promotes. But this demands acts of renunciation. And these actions will be different for each person, the NO spoken in each one's unique voice, place and time. For me, it might begin with the refusal to take an aspirin for a headache; for another, the rejection of a bypass operation. For yet another, with something as complex as the struggle to define oneself over against the diagnosis of a physician . . . or the decision to die one's own death.

For the person of faith in the transcendent, this NO is an initial step in leaving the world of blasphemy. Blasphemy is predicating something of the divine goodness that does not belong there, or denying something that does, usually accompanied by contempt. But that which is constitutive of the contemporary world—reality conceptualized and manipulated as a system—is just such a predication and denial, colored by a peculiarly modern arrogance.

Ultimately, blasphemy is a sin against faith. Through faith, what I see and feel I *know* to be creation; I know that I, as much as all the universe, am in God's hands. What I believe to be real exists only by participation, by sharing in the being of the divine goodness. Through faith, I know that the world is, that it exists, only contingently. Nothing has independent existence—except what I call God. But the "everyday" world in which I find myself acting is more and more an artificial world, a manufactured "reality" ever further removed from Creation. Through this construct, men—and today, women, too—deny Creation, accepting without question the pronouncements of professionals and the hype of publicists, handing themselves over to the inventiveness and manipulation of the more clever and unscrupulous among us. In an efflorescence of vanity, the more enlightened, viewing Creation as a system or set of systems, claim that they understand something called an "ecological problem." Rather than beginning with Creation on one hand, and the fact of vicious behavior, individual and social, on the other, they look to political fixes guided by current views of science and implemented by technological ingenuity.

Formerly, people humbly or arrogantly, trustingly or fearfully, accepted Creation as a gift, as the primary gift, the original expression of the divine goodness, the outpouring of divine love. But the world viewed as a global system, and humans seen as immune systems, deny this ancient belief. Aquinas teaches that blasphemy is a most serious sin because it attacks what basically establishes one in what is— through faith I place myself *in* Creation. Accepting the placement of myself *in* systems is to deny this, is to be blasphemous. And this is why, for the person of faith, the most fundamental question today is: How do I act, vis-à-vis the systems construct? For this is precisely where the denial of faith occurs.

As my friend Mark found, a free life requires a certain self-denial. For some in the affluent sectors of society, those who are most distant from the possibilities of virtuous behavior, such renunciation may seem too drastic, too frightening. It definitely means withdrawal, in some way, from the embrace of institutional supports that act as blindfolds and straitjackets. I firmly believe that one aspect of Mark's behavior is directly and necessarily imitable: to join with one's friends in the search for the places and times to say NO.

8

To Die My Own Death

Socially approved death happens when man has become useless not only as a producer but also as a consumer. It is the point at which a consumer, trained at great expense, must finally be written off as a total loss. Dying has become the ultimate form of consumer resistance.

Ivan Illich

First I see his hands, gripping the bars tightly. Old hands, hands scarred and marked by nearly fourscore years of labor. The fingers are not delicate, the nails not pampered. A remark of my mother's, remembered from a distant childhood, comes to me. "Clean your nails," she gently reminded him, as we got ready to go to church on Sunday mornings. And then he did something that shook my youthful and tender sensibilities, he cleaned and pared his nails with his sharp pocket knife!

My eyes return to the silent figure, confined behind the bars of a hospital bed, hooked up to various machines—*I* feel sick. What have they done to someone who has lived honorably among us? What is this treatment called care? Is there no prophetic voice to scream out to the world: This is not just! This man is owed the dignity his life and work merit! Who is guilty of imposing this shameful end on a praiseworthy citizen? Overwrought, I am unable to look calmly at my father in this strange, new place. I never before felt so strongly my affection for him.

He opens his eyes, sees me, and closes them again. I am unable to speak. Did he recognize me? Why doesn't *he* speak? What is he thinking? A kind of terror slowly envelopes me. But I am too confused to do anything except stand there in dumb silence. What could I do anyway? I need time . . . no, I need knowledge . . . perhaps understanding . . . or, better yet, wisdom.

Later—was it minutes? hours?—the room darkens. The hospital noises, the racket of efficient technology, become somewhat muted. I sit and stare, my mind a jumble. When I first arrived here, after traveling several hundred miles from my farm, the physician gave me a report. I recognized it immediately: a series of categories strung together in the desiccated nonlanguage of a textbook, what passes today in some circles as value-free objective reality. But now I ask myself: What has that description to do with what I see before me? Unless . . . Is this *not* my father then? Has my father been transformed into some other creature, one that fits the needs of modern medicine? Is he already gone? But not yet dead? Creeping terror again.

I stay on through the hours of the night, searching for light in the darkness. I hope to run into him there, among the shades . . . I wait . . . I am quiet . . . then, slowly, images float up before me, some vivid, sharp; some still opaque, playing with me. I have been in hospitals before, many times. I thought I was overfamiliar with these places, skeptical of their promises, hardened against their illusions, confused by their personnel . . . so often I found decent people working there. But now I feel something new. I appear to be lost in a labyrinth; the shadows advance and recede. Then, a startling scene, with its story, comes into clear focus.

I had been here in my hometown some weeks earlier with my son, Ben—a regular trip to see Grandpa and the family. One day we went together to visit an old aunt in the nursing home. She had no children, her husband was dead, but family members regularly dropped in to see her. Entering the main door, we discovered that it was lunchtime. So we headed for the dining room where we knew we would find Aunt Frances with the other ambulatory people. There they were, all seated at their assigned places, four to a table, looking down into their laps, waiting quietly for their meal. I had noticed, during previous visits, that the same old people faced one another at the tables three times a day, until death, but seemed never to carry on a conversation, and often never spoke a word to one another. As Ben and I came into the room, a slow-motion electric shock hit almost everyone. Like Pavlov's dog, each hoary head raised and bleary eyes sought us. The pathetic exchange was familiar to me; it was repeated every time I visited the institution. As I walked past the glassed-in TV lounge on my way to Aunt Frances's room, the eyes of each person, expectant, tried to focus in and hold on to my eyes . . . they mumbled, pleading, Are you coming to see me? Are you my husband? My son? Have you finally come? Guiltily, painfully, confusedly, I turned and forced myself to look straight ahead, down the corridor, until I reached Aunt Frances's room.

Today, making my way through the tables, I seemed to be walking away from rather than toward our aunt. The room moved out, the pitiable creatures rose up to become vague figures in a distant panorama, like faded and unrecognizable clones of Munch's *The Scream*. I felt troubled, anxious. But I knew from previous visits that the dining room population represented the most "presentable" patients. If one were to peer into the rooms of the bedridden on the second floor, a much more shameful sight awaited. There, one really doubted: Is that still someone's mother?

Once, another aunt was on this second floor, and my sister and I came at lunchtime to help her eat (my sister and brother took turns doing this every day). Some of the old folks could be put in wheel chairs and brought to a common room for their meals. While my sister helped our aunt eat, I noticed another old woman being fed by one of the aides. The aide filled a large plastic syringe with what appeared to be mashed up baby food. She then forced open the old woman's mouth, stuck the syringe in, and pressed the mouth full with the pap. After the woman swallowed, the procedure was repeated . . . until she was sufficiently stuffed. I had to work at controlling myself so as not to retch. It seemed obvious to me that the creature sitting there had long ago understood, somewhere in her soul, that her time had come. Instead of a vain struggle against the timely opportunity to embrace death, she stopped eating; she did what her nature and person required. Perhaps she was unable to explain this prudent action in words, but she knew what to do, she understood the laws of the universe, she was ready to obey them. But a recent invention, the caring system, intervened, transforming her from an obedient child of God into an object for the consumption of services; her body was still of some use to the economy; it helped support a huge new growth industry, nursing homes.

Seeing this woman I understood, then, that it is necessary that the society invent a Doctor Kevorkian, necessary that people find a way to have doctors kill them. Techno-medicine has created a race of freakish prodigies far beyond the imaginings of science fiction and Hollywood —for these creatures were truly human at one time. Some people, finally, begin to revolt, begin to demand death in place of suffering monsterhood. However, the pattern of technological death is too deeply engrained. People have had their knowledge of how to die obliterated by a lifetime of treatments by professionals. Now comes the final request, the solution: "Through your propaganda and interventions, reaching back to before I was born, you have made me what I am. . . . I am your invention, your product. Now, I've had enough; it's time to die. Kill me. That's your obligation . . . since you have created me. . . . Into your hands I commend my spirit."

But modern life is not wholly determined by techno-science; bureaucratic procedures are still required; other experts must be consulted; rationales must be devised; the appropriate poison or instrument must be selected; papers must be filled out; all the requisite signatures must be obtained. Only then can the killing take place.

It is fitting, I suppose, that death in the technological society occur in this way. After all, one of the principal effects of modern science is to make each person more and more helpless, to increasingly remove any vestige of autonomy. Death should fit this pattern, should be totally under the control of caring professionals and conscientious bureaucrats. Compassionate doctors cannot renege on their responsibility at the last moment. No one should be permitted, simply, to stop eating and drinking.

I was gazing upon the final scene in modern institutional care— the inevitable result of Western scientific progress, the success of accepted medical intervention, indeed, the picture of what is today called a right! If only the ideologues and technological fanatics could stand here and *see*. They think of time as an irreversible line, at times interrupted, at times continuous. The line proceeds through discoveries and inventions. So, in time, because of progress, we are always at the summit, always on the cutting edge, always enjoying state-of-the-art performances. And, of course, we are never wrong for the naive, banal reason that we are living in the present moment. Therefore, we are *permanently* not only right, but righter than was ever before possible. How neat! How logical!

But I have a feeling that something miscarried terribly. This scene was never imagined. No one had thought it necessary to meditate on Dante's Inferno before going off to medical school, before inventing yet another wonder drug to prolong life. As I looked at these figures, I saw a new race of technological zombies, pathetic Frankenstein monsters in wheelchairs and beds, each one artificially kept alive to a great old age through a lifetime of medical treatments, beginning before birth and generally intensifying as the person becomes ready to die. Someone's father, or grandmother, an individual with a name, now lived on as an abstract example of longevity. So this is what the statistics tables refer to! Apparently, however, no one can see these cruel crimes; people are blinded because they are participants. Everyone shares in the guilt because everyone lives off the industry—believing in its science, buying and ingesting its products, getting rich off its profits. So no one is free to step aside, to stand outside the illusions of modern medicine, to find an independent place from which to see what is there.

I stop myself. Perhaps the shock of seeing my father in a hospital bed has unhinged me. These thoughts might be only the bizarre associations of a promiscuous imagination inflamed by an emotionally-heightened night. Perhaps I just need some sleep. St. Clara Manor, where our aunt now lived, is in many respects an exemplary setting. A new building, designed for this purpose, filled with light, color, and efficient arrangements for the latest technological treatments. Various activity programs were offered each day. Volunteers came to entertain, clergy to minister. Since this was a small town, many of the employees knew the patients and their families. Every time I went to see different relatives over the years since the institution was founded, I ran into others also visiting elderly members of their families. Many of the younger generation, like my brother and sister, remained in the town of their birth and were able to maintain close contact with their old. Perhaps I just do not understand how care functions today.

But why do I feel so badly, if my father is receiving the best that an enlightened profession can offer him? Why does the well-run nursing home upset me? Why does this hospital make me sick? Is there some insight here beyond the realization that those I love are getting close to death? Am I on the edge of some perception that I must desperately attempt to comprehend? . . . out of love for those near me. I cannot believe that this is a good way to die. Death should not take such grotesque forms. Is there some relationship—the more control the more horror? Or, is technological death only the modern version of what all humans have had to face? Death, in any form, is always cruel, or senseless, or unjust, or painful, or lonely, or terrifying; perhaps I don't understand anything about the Christian prayer for a good death. It is claimed that with modern medicine one lives longer. Yes, something continues. But what is this creature that hangs on? Anyway, length of life has nothing to do with a good death; of that I am certain. Further, I strongly suspect that a so-called longer life is used (unconsciously, I hope) by the medical profession to extract yet more money, more power, from the public; old peoples' bodies are used to promote the project. But I must concentrate on what is taking place in front of me. The truth of my life at this moment will be found here.

What I see, in and around my father, is the noisy drama of a technological death. But isn't that a matter of more or less, just like life in today's world? No one is completely free from the possible distortions and perversions of technological intrusions. How judge? I've heard that the Amish use a rule of thumb: How will the adoption and use of this technology affect our local community? But almost no one among the rest of us belongs to such a community. We must seek another touchstone. That can be found, I came to think—even today—in the notion of a self. How will the technology affect the self, my self?

The self exists to the extent that the subject is autonomous, not heteronomous, in sensing, perceiving, imagining, thinking, knowing, speaking, and acting. The critical task, vis-à-vis technology, is to determine whether, how, and how much technological devices are corrosive of selfhood. In this sense, I can hold that the self is precious. This self is also given a measure of time on earth, independently of my thoughts or desires. Years of medications and therapies, however, frantically intensified at the end, can alter my time. Is this a particularly serious technological seizure or theft of my self? Is this one of the great sins of our time?

The hours pass; I watch my sleeping father. I immediately left my work and came when my sister called me. She lives with him, caring for him in the family home. Although he became less and less active in the last few years, he required almost no attention. He was accustomed to look after himself, especially after the death of our mother some years ago. The morning after my arrival, I again met with the physician, a new man in town, but my sister liked him. Our old family doctor, with his fingers yellowed from chain smoking, was long dead. The young man spoke to me; he gave me a conscientious report. But it was the speech of an ex-medical student, mouthing the logic of his textbooks, skirting infantile fantasies of omniscience. Then, with obvious feeling and concern, he ended, "Unfortunately, we cannot predict the exact outcome."

"Thank God!" I countered—impulsively, passionately, almost shouting. "Thank God the world and its creatures are such that you cannot predict what will happen!" Startled, his eyes revealed a mixture of fright and puzzlement. Who was this wild man irreverently confronting him? But then the entire expression on his face changed—he understood the meaning and implications of my outburst. He looked down at the floor, turned, and slowly walked away in silence. He gave the impression of being an honest man.

I walked the few blocks from the hospital to my father's house; the town was a comfortable size. When I grew up there, I seemed to know a lot of the people. But now so much had changed; now so many were strangers to me. I recalled a recent visit. Dad asked me to take him around to pay his bills. Never in his life did he have a checking account. He believed credit cards to be some kind of financial deception, designed to trick you into buying and to keep you in debt. Each month he personally visited the various offices to pay his bills: telephone, electricity, gas, water and sewage. He had only utility bills, since he always paid cash for everything he bought. He believed that if he didn't have the money, he shouldn't buy it. Formerly, he rode his old bicycle in this monthly ritual—it would have been a waste to start up the car for such errands. But now he was too feeble to ride his bike— he had already sold the car a couple of years earlier—so I drove him around town that day, substituting for my sister.

I arrived at his house. It was surrounded by large trees, all planted by him years ago, now covering the yard with shade. How many trees he had planted for the neighbors, for different members of the family! He found almost all of them in the few wooded areas still left around the town. He believed that he should look there first, and only pay for nursery stock if the kind of tree he wanted could not be found. He knew all the local species of trees, knew how to dig up one in "the wild," and how to transplant it successfully. How attractive the property looked! But as I approached the house I saw that the shubbery needed trimming; this kind of chore he could no longer do. Neglecting such work, though, was not the significant fact. Rather, in the last years, he had lost interest—in almost everything. I realized that this was a fundamental change in the way he had always lived. I had no recollection of ever seeing him idle, doing nothing. Nor did he ever go to a movie, or any other amusement event, never to a restaurant. Apparently, he felt no need to be entertained. During his vacations, he worked on our or some family member's house—there was always some painting or electrical work, landscaping or gardening to be done.

During the past few years, he spoke progressively less each time I visited him. But I went to see him regularly. I liked to visit his home; it reflected a life I came more and more to respect and admire. I also wanted to hear what he had to say. I believed that he had a certain repertoire of stories, memories from his life, which he would tell me. But he was not the kind of person who, on any certain day, would sit down with you and relate one or more of his stories, if you bluntly asked him. Like other people I know who have good stories to tell, he seemed to follow some secret, idiosyncratic inner rhythm; one could not command or force such a memory. I had to be prepared to wait, to practice a great patience. Genuine stories are not commodities. He told them, one at a time, when he was moved. I could only come, sit, and relax. When he was completely silent, I would know that it was the end; he had finished the last story . . . it was time to die.

Later, I returned to the hospital to keep vigil. He was awake. Seeing me, he asks whether I got the corn grinder; then he seemed to sleep again. He had a grinder that he used to crush corn to feed the birds in winter. The corn he gleaned from a farmer friend's field each fall. He wanted me to take the grinder to prepare corn and grain for the baby chicks on my farm. It would be difficult for him to imagine buying ready-prepared chick feed, which, I guess, all farmers do today. Strange, that he should think of that; it was weeks since he had asked me to take the grinder. How could he come out of the medication, the drugged sleep, find himself in a truly strange place, he who had known only his own bed almost all the nights of his long life, and speak nothing but words of concern about literally helpless creatures, day-old chicks without a mother hen? I had expected to hear some complaint, or the pitiful meanderings of a disoriented old man. I sat down, and emptied my imagination and mind. Perhaps he had yet another story to tell me. As the noise of the hall traffic, the machines, the loud-speakers, died down, a kind of silence settled on the small hospital. In this quiet darkness, I saw something about the truth of his life . . . and his death. There was a last story! When the physician arrived on his morning rounds, I told him what I had heard and seen:

> He is obviously more in our hands than his own. For him, this is a violent change from the way he has lived; this places a direct responsibility, first of all, on me and the rest of the family, but also on you. You have the opportunity to actually do something for him, for this man. That means to be a physician here you must ignore many of your simplistic textbook concepts and formulas; you must try to look at the man before you. He is not a patient, that is, not a generalized, categorical abstraction. Let me give you one small example to illustrate what I'm talking

about. This is something altogether typical of his life; I've just spent all night reflecting on it.

Many years ago he bought and single-handedly tore down a large, old, two-storied frame house. He did this in his spare time after finishing work at the post office each day. Then he tried to salvage all the materials; if possible, nothing would be wasted. He intended to use everything he could in the construction of a new house.

The old one had plastered walls, with old-fashioned laths underneath. He carefully cracked all the plaster, removed the rough-sawn laths without breaking or splitting them, and took out all the nails. He tied them up in bundles and stored them—I don't remember where; there were many bundles.

Over the years, with a hand plane, he turned those thousands of laths into smooth, finished strips of thin lumber. Out of these he made lattice fences, for our yard, and for the yards of relatives and friends. It is almost inconceivable that one man could stand over his workbench the countless hours, slowly doing all this hand labor, all those years. But he could do it because that was the shape he gave to his life, that was the kind of active life he chose to lead. He understood the quiet satisfaction and joy of making something. He was practicing an imaginative recycling long before the concept was invented. His kind of recycling meant that he himself, through a highly labor-intensive action, found a way to turn waste into a useful and attractive artifact for many others. With his finely cared-for hand tools, he stood at that solid homemade workbench during many hours of his lifetime, turning out everything from bird houses to doll houses for family and friends.

Several years ago, you people said he had a cancerous bladder and it should be removed; you took it out. Then, about a year ago, some specialist claimed he needed a pacemaker; you installed it. I suppose you would claim that modern medicine extended his life. Well, it did *something* to him. In this time since you people have interfered in his life, he has drastically altered the way he lives. At eighty-eight, he gets up each morning at six o'clock and cooks some oatmeal for breakfast, the practice of a lifetime. But then immediately returns to bed! This he has never done before. In these years you have given him, he arises at midday and in the evening to eat what my sister prepares. The rest of the time, he sleeps or lies in bed—all day, all night, with one exception. He gets up to go to church on Sundays. He has stopped his lifetime habit of reading in the evening; he no longer watches television. He has become a different kind of being; he is not the same man he was; I cannot recognize him. We—you people, my brother, sister, myself—have made him into what we see lying there in that room. Who or what is that?

He has never been articulate in a conventional sense. But he has always spoken, in his own time, in his own way, and he speaks now, clearly, unequivocally. He's trying to tell us that it's time to die. He's been telling us that for the last several years. What could have been more obvious, more indisputable? Yet I was too blinded to see . . . too much wrapped up in myself, I suppose. We have artificially, probably sinfully, lengthened his life. Doing this, we assaulted him; we violated him. We've turned him into a creature fit only for suffering and the consumption of medical treatments. Now you people would like to try something else! To intensify and prolong the infliction of pain!

Well, he's had enough. There will be no exploratory surgery or any further invasion of his body. When he says he is in pain, give him an anodyne—immediately. No waiting. Is that clear?

He has lived in pain, for years. One had only to see the grimace on his face when he got up out of a chair—always silently, never complaining. Sometimes, when I saw this, I would ask him, "Does that hurt you? Are you in pain?" he always answered, "No." If he says he is in pain now, then simply accept his word. You have no way of imagining his agony. But from the way he has consistently lived, if he now speaks of pain, then he is indeed *in extremis*, and it is our duty to help him. Once, when visiting him at his home, I went to the medicine cabinet looking for an aspirin. There weren't any. None in the house. No medicine of any kind! He was then over eighty.

There is an ominous and terrifying thought: What he suffers now is the unmistakable result of repeated medical interventions, these modern wonders of up-to-date care. Such misery is utterly unnatural, horrifyingly perverse, way beyond what is man's lot to suffer in this life.

I can't expect you to truly see this man. It would be necessary to have lived with him, observed him over many years, to see him. To see another is a wondrous thing, a grace, something quite outside the realm of the professional gaze. So you'll have to look at him through my eyes. Then you'll see him, insofar as

it is given to you, and you will no longer be dealing with a patient, but be looking at someone's father. Your responsibility
now is clear, unambiguous: your job is to help him die, that is,
to leave him alone.

I did not speak calmly, and I probably made harsher remarks than I
remember about medicine today, but at the end of my tirade I offered
something of an apology. I told him I was speaking principally and
directly about the world from which he came, the world of so-called
care systems that endlessly multiply monsters, not about him personally. By this time, I imagine, he was quite bewildered by the polemic.

The darkness and silence of my nocturnal watches turned out to be
radiantly eloquent. My father made himself known to me, and revealed
something about the world in which I live. I now saw more clearly,
because he led me into the experience of it, that the high-tech medical
industry, in its beliefs and ambitions, practices and myths, incarnates
what I have traditionally understood as hellish, fiendish. My father had
become one of the countless victims of the madness that is modern
medicine; he was imprisoned in a demonic torture chamber. With an
anguished, sick feeling, I realized that he had indeed become a patient.
Now anything was permitted.

It is generally believed that the actions of the Nazis were evil. I have
heard of the extermination camps, and I visited one, Auschwitz. After
slowly walking through the gate, under the words in iron letters over
my head: *Arbeit macht frei*, across the yard, into the buildings, I sat
there, alone in the late afternoon of a somber, overcast winter day, in
silence, and wondered . . . Hitler's program of hatred and horror selected only certain well-defined individuals; one could see a frightful
rationale in it; it was not mindless mass murder. But a technological
death makes no such fine distinctions. Everyone might just as well be
a despised Gypsy, a hated Jew or an intransigent Jehovah's Witness.
Everyone in the affluent sectors of our world, even before birth, is a
potential guinea pig for genetic screening and other medical intrusions; after birth, for organ transplants and an ever-lengthening list of
scientific manipulations and experimentations. Everyone, unless the
money runs out, is coerced or pushed, throughout life, to become a
technological construct, a suitable subject for a scientific death.

The rational Nazi order helps greatly to understand what all people
have most in common today: a greater or lesser encirclement of their
ways of perceiving, feeling, thinking and acting by ever more inge-
niously complex and unintelligible technologically generated instru-

ments and organizations, monitors and agents. What I saw in the nursing home, what I see here in the hospital, is of another order, significantly distinct from that of the Nazis. In a sense, there can be no comparison because the differences are too great. Today, the torture is inflicted for the other's good, and with almost everyone's approval. The action is honored by the society, the technologically-supported institutions praised and celebrated by nearly all reasonable people. Few, however, note the extent to which all are increasingly rendered helpless by the technological project, that the interventions are now necessary, an integral part of the megamachine. Further, one's final days come out of the very organization of society, this is the way the society works. Death comes, not by turning on the gas, but by turning off the apparatus—ultimately, according to the indications of the machines and only secondarily from the judgment of the technicians.

In the last few years, I had learned something about political policy, about industrial farms and schools, and now, technological medicine. All actions related to these notions come out of an institution. Are these institutions, then, some kind of lie? All of them equally? Are they an unnatural project? Is this one of the principal sources of evil today? Is this where I should look to see the contemporary forms of the principalities and powers St. Paul warned us about? All these institutions owe their growth partly to the idea of rights. Arguments about the denial of rights, claiming that people have a right to education, to an efficient food system, to health care, to employment and so on, in addition to their dubious character with respect to the concept itself of right, may be a deadly distraction. There may be much more pressing social imperatives: for example, to submit to critical examination these institutional forms, together with the so-called need for such all-encompassing intrusions in peoples' lives.

At the hospital, I quickly learned that constant and alert observation was necessary to protect my father from the normal care procedures. For example, a young woman came in the room to take a blood sample, a routine practice, often repeated, I'm told. My father winced and groaned as she sought yet again to find and puncture an old vein. When I saw what she was doing, I jumped up and demanded, "Why are you doing that?" "We need blood samples for the lab tests"—what could be more obvious? "No, you don't," I shouted angrily. "You'll never take another blood sample from him."

I strode to the nursing station, peremptorily gave them the order, and asked to see the physician when he appeared. Later, confronted with the stupidity and cruelty of the procedure, he admitted that it was unnecessary. And so it stopped. By staying at the hospital as much as possible, and questioning everything they wanted to do to him, I was able to prevent further useless torture. Finally, he was left in peace—to die.

Most patients, regardless of the number and frequency of family visitors, have no one to question the sense of *every* procedure and pill, no one to defend them. But what must be the cruel loneliness of those isolated patients who have no loved one to sit with them day and night? For long hours they are alone with the rhythmic regularity of the beeps and blinks, the maddening absurdity of a machine's cold company.

While waiting for my father's death, the physician and I had several good, "clearing the air" conversations. Speaking together shortly after our early meetings, he presented me with two questions that, he pointed out, are quite different before and after the procedures involved are begun. "Do you want us to feed him if he stops eating and drinking? And, do you want us to use resuscitation measures?" As the eldest, I discussed the matter with my brother and sister and, getting their agreement, I told him, "No resuscitation measures of any kind, and no intravenous feeding or hydration." Since we were not always there twenty-four hours a day, it was necessary to be quite explicit before the occasion.

Once, he expressed his fear, implying that we might sue him because he had neglected to carry out some possible test or procedure. He was confused by having to deal with a family that wanted no unnecessary medical treatment that, in this case, meant no further "curative" measures at all. At another time he worriedly explained how government bureaucrats review physicians' records, and he might be penalized by them for failing to utilize available means to treat this patient.

Toward the end of our vigil, the physician confessed that if it had been his father, he would have acted in the same way. As I suspected, he wanted to be a good man; in his work he still retained some shreds of decency, in spite of the training, in spite of the nefarious business that employed him. This is something quite different from the Schindler phenomenon—the actions of a very *worldly* man who, at great personal risk, saved several thousand Jews from the gas chambers. In the hospital, I regularly noticed bits and pieces of cheer or kindness, in the actions of other employees, too. Can one here speak of some kind of balance? Do these remains, these vestiges, of a gentler way of living, where one person touches another, takes time for another, attempts to see another, prevent the malignant forces of modern institutions from plunging the world into an organized hell? Interestingly, and perhaps importantly, in my experience of hospitals, universities and other such places, it is generally the employees at the bottom who most often act in ways that acknowledge the client or citizen as a singular person, someone with a name, a face, a history different from that of everyone else. From what I have heard, this is not true in another American growth industry, the prison system.

The central question of this experience then appeared before me: How do I protect those I love from the demonic in its specifically modern forms? The answer lies, I believe, in the practice of loving familiarity. This requires time, patience; one must learn to see, to listen. One needs to acquire the habit of being aware of the other, sensitive to the other's nuances. In my case, after a lifetime of casual indifference, I was somehow moved during his last years to be more attentive to my father, repeatedly visiting him, waiting for him to speak, listening to him, attempting to learn the shape of his life. When I knew this, when I knew *him*, I would know how to help him die. I would also find the courage to confront the professionals. So much depends on the intensity and accuracy of this very particular, personal knowledge. One has to know the other intimately. For example, while sitting there beside him, letting the images and events come up out of my memory, hour after hour, I saw something I had forgotten, and I saw it in a completely new light.

My father was born in a rural area of Poland, but his parents emigrated to America when he was two years old, and he grew up in the small town where he remained all his life. The pull toward the soil, toward working in the soil, was strong in his peasant blood; the experience of living on the land had been there for many generations. All the time he was married, a time when he had sufficient income, he wanted to buy a small farm.

His first full-time job, which he began after finishing grammar school, was in a local greenhouse, working with plants. I remember, as a child, helping him in his garden, which took up two city lots. I see now that he and my mother tried to be self-sufficient in providing food for the family. They had the help of others, too. My maternal grandmother still lived in the country and had chickens. Fried chicken was a frequent Sunday dinner. When hogs were butchered, farmers on my father's rural mail route gave him gifts of fresh sausage.

But this was not enough to satisfy his longing for the land. He located a small farm not far from town that was for sale, and wanted to buy it. He would keep his job, but we would move there to live, and he could become a part-time farmer. He carefully explained his plan; the seriousness of his desire was evident to all of us. But our mother said no; and she was adamant. She grew up on a farm, the eldest of four daughters. No sons who lived were born to my grandparents. So the girls had to work hard that the family might pay off the farm mortgage. Now Mom had married a man in town who already owned a house there—he had first built a house, then looked for a wife. She was happy with town living and never wanted to return to the country, except to visit. So, Dad denied what was probably the most powerful longing of his life out of love for his wife. After once bringing up the idea of moving to the country and seeing it shot down, he never mentioned it again. Nor did he ever manifest any resentment. On the contrary, insofar as I could remember, he threw himself single-mindedly and conscientiously into giving his wife, all of us, the best kind of home possible.

With three children, the house he had brought to the marriage proved to be too small. So they bought the old two-story house because of its location, intending to tear it down in a few years. Together, they then designed, and hired a contractor to build, a new house on that property, utilizing much of the material from the old place.

As the children were leaving home, Mom talked about yet another house, a kind of "dream house" with everything conveniently on one floor, and in a better part of town. She was unreservedly and patently untroubled about her vocation. Before marriage, she had worked as a bookkeeper in an office. But from the day of her wedding, she devoted herself enthusiastically and joyfully to the jobs of homemaker and housewife. Although as a young woman she knew how to drive a Model T Ford, she never once drove the newer models that came out after she took up housekeeping. Although I don't know the kind of excitement Dad felt for the new house—I was away in the Marines and then in college—from the results I could see that he thoroughly threw himself into making the new home one of the most attractive properties in the neighborhood.

I also remembered other such actions—the ways in which he repeatedly and consistently reached out to his children, relatives, friends, and neighbors, in light of the respective ties that bound him to each of them. I had no memory of him acting in terms of self; he seemed to have nothing of a modern self about him. But I also remembered many small ways in which he asserted his independence. For example, his first automobile, purchased before his marriage, was a

Model-T Ford. And he stayed with black Fords all his life, in spite of our arguments in favor of some other make or color each time he bought a new car.

In so many ways, he appeared to reject the modern world, the world that, finally, turned against him and attempted to rob him of his death. Reflecting on the actions of his life, I searched for their pattern, their meaning. Then the concept came to me, from out of the Middle Ages. For a thousand years, philosophers and theologians had tried to talk about the Trinity. One of the ideas that some of them came up with was that of a *relatio subsistens*, a subsistent relationship. According to the tradition in which they worked, the two words were contrary to one another, the expression was illogical, nonsensical. A relation only exists between two things, it has no existence of itself. And *subsistens* means totally independent existence, neither needing nor admitting anything else. These men used the notion of a *relatio subsistens*, then, to talk about the Persons of the Trinity—each existed only as a relation to the other two. No one could exist for itself.

Since my father was a man of deep faith—which I noticed, for example, from the way he prayed—I would expect him to express his faith directly in the way he lived; and he did. His life made the ancient concepts sensible—accessible to my sense experience—as the ideas in turn marvelously illumined his life. His final gift to me, then, was this: to some small degree I was enabled to act as he had acted, to focus my attention on someone else, not on myself . . . I helped him die his own death.

9

Childhood as Addiction

I also committed thefts from my parents' cellar and table,
either under the sway of greediness or to have
something to offer other boys who would sell me their
playthings, in which, of course, they took equal delight.
Often beaten at games, out of a vain desire for
distinction I tried even then for dishonest victories. . . .
Is this boyish innocence? It is not. O Lord, it is not: I
pray you, my God, that I may say it.

Saint Augustine

A few weeks after my eighteenth birthday, having just graduated from high school, I left home secretly vowing never to return. I had stuck it out to graduation and could now, I thought, leave in good conscience. Feeling as if I had been narrowly confined too long to a small town, under the control of very provincial parents, I sought to get as far away as possible. I joined the military, attracted by the recruitment promise: "Join the Marines and see the world." Now, fifty years later, I see my parents and that town very differently . . . of course! Long, quiet winter nights in a remote nonelectric farmhouse are one of the great gifts of my life. Watching the constantly changing flicker of the fire, hearing it crackle in response to the moaning wind outside, I now see aspects of my life that were previously hidden from me. For example, I think I finally understand something of who my parents were and what they tried to do, as parents. In those years before leaving home, I was consumed with great anger toward them, especially toward my father. Many times I would end a conversation with him, shouting, insulting him, condemning him for what I judged to be his ignorance and prejudice. After having exploded spouting my adolescent wisdom, I would storm out of the room, not waiting to hear any answer from him. Vanity and arrogance fueled my anger, but I also felt seriously deprived: he had denied me a childhood.

When he and his parents emigrated from Poland in 1900, he was two years old. They settled in Lincoln, Illinois, a small town where his father found work in a coal mine. This was a place and time when one could still keep a cow, chickens, a pig, and cultivate a large garden in the town. Today I understand that the ways of viewing the world and self, the manner of thinking and acting, were for the recent immigrants the heritage of hundreds or thousands of years' experience—the experience of subsistence, the *lack* of experience of living wholly in a money economy. Although my grandfather gratefully accepted the necessity of employment, and went to a job every day to support his family in comfort—as a child I thought their house, with two (rather small) parlors, was enormous and sumptuous—he kept to customs that were anomalous in an industrializing America. For example, for him and my grandmother, part of the joy of begetting children flowed directly from the way *all* participated in the life of the household. Quite young children early took on the responsibility of caring for their younger brothers and sisters. Everyone had his or her job in the domestic economy, that is, everyone was needed. There was a large garden and orchard. The cow had to be taken to pasture at the edge of town and milked twice every day; the milk was sold and delivered to neighbors. A flock of chickens required some care. All the youngsters, both boys and girls, as soon as they were old enough, found part-time employment. In this kind of life, young people were not an expensive nuisance, could not become what John Holt, that marvelous critic of educational mischief, recognized as middle-class "super-pets."

In the new land, my father completed grammar school. He was not sophisticated enough to reject all schooling, but he was smart enough to know that he didn't need more. As the oldest of six children, he immediately became employed full-time in a local greenhouse. He was thus able to help support the family and allow his brothers and sisters to go to high school. He was the only child who remained continuously in that town until his death, the one who seemed to have the strongest sense of place, of the importance of rooting himself in a familiar place.

When I was growing up, the town and its inhabitants had become more urban. My grandmother still kept chickens, but only a few people on the edges of town had cows, horses, or pigs. One man, with his wagon and team of horses, would go down the streets and alleys each day to pick up garbage and damaged produce for his hogs. Since these were the days before the widespread use of chemicals in agriculture, he could confidently feed these slops to his livestock. I suppose one could view this as an early version of modern garbage disposal. But it was very different from what came later. At that earlier time, very little went "to waste," as the expression used then put it. There was almost nothing to pick up except for edible leftovers. Such was the way people still lived in that town. Elaborate packaging had not yet become universal. People had next to nothing to throw away; there was no regular trash removal.

By the time of his marriage, my father had a better job as a rural mail carrier in the post office. He went to work early and was usually home by noon. I now realize that the rest of the day was largely devoted to what can only be called subsistence activities, that is, as tending toward this kind of life. For example, he salvaged parts from a couple of wrecked Ford Model A cars and made a four-wheel trailer that he pulled behind his car, connected with a hitch that he himself designed and made from scrap metal. He was then able to use the car cum trailer as a kind of truck for hauling things.

Once, some professional lumber people cut down and removed the "saw logs" from a grove of black walnut trees a short distance outside town. From what they left behind as useless or worthless, Dad and Grandpa, with a large two-man saw, cut logs, and transported these to a local sawmill in the trailer. Then he hauled the lumber to my maternal grandfather's barn in the country, where he let it dry and cure for some years. When the boards were ready, he delivered them to a highly skilled cabinetmaker in town, a German immigrant. After looking at pictures in catalogs, my parents showed the craftsman the design they wanted for their dining room furniture. Although I was a very young child, I can still remember what the man told my parents in his halting English. He explained that he had a secret formula for making his own glue, and it would never fail. Over sixty years later, the handsome furniture is still in perfect condition. I suspect that it is the only solid walnut dining room suite in the town.

Although not possessing cabinetmaking skills, Dad knew how to do carpentry, plumbing, and electrical wiring. From him, I learned to use all the basic hand tools, from a spirit level to a pipe threader to a blowtorch (fueled by gasoline and hand-pumped compressed air, used to heat a soldering iron—he never bought an electric one). I cannot recall him teaching me the difference between a claw and a ball peen hammer, between a cross-cut and a rip-saw, or their respective uses. But I learned those things, together with much more, which only now have I begun to understand and appreciate. Today I know how to use these tools for various building projects.

When I was quite young, he made me a child's wagon. The manner of making it was a typically characteristic action. He never bought something when he could make it himself; he never paid for some service when he could do it himself. But it was only when I saw him making a wagon for my children that I learned how he did this. He salvaged the wheels, axles, and handle from the local city dump. He also found usable lumber there, from which he made the wagon bed, and many other things. I remember seeing an old photo of myself when I was three or four, with one foot on the running board of a homemade scooter. I most probably never owned a factory-built one, not because my parents could not afford it but because such a frivolous purchase did not fit their idea of how to live.

I don't remember how it happened, but he gave me an idea on how to make good use of my new wagon: I could go up and down the alleys of the town, knock on doors, and ask for old newspapers, metal, rags, and glass. I then took the newspapers to the greenhouse, which bought them for use in wrapping plants and cut flowers (today, I have seen the custom continued only in "Third World" countries). The local junkyard bought everything else. I remember both places as huge, fascinating complexes into which a small boy could only get a glimpse. But the junkman accepted me and my little wagon on equal terms with the man who hauled a ton of scrap iron on a truck. We both received payment according to the weight we brought him. Between kids learning to live in an economy and a friendly junkman, the town had little need for professional trash removal. With the money earned, I was able to open a savings account. My introduction to money and banking was through entrepreneurial work, not through an allowance. I don't remember ever being given money by my parents, but one grandmother usually gave us kids a dime when we saw her.

I also learned to look for jobs where a young person would be hired. For example, I remember getting up before dawn, riding my bike to the edge of town, and picking black raspberries in a large patch there. My earnings were in direct proportion to the time I worked and the speed with which I picked—an exciting experience. Many years later, I learned that this was called piece-work, and a method used to exploit factory workers. But in that place, with that owner, I thought I was being treated with singular generosity. When it was time for the stores to open, the owner himself loaded the berries in his small truck and delivered them to the locally-owned grocery stores. The entire operation, in retrospect, appears eminently sensible, good for all whom it affected.

Then, while still in grammar school, I was introduced to the machinery of the State. My father took me to an office where I obtained a social security card—of which I was quite proud! Another proof that I was no longer a child, that I was grown-up; I could officially work as an adult. Almost immediately, I found a job—my first employment with a regular business that kept records and required its workers to have social security cards. A local print shop hired me to deliver their free weekly paper, *The Lincoln Shopper*. I was not yet old enough to deliver the town's daily newspaper, a job for which there was keen competition among older high school-age boys.

I paid my own way to the movies—Westerns—every Saturday afternoon, but I have no memory of using my earnings for any other personal pleasure or recreational consumption. I noticed that I differed from my friends in these habits; when they got money, they spent it. But I never reflected on the differences between us. They were given money, as they were given clothes and food, affection and rules. They were dependent adjuncts to their parents. Now I see that my parents lived very differently. Each person in the family worked and saved; it was somehow indecent to be too dependent, sinful to waste. Reflecting on my seemingly automatic actions today, and looking back at my parents' lives, I get some idea how strongly their pattern of living affected me. A connected series of routine acts, repeated daily, illustrates an aspect of the pattern. My father needed a car to deliver mail on the rural mail route. When he came home, he drove the car directly into the garage—where it stayed; he never parked it on the street. If he needed to go out again, he walked or rode his bicycle, a rather ancient model. He took the car *only* when strictly necessary. I, too, had a bicycle, a very plain, used, "unfashionable" design he picked up from a friend. I never owned a new bike. But I don't remember objecting to any of this.

I do recall a much later discussion with my sister about Dad's bicycle after he had sold the car and given up driving altogether. She begged me to intervene, to tell him that he could no longer ride the bike; at his age, it was far too dangerous; she could easily drive him wherever he wanted to go. "He'll get killed out there on Seventeenth

Street one of these days," she lamented, referring to one of the busiest streets in town, a street on which he often rode. I said, no, I would not interfere. Without understanding what I was saying, I told her that that would be a good way for him to die. Somehow, I did comprehend the importance of allowing him as much freedom and independence as possible . . . to treat him in his old age as he had treated us when we were young.

All my recollections of this early period are good; there are no unpleasant memories. I remember the excitement of being taken out and taught how to fish, with homemade equipment. Another day, in the winter, I was allowed to accompany my father and Grandpa to a nearby forest where they cut down a huge tree with their hand tools for use as firewood. While watching and waiting for the tree to come crashing down, I warmed myself at a small fire they had made. On Sundays, we would sometimes visit the zoo in a neighboring city, or a park in another. I became an avid model airplane builder. During the summer, there were "meets" on Sunday afternoons in the surrounding larger cities. Whenever one of these occurred, he would drive me and my models there to participate. Mom would make us a lunch and a large jug of iced tea. It would not have occurred to any of us to *buy* soda pop, sandwiches, or snacks. I thought we made long journeys then, but I realize now that each city was only about thirty miles away.

Since that time I have wondered about these excursions. My father was very strict with himself on the use of the car. For example, he never traveled any place on a vacation trip in his life, except that once we visited relatives in a city about a hundred miles away. This was considered a major trip! Such was the extent of my geographic world; I never traveled farther until the time I left home. But he was always eager to take me to those model contests. I was a good builder of airplanes, and won prizes. Perhaps he respected this activity because, starting with delicate pieces of balsa wood, glue, and tissue paper, I ended up with something well made, something whose artistry and beauty he could appreciate. Today, it's called a hobby and I've noticed that one makes almost nothing. All the pieces are already cut and shaped; one only assembles them.

At that time, I never felt deprived, I never had any resentments—that I can remember. The work was meaningful, rewarding. I knew how to do things; I earned my own money. I experienced a certain independence. In some significant ways, I lived as an adult. I also joined the Boy Scouts and was an enthusiastic camper. I found a cheap, used tent but otherwise had almost no "store-bought" equipment, nor a complete uniform. I made my own back pack with a padded wooden frame. When we lost our scoutmaster, and could not find another, Dad stepped in and took over, although he had little talent for the organizational regimen of scouting.

I think it must have been about the time I entered high school that I began to feel differently about my parents. With an interest in girls, I became extremely self-conscious. I took some kind of special injection from the family doctor because I imagined that I had acne. At the barbershop, I could get a face massage, which was supposed to help keep one's complexion clear. I began to feel a certain embarrassment; Dad did not use "correct" grammar, he always wore "farmer" overalls when at home—except for Sundays. He was the only person in town to be seen pulling a four-wheel homemade trailer behind his car, always hauling something or other. He would buy only a black, "practical" car. Of course, he himself changed the oil and did the lubrication, buying the oil and grease "in bulk," that is, filling his own containers at the supply store. Today, I doubt that one can buy oil and grease in this form; they only come in small throw-away packages.

Whenever I wanted to drive my friends to a football or basketball game in a neighboring town, or had a date, Dad always let me have the car. This was during the war, with gas rationing, and he would sometimes remind me of that fact. He had a "C" ration card, because of the mail route, and could get all the gas he needed. But for himself, he would never use the car except when strictly necessary. With me, he was much more liberal, although he would mention that I should think about the war, too. But I was too wrapped up in myself to worry about a distant war. My great concern was the gnawing fear that I could not impress the girl I was dating with that black Ford. Also, how could I bring her home to meet the family when he would be dressed like that? speaking like that?

I had a regular after-school job that allowed me to skip the last period in the class day. At first, I was proud of this—I had the kind of serious job that gave me, and a few other students, this privilege. But then I noticed that all the other kids in my social circle strolled downtown every day after school to have cherry Cokes at Gus's, the local soda fountain. On Saturday nights, there was often a dance. I had to work all day Saturday, until about ten at night. This was a farm town and all the farmers came to shop on Saturday, the one day the stores stayed open late. I either could not go to the dance, or had to arrive very late, since I had to go home and shower after the day's work. Then I began to feel really victimized . . . and smolderingly resentful.

Now, however, I recognize that my own selfishness and vanity had much to do with the rage building up within me. I imagined that my father had trapped me in this work situation, had kept me from enjoying the carefree freedom of my friends, and I turned against him. When I could legitimately escape his control I did so. And I got what I wanted: the Marines sent me to China immediately after boot camp!

Now I see that my parents were trying to save me from childhood, from *modern* childhood. Of course, they would not have said this, could not have explained it. Their attitude and action flowed directly out of their respective histories: centuries of young people growing into adulthood without the debilitating indulgence of a childhood. Neither parent had known a childhood themselves. My mother grew up on a farm, the eldest of four daughters, and had to participate in the domestic economy of that household, that is, work, as soon as she was able.

John Holt believed that the unique character of modern childhood lies in this: it cuts off the young from the adult world, making young people—especially in middle and upper income families—a mixture of expensive nuisance, fragile treasure, slave, and super-pet. Well, neither my parents nor I ever experienced any of this. As the historian Philippe Ariès showed some years ago, the modern phenomenon of childhood is a social construction that has its origins in the "rising" middle classes of seventeenth-century Europe. It was a creation of those we now understand as ideologues, and did not extend to the "lower" classes or peasants. Its rise accompanied the destruction of a gendered society, a society where men and women occupied separate spheres of thought and speech, worked with different tools, and acted according to the appropriate male or female behavior. When the culturally created and approved patterns of gender no longer existed, young boys and girls had no exemplary figures to follow. They could not become adults, as had previously been the case. Childhood, and then adolescence, were created for them. From what I see all around me today, many experience great difficulty in freeing themselves from the trivialities and inanities of affluent teenagers. They are stuck; they cannot get beyond being ex-children.

My father was not an articulate man. He did not sit down with my mother and discuss what would be best for me, my sister, and brother. In his world, such a question could not come up, indeed, would be considered silly or gratuitous. The wisdom that guided his and my mother's attitudes and actions grew out of centuries of experience. It was a cultural, moral stance prior to thought, more fundamental than the literate imagination. Their configuration, as man and woman, was somewhat like the basic place in which tribal peoples in India live. A friend who works with them told me that these people lose their ability to live within their natural and cultural world as they are inducted into the world of literacy. My parents, although literate, had managed to retain their traditional belief and behavioral formation.

My parents' ancestors, people called peasants, were never infected by childhood, this early modern form of an immune deficiency produced by intellectuals. Both parents, strongly rooted in ancient practices, also possessed the strength of character needed to resist the blandishments of an easy accommodation to a consumptive mode of living. Although we lived in town, and Dad earned a decent salary throughout the Depression, both parents nevertheless sought to be as independent as they could, that is, to live as far outside the money economy as possible. Dad only abandoned his large garden when he was too old to do the work. Mom continued to can and preserve food, darn socks, make the bread, pies, cakes and cookies that we ate, until her death. I seem to remember that our principal meat in the winter was wild rabbit. Dad made wooden box traps out of old, discarded lumber (best, he said, because of its smell), and supplied both us and the neighbors with fresh rabbit. He did not need an ideology of animal rights, or a sentimentalized feel for little furry beasts, to dissuade him from using cruel steel traps. The traps were manufactured; you had to insert yourself more deeply into the money economy, making yourself more dependent and vulnerable, to buy them. He brought his rabbits home alive in an old gunny sack. I still recall my fascination watching him expertly and quickly slit a rabbit's throat, instantly killing it, then hang it up on two nails so that he could cleanly skin and gut it.

Each Saturday night my father churned our butter with cream from my maternal grandparents' farm. On Sundays, we often ate chicken from the same place. On our way home from church, we always stopped at the ice house for a chunk of ice to make ice cream for Sunday dinner. We children participated in the tasks of the family rituals. Turning the crank of the freezer until the custard felt hard enough indicating that it was ready for packing with ice and salt was only one of the many activities where we children actually felt something happening under our hands, due to the work of our hands. We lived in a world largely devoid of packages, of commodities, of nouns. We actively affected and made the substance and rhythms of our daily lives; it was a life of verbs.

We never bought anything—neither goods nor services—that we

ourselves could supply at home by our own work. I never ate in a restaurant until after I left home. But we "ate out" frequently—at the homes of grandparents and other family members. It seems to me now that my parents had no inclination toward, no desire for, modernity as a way of living, as the sort of life where one constantly consumes— things, services, culture—and produces mostly trash and neurotic symptoms.

I do not remember being encouraged to do well at school, and no mention was ever made of going to college. I do remember the oft-repeated advice of my father, "Whatever you do, learn a trade. That is always useful." By this he meant something like plumbing, carpentry, or auto mechanics. We never "broadened" our horizons through travel. But we often visited relatives, and never missed the annual family re-union—a full day's outing to a neighboring city. There was no attempt by our parents to feed us culture through visits to art museums, thea-ters, and concert halls; there were none in our town. But I was given piano lessons—which was an extra expense—until I refused to con-tinue, at about the same time that I found "deficiencies" in my father.

From observing those around me in the various subcultures through which I have moved, and in which I have lived in different countries, and from my reading of Western literature, I now see that I learned something in that small town infinitely more precious than the con-sumption of "high" culture, a truth that precedes all genuine expres-sions of artistic beauty: I learned the necessity of hand labor. Wendell Berry believes that the experience of hand labor that good farming requires is the source of that confidence and independence of charac-ter that underlie what is traditionally understood as a virtuous life. In spite of an apparently successful academic life, far removed from any hand labor, I immediately recognized the truth of what Berry wrote when I first read it. I then came to believe that I had to make a change, to fill this emptiness in my life. But I strongly doubt whether I would have been capable of the recognition or the move without the strong and unwavering example of my parents, and the initiation into real work—at a very young age.

I have no memory of my parents telling me how to live my life. This seems somehow related to the unspoken but quiet certainty of their own lives. Without any reflective rationalization, any justification or mystification, they *knew* how they wished to live. Their strictness with themselves and me, however, also allowed a remarkable spirit of per-missiveness. In my third year of high school, I started smoking when out with my friends. But almost immediately, I decided to announce that I was going to smoke in my room at home. Although neither parent had ever smoked, they quietly accepted my declaration without comment. But I didn't risk pushing what appeared to be my good luck too far; I never smoked in the other rooms of the house, until I returned from the Marine Corps.

About the same time, my friends and I began to experiment with taking a drink. In that small town we were able to get the town drunk to buy us a bottle of whiskey now and then. One day I asked my father to buy me and my friends a case of beer. I wanted to invite them over to my house for an evening of poker, a real all-male party. He immediately did this without discussion, although he himself seldom drank beer and liquor never. The other boys had to be careful to hide these parties from their parents. They would never dare ask for such liberal treatment in their homes. Why was it, among my circle of friends, that my parents were the only ones who insisted that their children "earn their own way," and were also the only ones who permitted their children to do things like smoke and drink at home?

In childhood, as it is generally lived among the middle classes today, young people never actually live connections—between work in a field and the food one eats; between thought, construction and the enjoyment of shelter; between activities and a place, leading to the bonds tying one to that place; between themselves and the adults in their lives. Most young people have no daily experience of being needed, of genuinely feeling that the work of the household could not be done without them; of knowing that not to participate in this work is to cut oneself off from oneself, that is, from one's integral self, from one's immediate community, the family.

About twenty years ago, thinking these thoughts, and looking at our two young children, then about seven and eight, I came to see that we were giving them a childhood, searching for the best school, looking out for cultural events in the city for very young people, always on the watch for enrichment experiences to feed them. Although I did not understand very well what was happening, both to them and to us, their parents, I felt that something was wrong, something was not good. In spite of what I had learned as a child, in spite of my father's advice, I had acquired not a constructive skill but a Ph.D., and worked not in terms of anything remotely resembling subsistence but for a university. Our children were being corrupted by childhood, I was becoming ever more helpless by employment, but I was not perspicacious enough to see this clearly. I only had my suspicions; happily, they were just barely enough.

This was when I quit my job as a professor of political science and gathered up a collection of my father's old but well cared-for hand tools—he seemed to have two of everything, and insisted that I take what he was not using—and set out to practice those skills I first learned as a child: how to use a square, hammer, and saw, how to work with chalk lines and a plumb bob, which wrench was required for which task.

We wanted to make ourselves as independent as possible of the economy. Taken out of school, going to live in a tent until a house was built, the children saw what had to be done to protect oneself from the rain, to dispose of human waste, to plan and construct a dwelling. To the extent they were able, they learned carpentry, brick-laying, plumbing, how to grow food, how to care for livestock. Our new home was a passive solar design—which worked out well—but when cold temperatures were accompanied by an overcast sky some supplemental heat from a wood stove was needed. We prepared our food on a beautiful old-fashioned cook stove that also required wood. So logs had to be cut up and split. I had two saws, a one-man and a two-man crosscut. I suggested to the kids that they take turns on the other end of the two-man saw. They had no objection! So each day after lunch we sawed two or three logs. They apparently recognized that they were not just being used, that the work was necessary. Later, they enjoyed sitting in front of an open fire in the heating stove, directly enjoying the fruit of their labors.

One aspect of what I did, though, was not good. I did not sufficiently trust the kids. We tried, in subtle and sometimes direct ways, to organize their learning. We suggested they do some math each day; I studied annotated bibliographies of children's books published at the University of Chicago and picked out some "better" books for them to read. Each week we visited a local public library, where they themselves were allowed to select most of what they read—a rather large stack of books each week. I suppose that, seeing their parents read, and having no television, they naturally picked up books. I had not yet read Jean Liedloff (*The Continuum Concept*), and had no knowledge of what she found among the Yequana in Venezuela—roughly, parents acted out of an "instinctual letting-go" based on touch, rather than rational theory based on some anthropologist's interpretations. I now see that this book helps to explain what my parents knew about rearing children. They acted out of pre-rational cultural patterns on which I could not call because I was corrupted by modern ideas and books on socialization processes and child-rearing practices. Mom and Dad understood that after the "age of reason"—which most peoples fix at about seven or eight—the young person should generally be treated as an adult, treated seriously, that is, neither as a love-object nor as an annoying and expensive pain-in-the-neck. A friend of mine, out of her reflective experience, believes that the projection of childhood onto young people contributes significantly to child sexual abuse. If the very young person were treated as an adult, he or she would be much better prepared to resist unwanted sexual advances, would have habitually experienced him- or herself as a person with some measure of independence, autonomy, a real ability to stand on their own feet and defend their own integrity.

At this time, I still did not know John Holt's *Escape From Childhood*. After reflecting on my own experience as a young person and on that of my kids out there in the countryside, I now know that Holt's position must be seriously considered:

> Young people should have the right to control and direct their own learning, that is, to decide what they want to learn, and when, where, how, how much, how fast, and with what help they want to learn it. . . . A person's freedom of learning is part of his freedom of thought, even more basic than his freedom of speech. If we take from someone his right to decide what he will be curious about, we destroy his freedom of thought, we say, in effect, you must think not about what interests and concerns *you*, but what interests and concerns *us*. . . . It did not occur to them [the framers of the Constitution] that even the most tyrannical government would try to control people's minds, what they thought and knew. That idea was to come later, under the benevolent guise of compulsory universal education.

From looking back on our growth, I now know that both I and my children learned best, and selected better things to learn, when left alone, to be on our own. Holt was right: Kids are naturally curious, eager to learn, will learn by themselves, and generally need no teaching until they ask for it. For example, I once noticed the kids, ours and the neighbors', busily at work on some project. I asked them what they were doing. "We're putting out a newspaper," they said. The paper had pen drawings, rubbings (which they had themselves discovered how to make by placing a piece of paper on a surface having a bas-relief, then "rubbing" a pencil or crayon across the paper), and various categories—news, feature story, comics and sports, with each person responsible for one of them. I was not aware that the kids had ever looked at a newspaper. A local weekly arrived in the mail, but I never suggested that they read it or study its conceptual order. Since we lived at great distances from most neighbors, they could deliver only three or four copies of their paper. But each one was individually handmade; it would have been difficult to produce more. Further, they expressed no desire to do so. A calculation of number did not occur to them (How do we get this out to more people, and more efficiently?!). They showed no trace of a modern ethos. A day or two later, they were busily involved in another venture, which they themselves had thought up. For the various activities and projects, they seldom came to ask for special materials, and never sought to be taken someplace. They always managed to exercise a great deal of imaginative improvisation. In all the time we lived in the country, I do not remember them ever coming with the complaint, "What is there to do? I'm bored."

John Holt believed that his proposals on the rights of kids

> could well take place in any reasonably intelligent, honest, kindly, and humane country in which on the whole people do not need and crave power over others, do not worry much about being Number One, do not live under this constant threat of severe poverty, uselessness and failure, do not exploit and prey upon each other.

Such rights could be exercised—*then*—in towns like that in which I grew up, but only if one had a certain kind of old-fashioned parents who were insightful and courageous enough to act on their inherited wisdom. At the farm, we tried to give our own kids a setting in which they could learn not only how to work, but the necessity of doing what most people seem to regard—Wendell Berry was not afraid to name it—as "nigger work," and a place where they could also "run wild," finally, a household where they were truly needed.

We were fortunate, or blessed: we found a piece of land in a remote area, constructed a house built according to my wife's design, provided our own food, obtained water, all without electricity. The kids saw that the parents worked hard all day, almost every day, that we might eat and be sheltered. But they also saw that we read many books, that we thoroughly enjoyed visiting the neighbors and participating in local church activities, that people often came to see us, some just to talk, some to look more closely at the way we lived. Essentially, I don't think they needed anything more. They certainly did not need any planned lessons, or a curriculum, or programs to broaden their sensibilities or minds. As Berry writes, to the extent one feels the small pleasures of one's place, one is strong; to the extent one needs other pleasures, the ones for which money is necessary, one is weak.

After the kids were grown, I heard talk about something called Lyme disease. The ticks that are supposed to cause such a feared malady are common where we lived. But the kids were never given elaborate warnings or clothed in anything except what they chose to wear— shorts or long pants, depending on the season and their whim. They did become expert, however, and quickly, in searching for and immediately removing ticks from their bodies. They freely explored the surrounding fields and forests without ever being bitten by the poisonous snakes of the area, the dangerous and aggressive copperhead. They knew such snakes existed, and would often tell me, when they arrived back at the house, that they had seen one. I usually smiled to myself, thinking that their imagination probably had something to do with the sighting.

When I read Liedloff and Holt, I finally understood what my parents were valiantly struggling to do: save me from a modern childhood— what I later tried to do with my own children. I feel now that my instincts for how one treats kids are not as thoroughly corrupted by modern thought and practice as they were when I was still closely involved in accepted institutional living. I was also greatly helped to understand these things when, a few years ago, I saw a documentary film in Chile. That year the IRS surprised me with a check of just over a thousand dollars. As a divorced "head of household," I did not earn enough money, or so they judged, to support myself and my son who was living with me at the time. I felt no need for more income that year. What to do with the money? I then recalled that, for about thirty years, I had been hoping to find a way, somehow, to visit old friends in Chile. But I never had the money for such a trip. Suddenly, I could do it! My daughter, paying her own way, wanted to go with me. There, my friends urged us to see this documentary, which had won various prizes, including first place at the Cuban Film Festival that year.

It told the story of some upper-middle and upper-class university students voluntarily working with kids in a *barriada*, a slum in Santiago. To show the reality of the youngsters' lives, that is, to show how "deprived" they were, the moviemakers focused on the daily activities of two, a boy and a girl about nine or ten years old. They followed the little girl as she pulled her homemade wagon around the city from one garbage can to another, gradually filling it with the "treasures" she rooted out from the trash. At the end of the day, she proudly and smilingly held up what she had salvaged for herself and her family. The little boy showed how he started with a rag, a can of shoe polish and a simple homemade foot rest, taking them downtown to shine shoes. Later, he was able to get a greater variety of polishes and brushes. He displayed all the household items he had purchased for his mother, and the school supplies for himself, out of his earnings. An evident confidence, self-reliance, joy and pride shone out from the faces and posture of these kids as they stood before the pleasant strangers with their fancy cameras. These kids would never enjoy a childhood. But, on their own, they had quickly become mature persons; their self-respect was evident in the unstudied ways they moved in front of the camera. I know something of the life of the privileged students, that is, how they are brought up, surrounded with toys matching their age level, right up to senility and death. With a surprised shock, I saw that the very excellence of the moviemakers' art let me recognize which group of young people were deprived and which blessed. Of course, this interpretation was radically different from that given by the Chilean and Cuban critics.

In their bones, in their flesh, my parents knew that modern childhood is bad; it serves today as an efficient and effective training ground for addictive-like dependence on consumption, and for learning to demand various packages from professional experts and government agencies. This kind of rearing of the young almost infallibly produces grown-up ex-children who continually need new toys, who are never satisfied, who have no sense of what is enough, who see no wisdom in Thoreau's ideal of seeking the minimum, who cannot find happiness in a lifelong dwelling in one place, rejoicing in an ever deeper appreciation of its wonders. The universally popular American childhood is programmed to produce ever new generations overpopulated with overgrown spoiled brats. Today's child-adults are mobile, continually moving, always seeking a new job, a different city, and then buying travel packages to break the routine. But they can never cure their itch. They are driven to earn enough money to visit "exotic" and "interesting" vacation spots continually, to relieve ever-pressing boredom and affirm their social status among peers.

When I quit my job, I believed that I had to reject all modern institutions—educational, health, employment, cultural—in order to live a good life. I now see that my parents' peasant parochialism was at once more daring and more audacious. No voices in their surroundings questioned the conventional wisdom of a middle-class childhood. I am a slow learner, but I have finally recognized that their wisdom enabled them not only to live well, giving their children the daily example of virtuous lives, but to resist, quietly and bravely, all the respectable currents that would suck their children into childhood.

10

A Job To Find

There is no issue in society that is not a moral issue in
both the transient human sense and also as one that
God judges. In a fallen world, all human beings live at
each other's expense, and every decision and action,
even those that seem trivial or only private or
unambiguous, is consequently related to the lives of all
other human beings.

William Stringfellow

Trying to live on the edge of the economy can
sometimes require sharp and sudden shifts.
Once, a few years ago, when I was beginning to believe that my life on
a subsistence-like farm was reaching a certain rhythm and regularity, I
unexpectedly found that I needed a regular, "real" income, a check
every month. Unforeseen and unavoidable circumstances demanded
this. The good work of the farm was not producing enough income to
cover some new bills. Well, I was not facing anything so unusual. A
large number of my fellow citizens, on any given day, were out there,
broke, in real need of money. What did they do? Many turned themselves into the specific *homo economicus* found at the bottom of the
heap: they searched the job market for employment. In my unemploy-
ment, I had become rather complacent, even self-satisfied; I had successfully escaped. Well, almost. It appeared that I had not sufficiently
"paid my dues." I had fled from the common lot too soon. . . . I had
achieved my independence too easily.

However, the task should not be so difficult. I had heard many reports, both anecdotal and "analytic," on the need for conscientious workers in all sectors of the economy. Good. But I lived in a part of the country where job opportunities are extremely limited, and I was not willing to relocate. So, looking around my area, I found that the two major employers were the large state university and several prisons. I remembered reading about the life of a writer I admired, John Cheever, who had recently died; he had taught prisoners at Sing Sing. I was impressed by the story, and intrigued by the possibilities of such work. Perhaps this kind of job would be something other than mere employment, a kind of *good* work.

I immediately started making inquiries. Yes, there were educational programs for prisoners; and, yes, they hired teachers. With a certain feeling of excitement, I filled out application forms—and started fantasizing about the work, knowing almost nothing about prisons. For years, I had been haunted by a statement of Thoreau: "Under a government which imprisons any unjustly, the true place for a just man is also a prison." I have heard the claim that people are imprisoned unjustly in America today. What is the truth about this? Getting inside a prison, I would have the opportunity to know actual persons there, rather than have my mind cluttered with the pseudo-knowledge of statistics. Perhaps I would now come to know a world that was foreign to me, but somehow—because I lived in the same state with many prisoners—one very near.

I soon discovered a few practical, discriminating facts about institutions bureaucratically organized: to work in them one must have the proper credentials; these are obtained from another bureaucratically organized institution, recognized as legitimate by the first one. Actually, I should have remembered all that from my last employment at the university. I quickly learned that all my many credentials counted as almost nothing. A Ph.D. from a prestigious university with the other degrees that precede it, studies at various specialized academic institutions, teaching experience in two languages at several levels in a number of different countries were of no use at all to gain entry to a prison. I needed a certain number of credit hours in appropriate methodology and theory courses in primary and secondary education—such as Behavioral and Psychological Aspects of Classroom Management—together with a period of approved experience in supervised student-teaching. Since I needed the job immediately, I could hardly devote a couple of years to fulfilling these requirements.

I suspected, however, that there were ways around the letter of all the rules. The most certain, of course, would have been a powerful friend in a high place. But I knew no such person. Most of my friends were modest farmers. Their voices would carry no weight, and they could only speak about my character and work habits, not about teaching ability. So I began exploring various channels through correspondence. There followed a series of letters to and from officials at the prisons and in the state capital. But as these multiplied, I came to believe that the labyrinthine ways of these bureaucracies would, in the end, defeat me. As the paper piled up, the situation appeared more and more hopeless and I began to feel like a lonely and despondent figure out of Kafka.

As a rational calculator, I had been pursuing other possibilities simultaneously, but not enthusiastically. When moving to the area, I had obtained adjunct faculty status at the university in order to use the library. Since this appointment created no obligations for the institution, and I never asked for anything except a faculty library card, they readily granted me the privilege. But now I appeared, asking for a job! I felt certain my credentials would be impressive and broad enough so that I could fill some need in the department. Teaching one course each semester would provide me all the income I needed. I was not asking for anything like a regular, full-time, tenure-track faculty appointment. Nevertheless, they told me that nothing was available. I was quickly learning what people sometimes face when they look for a job.

At this very time, I saw an announcement of an opening, a part-time position as an advisor in a newly instituted Honors Program. Looking at the job description, and following a long conversation with the man responsible for the hiring, it appeared to me that I was uniquely qualified for the job. I submitted my curriculum vitae, a job application form and two very strong letters of recommendation from respected faculty members who knew me. The administrator hired someone else!

Beginning to feel a touch of panic, and growing more desperate in my need, I tried to figure out what had happened. Why had I failed to get the job? Reviewing the meeting with the man hiring for the part-time position, I suddenly realized that in our lengthy interview he did almost all the talking, and did not ask me a single question about my experience or background. It was obvious what had occurred: He had already picked the person he wanted, but went through the motions of interviewing more than one candidate without, however, considering their qualifications—a not unusual practice in academic life. A friend at the university told me that such positions are said to be "wired."

Whatever may have been the truth of my suspicion, the atmosphere of both offices seemed to contain a similar definable character. I had the feeling the respective administrators asked themselves, perhaps not so bluntly, nor so clearly: Why does he come to us? What does he seek here? Didn't he abandon the university ten years ago? I suspect they sensed that I had made a judgment on the academy and the way of life it permits and encourages. Therefore, I should now live with that judgment. From their perspective, there was a certain lack of propriety in my present action, a kind of moral flabbiness. On reflection, I would have difficulty arguing with that interpretation.

But at the time I was not willing to accept such a cold analysis. I was especially angry, really upset, about the Honors Program job. The hiring process was grossly unfair. My qualifications were not even considered. There was no thought given to what my training and experience could bring to the lives of students. Almost immediately, however, I realized how foolish were my sentiments, how vain my reasoning. I was chagrined to see what lay behind the kinds of employment I had sought. Working at a prison, I would appear before my children and friends as doing a good work, a bit odd perhaps, but certainly helping others who had taken a wrong turn, made a mistake, or been disadvantaged in the society. Holding a job at the university, I would return to the respected sector of society I had quit . . . albeit only part-time and at a second-rate institution.

I then saw that from both an intellectual and moral perspective—if one can so categorize and simplify—my behavior was actually reprehensible. How could I have been so misled by my pride and pretensions? Accepting payment for teaching in the prison would make me an integral part of that institution, one that daily, in so many ways, violates the courtesy and respect due the prisoners as fellow human beings. How could I so thoughtlessly participate in such a system? On the other hand, I knew men, upright and conscientious heads of families, who worked as guards in the prison. Society, through its leaders, had categorized the prisoners as incorrigibly dangerous outcasts, and a kind of wage slavery maintained an unrelenting power over people in that part of the state. These men found it impossible to refuse the jobs. If I were more honest, I would admit that I had more in common with them than with Cheever.

Being paid to assist students in an Honors Program would be something like working in a more humane alternative school. Such places, I had always believed, might be more injurious to young people than a rigid institution run by people who mechanically hew to the letter. In the enlightened structure, it is more difficult for the students to see how they are being used and exploited; hence, they are more deeply corrupted by the experience. The Honors Program was only a tiny piece of a huge institution; I knew nothing about its administrative background. Who was really interested in establishing this program? and, Why? The advisor job might be the position of a flunky in an image-producing program thrown as a sop to some legislative aide serving a powerful politician in Springfield; in short, a ploy to maintain or increase state appropriations to the university. I was brought to my senses and saved from my own folly, not by any action of personal insight, not by moral reflection, but by the "unjust" behavior of bureaucratic administrators!

I was familiar with some of the literature on jobs and employment in contemporary society. But except for certain outstanding authors like C. Wright Mills, people who researched and wrote in this area did not greatly impress me. I always felt there was something more to the story, something they missed, or that the entire account was out of focus, somehow distorted. I was also intrigued by certain hints I had picked up. For example, the efforts of the Castro government in the early years to alter drastically the reward structure for the various jobs in Cuban society, establishing much greater egalitarianism. I also read of persons in America, highly educated, who nevertheless chose to work as night watchmen, or garbage collectors. I had learned something from French and other historians who sought to write history from the perspective of those at the bottom. A question, then, slowly pressed itself on me: Why not go to the bottom and find out what is there?

I already had some job experience near the bottom of the pyramid. While a private in the Marine Corps infantry, I spent many hours cleaning heads (toilets), scrubbing pots and pans, walking around military installations on guard duty. The ideology constantly drummed into us was that we should be proud to be at the bottom—only the toughest could survive there. In high school, my part-time job included daily janitorial duties. While in college, I worked as a laborer on a construction crew one summer, and in a glass bottle factory during others. But this was temporary, summer employment only, and I did not desperately need the money. I benefited from the original G.I. Bill, and that covered all college expenses. My attitudes about money, employment, and social status, however, were very different then. The jobs were little more than means to achieve something I wanted: the freedom and leisure to study. Each night I returned to the comfortable family home. Now, however, I had the chance to travel to a largely uncharted world, the world of those permanently stuck in the cellar of the employment hierarchy. I felt a consuming curiosity to learn more about the place, to go there, not as an adventurer or tourist but as some kind of genuine participant.

In spite of all the talk about post-industrial society, and the growth of high-technology, I knew there had to be a bottom everywhere; one only had to look. I suspected, from my knowledge of what the research did not say, that the people there were like Ralph Ellison's *Invisible Man*—invisible. Physically, many only appear with their brooms and mops and vacuum cleaners after the important workers have gone home. I was also suspicious of the concepts I found in conventional reports, such as "dead-end jobs" and "unskilled labor." What do they mean? What's it like to be a person in a dead-end job? At the time, I knew no one there, nor anyone who had gone there to live with such people, to tell the literate public what it is like, except for the great French witness, Simone Weil. Her diary/report, about factory work in Paris before World War II, was recognized by American thinkers like Dwight Macdonald as the most biting and profound account of such labor ever written. She truly had something to say about what that kind of employment did to people, to their dignity and spirit. But "the bottom" in the United States of today is very different from a Paris factory in the 1930s.

Weil attempted to share, as fully as possible, the working and living conditions of her companions in the factory. The comprehensiveness of her experience contributed greatly to the veracity and richness of her journal. Her powers of observation, both of herself and of her fellow workers, were quite remarkable. No one would ever be able to lay down her account unmoved. I had heard of others, too, for example, the Little Brothers and Sisters of Jesus, a group founded in France after World War II. Inspired by the life and writings of Charles de Foucauld, these persons go to live and work quietly among the "lower sectors." But I knew none of them well, and very little of their experience. I immediately understood, however, that I was especially fortunate: I would not go to the bottom as an observer, even a so-called participant observer. I was going for the same reason others go: I had to find a job, I needed the income, and this was one place—for me, maybe the only place in the area—where I could find employment. For the first time in my life, I began to feel options being cut off, doors being closed. . . .

I decided to look for the invisible workers at the bottom of the ranking at the university, the region's major employer. I found that, below administrators, faculty, and staff, there is a large and heterogeneous grouping of people, the blue collar workers, and that among them there is an order according to prestige and pay. Electricians, for example, higher, grounds keepers somewhere in the middle and, at the very bottom, a category called "kitchen helper." I had no idea what that meant, but the literature had said that jobs down there were all unskilled. So I certainly must have the qualifications! For I was beginning to feel a certain desperation. Ever since I discovered I needed regular income, I had been reading the Help Wanted ads, checking out various leads, but all my efforts ended only in disappointment and frustration. Was I participating further in the experiences of so many today? I *have* to get a job, and soon. What are my chances here? How should I approach them? Will they hire me? Each day my search became more anxious; each evening I returned home more discouraged.

At the university, I found the employment office. The first step was to undergo "job counseling." The nice young woman tried conscientiously to learn something of my experience and qualifications, together with my past job record. I suppose she would then match this information against the dozens of job categories available, and then point me toward the place where, presumably, I fitted best. Before she got started, I immediately tried to distract her; I didn't want to let her ask her questions. "Well, I have this crazy fantasy," I said, "I want to work as a kitchen helper; I don't want any other job." Trying to sustain this line of talk, I hoped to avoid any direct inquiries about my background, for I didn't want to lie. Is this what others, too, must do? Perhaps for very different reasons? I had no criminal record to hide, only a Ph.D. What might other poor devils have to disguise? In my case, it worked. She let me fill out a form without any probing, and told me the time and place for the next kitchen helper civil service examination. Fortunately, it was quite soon.

On the big day of the exam, I arrived at the proper place, as eager and nervous as any other job hunter. About twenty-five or thirty of us quietly took our places in school chairs, those with a writing shelf; the exam was written and timed. I looked around the room. They seemed to be quite normal people, appearing to be not so very different from many friends and acquaintances. But I had a distinct impression of deference—these people are accustomed to being told what to do, to stand and wait. They know the habit of deferring to their "betters." I wondered . . . how many authors, who write books about the economy and the job structure of the society have stopped to look closely at these persons who work at the bottom? To meet them? To come to *know* some of them? Who can imagine what each of them is feeling today, at this moment, waiting to be tested by a set of questions dreamed up by some expert in personnel management? A paradoxical meeting was taking place in this room: tests drawn up by those in the society who are the most successful test-takers, and those who have most egregiously and frequently failed.

Recalling my questions of that time some years ago, I am reminded of my recent puzzlement when speaking with a friend from Germany. I was telling him of my difficulties with a German locksmith who was not being very cooperative in making some unusual keys I needed. "Well," my friend, an academic, said, "you have to remember that these men are at the bottom of the economic ladder . . . they sometimes feel certain resentments." I was taken aback, but said nothing. I wondered . . . Has he never looked at his own society? at what appears to me to be the bottom? For example, all the men who sweep the streets regularly, cleaning up the trash that thoughtless people throw there, picking up the large amounts of dog shit deposited there, or the men and women on duty in the public toilets, keeping them neat and spotless. Are all these workers invisible?

As I waited for the test administrator to come, a disturbing thought upset me. I had heard that there would probably be one or two openings in this job category in the next couple of weeks. But there were also applicants listed who had already taken and passed the written exam. And here I was with another roomful of patient but expectant job-seekers. So I was in direct competition with all these people for the available openings—assuming there would actually be some. This, then, is part of what economists mean when they say that the system is based on the principle of scarcity! But who has understood this? Which one of us has had the opportunity to sit down in front of the other job applicant and say, "I am directly competing with you for this job. But I cannot look into your eyes, I cannot ask you about your need . . . I must put my own first . . . I must seek to take care of *my* family, not yours. Only one of us will emerge from this bureaucratic ordeal with a job, enjoying the wherewithal to stand on his or her own two feet . . . insofar as that is possible in this world of employment." Is this what lies at the bottom of our society? Is this the relationship between the other and me on which our society rests?

In some form, a similar situation exists throughout the economic system. But it has been my experience that there are great discrepancies between the top and the bottom. As I have explored the lower sectors, I find that the farther down I go, the options are fewer, the constraints more pressing; the desperation becomes greater, the dog eat dog character fiercer. People at the top, too, knife one another, but the warfare is generally quite different. There, one has more freedom to move; the necessity to destroy one's competitor for a job tends to result more from one's own character and ambition, not from the structure of available positions. As one descends the hierarchy, the image of the pit bull appears to illustrate the reality. Before being thrown into the ring to fight and destroy the other, these animals are bred to do this task well. With the people at the bottom, breeding is called socialization, the normal process for introducing people into the society's approved myths and behaviors . . .

The university official arrived and explained the way the test worked —it all sounded so rational, so matter-of-fact, so . . . natural. Feeling a little sick, I took up my pencil and read the first question. Undoubtedly the most experienced test-taker in the room, I would surely pass with high marks.

Later I learned that, for this specific job category, the principle of scarcity did not operate quite so ruthlessly as I had imagined. Some of the people taking the test were also taking tests for other, higher positions in the civil service system. They were using the kitchen helper job as a kind of fall-back application. Some already had low level jobs, but in the private sector. They hoped to make a move to the public sector where the fringe benefits were much better. Further, largely because it was the lowest job in the university, there was a continual and regular turnover of personnel. If one could afford to wait, an opening probably would turn up. I do not know how many of my fellow test-takers that day were like me, truly in need of the job—and as soon as possible. I imagine it's much better not to know the other dog.

Shortly after, through the use of some "political" pull, I was called for a personal interview, and then hired. Were others passed over or turned away that I might get the job? I never knew; and I did not want to find out. I did not then want to think about the question; nor about what was happening to me. I used to believe, with all my academic background and years of experience in "developing" countries, that I knew something about the economy and how it functions. Now I know that my knowledge was largely false. Not only were there huge gaps, but the very character of that knowledge was essentially flawed. This was true because I had seen and understood nothing of what an economy does to one's heart. I now see that my feelings of unease throughout the process of landing a job were sometimes gentle, sometimes forceful indications warning me of the hardening of my heart. I was coldly and determinedly turning against my unknown fellow citizens. The principle of scarcity is indeed real . . . and powerful; it was transforming my person. If I were "employed" only on my farm, I would find this new creature loathsome.

So this is what the principle of scarcity does! This is what underlies the economy. And the economy supports everything else, largely determining what and how one thinks, what one does, how—and whether—one reaches out to another . . . I have now come to understand that my action ten years before these events—an attempt to live outside the economy—had also been a flight *from*. I had thought of it more exclusively in terms of a movement *toward*, a reaching out to a good, a life of contingency, a resting in Providence rather than a dependency on institutions. Now I see that it was also a happy escape from a very bad life, a life in which one is strongly encouraged and pushed to walk over one's neighbor, thereby simultaneously destroying one's own heart.

I was assigned to work in a student dining hall. There, about three thousand young people ate every day. The kitchen helpers gathered up and carried out the garbage, which consisted mostly of large quantities of waste food that the students put on their plates but did not eat. We washed all the dishes, glasses, flatware, pots and pans, and cleaned the dining, serving, and cooking areas. Our crew, about a dozen people, were of all ages, mostly male, about half white, half black. My first day on the job introduced me immediately to an interesting aspect of this strange world. After the noon meal, I was told to take dishes and glasses out of the washing and sterilizing machine. A young black worker was put on the other side of the moving track, so that we worked together. Occasionally, he would disappear, leaving me with twice the work to do—a bit clumsily, since I had never done this before. The shift supervisor, when he saw what was happening, angrily reprimanded my co-worker and made certain that he did his share of the work. The supervisor was black. In nearly two years, working there and in another similar dining hall, I served under several different supervisors, all of whom happened to be black. Each of these—one woman, the others, men—working at the bottom of the heap, knew all the physical aspects of the various jobs well (they had done each of them before being promoted), and acted admirably as capable and habitually fair supervisors. I had previously worked at several universities, always with faculty and administrators. In no one of them did I ever find such a consistent level of both competence and fairness among my peers. Egregious examples of faculty and administrators lacking one or both qualities were always close at hand. Yes, I had indeed entered a strange world.

Occasionally, we had a middle-aged black woman as a worker on our shift, substituting for an absent regular employee. I asked another worker about her situation. He said that her "literacy skills" were not sufficient to pass the simple civil service examination. She had taken it several times, but could not pass. They hired her as extra help, calling her whenever someone was sick or when one of the shifts was short a worker. This had been going on for several years. As extra help, a defined job category in the system, she did not qualify for any of the fringe benefits regular employees received—only payment for the hours worked.

She was an excellent worker, and a person of good cheer, someone you enjoyed working with. For example, when I had been there but a short time, she spontaneously helped me out one day. Sometimes, when working on that washing and sterilizing machine, there was a break of a few minutes. I usually had a copy of the daily student-run newspaper in my back pocket, and would pull this out to read when waiting for something to come out of the machine. Fanny noticed what I was doing; she told me that the top kitchen supervisor did not approve of this and would give me a lower grade on my civil service evaluation (I was still in the probation period). Although I had been doing this for some weeks, and all the older workers knew the attitude of the supervisor, Fanny was the only one who forthrightly took the initiative to come forward and speak to me, to help me.

After learning about the employment situation of Fanny, I decided to try to do something for her. She was obviously being exploited. All agreed that she worked well on the job, but she couldn't be hired as a regular employee. The institution, however, was at liberty to use her whenever it was in a pinch, her lack of literacy presenting no obstacle. Since she needed the money, she would always come when they called, seeking a replacement for a sick or no-show worker.

We had a union and I went to the next meeting to present her case. The president and officers, all black, said they could do nothing: "The rules say." I was stunned; I could not believe their reaction. They appeared to have absolutely no feeling for the injustice being inflicted on this person. They had become wholly bureaucratized, identified with the institution, believing that the literacy test had some meaning, only because it was the rule, the way the system worked. They had lost the ability to open their eyes and see that this person actually did the required work as well or better than any other kitchen helper, and then to make the proper judgment about the obvious injustice wreaked on Fanny. Their own jobs would in no way be jeopardized by initiating some action; they were all certified civil service employees, and could not be dismissed without cause. I offered to argue the case with whoever had the power to make an exception to the rule, reminding them of the unjust discrimination against a model worker. No, they were not interested. From this and a number of similar experiences I came to the conclusion that ideas such as solidarity of the working class, of blacks, of women, and so on among other groups throughout the society are largely empty illusions created by venal and self-promoting ideologues who need to give the impression that they have a constituency, that they are actually leaders speaking for followers.

One day, at our coffee break, I noticed a story in the newspaper about university salaries. Since it is a state university, these figures are public. I calculated what the president was earning per hour and compared this with our wages (we were paid by the hour). I then talked about this huge difference with the others on the shift. No one of them felt that there were any grounds for criticism. But I could not determine what was in their minds. Did they believe that his job was so important as to justify the enormously greater rewards? Or that he was an especially competent person and was being paid for his superior intelligence and knowledge? Or was this just another of those societal enigmas—the "way things are"?

From working with the top officials of universities, I knew that their job is not usually very important. That, generally, the institution "runs itself," that most decisions can be handled by someone possessing good judgment and routine management skills. When some unusually complex or delicate matter must be decided, good administrators always consult others anyway. If one is looking for "vision," "new direction," or "distinctive character" for an institution, one will not succeed by meeting the high salary demands of coddled administrators. There is no necessary correlation between large sums of money and imaginative institutional initiatives. There is also the curious custom today that when some so-called important decision must be made, an outside consultant, highly paid, is called in. I also happened to learn, from an example of the president's work, that his job performance was seriously flawed. He had a degree in the same discipline as myself, political science. A few weeks earlier, he had passed around a syllabus for a course he wanted to teach. As adjunct faculty, I had a box in the office, and sometimes stopped by to pick up memos and junk mail. Some years earlier, in another university, I had been a department chairman, and had also worked on a committee approving new courses to be offered throughout the institution. So I had seen many syllabi. This man's presentation was a rambling account of half-digested ideas—on something he called "bio-politics"—with a laundry list of readings. It evidenced no coherence and reflected little intelligence.

I thought about this for some time because I had noticed that the kitchen helpers were uniformly good workers. They were busy the entire time for which they were paid, except for the authorized coffee break in the morning and afternoon. These were never extended a minute beyond the limit. Each knew his or her job and did it well. From my service in the Marines, I often had to prepare for a "white glove" inspection. That dining hall would have passed at almost all times. Nor was it an easy place to keep clean and orderly. Beyond the usual grease and dirt that a large institutional food facility produces, we had to cope with the behavior of the students. Scrubbing the place after they had finished eating, I often thought that I had never seen badly behaved small children make such a mess. From these years of mopping and cleaning up the waste and litter left by youngsters who seemed intent on establishing their credentials as overindulged delinquents, my generally jaundiced view of American college students was further confirmed.

I had come to know other administrators, faculty, and staff in the university, and the impression—at least from these examples—raised a question: As one went up in the hierarchy of jobs, the level of competence appeared to go down. I suspect that there is some general truth here, not only for that university, but for many institutions in the society. This is how I read Jaroslav Hašek's novel, *The Good Soldier Švejk*. I have always believed that the book, as great literature, is a powerful modern morality play revealing an important aspect of contemporary life, and suggesting an appropriate response. The story portrays all institutions as corrupt, but those that are more honored in the society are worse; their depravity is greater. Further, within any institution, the higher one goes, the more pronounced the corruption, encompassing both crass incompetence and moral turpitude. The question, then, is this: Is Švejk's response—to play the bumbling fool, to plead idiocy whenever caught out—the most sensible or reasonable? Perhaps my fellow workers on the job understood the world far better than I. My feelings of injustice and desire to "right things" might have been beside the point. Among those totally without power, the person with imagination is free, free to ridicule his betters, to exploit their weaknesses when possible, otherwise ignoring their antics and machinations, except to protect himself when they fall. I resolved to reread Hašek. The behavior of Švejk might have unsuspected affinities with the Holy Fool tradition in Russia, and with others, too, such as Lear's fool. My kitchen helper companions were opening up social forms I had never seriously considered, that is, as having a meaning and suggesting a direction for *my* life.

I smiled inwardly, considering the respective positions of faculty and kitchen helpers. The faculty here, *because* they were employed at this institution, were not free to move to a place like Stanford or Princeton. The recognition of such a fact is part of the inner structure of resentment and bitterness that poisons the vain and ambitious. But the kitchen helpers faced no similar obstacles if they wished to transfer to a more prestigious university. They could move to Yale any day. At the bottom of the employment structure, a marvelously democratic ethos reigned.

I have often thought about the motto expressing the spirit of Saint Benedict, *orare et laborare*, to pray and work. Various persons and groups throughout western history, inspired by this ideal, have attempted to put together, in some form, the life of the spirit and the life of the hands, contemplation and physical work. For example, one of the goals of the Catholic Worker movement in America is that "the workers become scholars and scholars become workers." These people have established farms where intellectuals, farmers and other workers can come together, to work and discuss their respective experiences and insights. While teaching at the university, I found that much of the "intellectual" work was reading and responding to administrative memos, sitting through long and boring committee meetings, engaging in various administrative or personnel disputes. When I came home, I could putter about in the garden or work around the house. But this combination came to feel depressingly unsatisfactory, both intellectually and physically. Then, working in the dining hall, I learned something altogether new. The tasks were such as to require almost no attention. I was free during all the day at the job, free to imagine, to think, to go where I wished, with few distractions. If I did not fully enjoy this time of the spirit, I could only fault myself.

I had acquired, over the years, a facility in what is termed a habit of recollection. I would quietly stand in the presence of some idea, image, or of someone, resting there, letting myself be led, be shown, be taught. Or I would actively pursue clear lines of thought, exploring some current interest. Over the garbage, I experienced a new sense of freedom, of lightness of spirit. I was employed, and yet looked forward to going to the job each day! The journey itself provided both peace and excitement. I had to drive for about half an hour, mostly through a national forest, to reach the university. Often, I would see deer and opossums; sometimes, wild turkeys or foxes; rarely, a coyote or owl. At the job, I always carried pen and paper in my shirt pocket, and would write down any thought or question that occurred to me in my meditations and excursions. One day Fanny and I were working together on opposite sides of the machine. Several times I took out my pen and paper to write down something. I noticed that Fanny was watching me closely and, finally, she could not contain her curiosity any longer. "What you doin'?" she asked. I tried to explain my behavior to her in terms I hoped she would understand. When I finished, she looked somewhat puzzled, and then broke out in laughter. She seemed to be saying, "What craziness! What odd people we have working here!" Of all the workers, she was the one with the greatest sensitivity to what took place around her, the one most candidly inquisitive, most spontaneous and generous with that eagerness one finds in children before it is destroyed by well-meaning parents and schools.

When I returned home at night, I would sit down, take out my notes, and "write up" the thoughts of the day. I always had a shelf or two of books from the library with which I could follow up my thoughts and questions with further reading. Such a regimen did not provide the deep satisfaction of farm work, of course. But if one must earn money, must seek employment, then the large modern institutions seem ideal places. One can usually find work at the bottom and move around invisibly, leading a quiet exciting life of thought and contemplation. One also meets honorable, fascinating people, some of them truly beautiful.

My duties between mealtimes included cleaning the basement area —a corridor, with the toilets and dressing rooms for all the dining hall workers. At various times in my life, I have found myself cleaning institutional toilets: for example, in the after school job during high school, and while in the Marines. Nothing unusual there, except that I learned how to clean such places well. Each of these work experiences also formed a certain mental attitude and inspired a specific kind of thinking. I was alone on the job, it occurred in a somewhat remote place, and I was always moved to reflection. I do not remember feeling and acting similarly in other places, that is, in a repeated, consistent pattern. Curiously, I also felt a certain attraction for this work; I never felt a temptation to shirk it, or an inclination to avoid it. At the dining hall,

I again found myself alone in a tranquil, windowless basement cleaning toilets every day. The various aspects of my thoughts and feelings puzzled me, especially the repetitive pattern extending over many years. Today, I think I understand better what I felt then. In this, I was helped by reading Wendell Berry's *The Hidden Wound*. He writes about necessary work, the tasks that have to be done for living. I take it that when population reaches a certain density, people must formally organize their evacuation, and this will require that someone clean toilets.

Berry claims that people need the experience of doing necessary work—for example, of preparing a piece of ground for cultivation, year after year, the same ground. Perhaps one needs the experiences over several generations. One needs this repeated work to acquire familiarity with a place, that is, to be able to dwell on the earth. If people wish to make their home on the earth, they need familiarity, and one gets it only through the repeated action of *necessary* work. But it is evident, upon reflection, that few people in modern society have this opportunity. Work is so clouded and distanced by machines, paper, throw-aways and hired help—all of which stand between me and most of the shit-work, the nigger-work, the necessary work—that nearly all affluent people are severely deprived and handicapped.

One day, simply enjoying my work, attempting to do a perfect job, I thought vaguely that this, of all possible tasks in the world, is *the* unique kind of work in which to do a perfect job—because no one will notice it, and tomorrow the place will be a dirty mess again. This is precisely the work one should strive to do supremely well. In some very special, initially enigmatical, but certainly true sense, this ephemeral cleaning chore can be discussed in the same breath as the creation of permanent art works such as the magnificent paintings and sculptures one admires in museums. Creating this brief moment of order and beauty, a clean toilet, which in all probability no one will ever notice—I have had a lot of experience to confirm this!—is to enter deeply into the nature of the world, into the truth of the world, the world as Creation, and into oneself as Creation; this is to know the natural experience of contingency: the making of purely temporal beauty. All attempts to create permanent works of art are a kind of hubris, attempts to escape the contingency of this world, dangerous temptations to play God. Thus, in the hands of talented artists they can indeed display an awesome beauty, a powerful but failed grasp for transcendence.

As these thoughts occurred to me, I had the distinct feeling that I was at the center, the center of the universe, that it would be impossible to be more at the center. I realized that the scientists of the Middle Ages who drew maps of the universe with the earth at the center were neither ignorant nor vain—as some modern intellectuals and scientists claim. The ancient scholars accurately portrayed a cosmic truth. The moderns, however, are often lost; they do not know where they stand; some are stupid enough to try to stand on the moon.

I do not now remember—and it is of no importance—but some so-called world-shaking events were taking place at that time. I recalled queer beliefs I had earlier noticed among many fellow academics: The odd thought that certain places were more at "the center" than others—in America, Cambridge or Palo Alto for intellectual life, New York for artistic life, Washington as the center of power, and so on. Since I had lived in these places—and other great "centers" in Europe, Latin America, and Asia—I knew that such an attitude was based largely on illusion. It was often the product of the journalistic hype of the media. With greater coverage and pervasiveness, the media now multiply the illusions.

Since my feelings were very powerful, unmistakably moving, similar in intensity to what I had experienced about twenty years earlier as I stood alone in Monte Albán, the ancient sacred site in southern Mexico, I made some effort to understand what I felt. I remembered that a few years earlier a friend had sent me a book on something called "centering prayer," and I had vaguely heard that people actually taught courses on this! But I knew little else about it. I then learned that "the center" is one of the four principal symbols found throughout the world, the others being the circle, the cross and the square. In many cultures, there is a rich mythology associated with each of these symbols. And, of course, they have a prominent place in some modern schools of psychoanalytic theory and practice.

The center is generally seen as the principle, the absolute reality. Some see it as the image of the meeting of opposites. Therefore, it is a place of dynamic intensity, where one sees a condensation and coexistence of opposing forces, where the one moves toward the many, the interior toward the exterior, the temporal to the eternal. The navel is universally regarded as the symbolic center of the world. Here, one finds both mystical and physical nourishment. The center of the world is also portrayed as an elevation; it is a sacred mountain. It is here where theophanies can take place. And people have identified such places/centers in many countries.

But such descriptive remarks, no matter how scholarly, are vague, highly abstract. The importance of center is found only in the *experi-*

ence of center, the experience of oneself meeting the power to transform self, giving one the ability to know, to love, to act. This is what peoples in all cultures have sought. I doubt that books promoting new "spiritualities," or methods purporting to introduce one to foreign, exotic "wisdoms" will give this transcendent experience. The many advertised Meccas and gurus, domestic and foreign, are perhaps even more dubious. But anyone can make a personal journey, a kind of pilgrimage, to sacred mountains in the midst of our cities. These many centers are often found in the "assholes" of the society, something similar to what I discovered in the sensible metaphor of the toilets. At precisely the moment when many are looking up—to the fantasies of inter-stellar or cyber-space—the real center is far below, in the bodily experience of necessary "nigger-work." It seems possible, then, to confirm in a way peculiar to our age the insights of Dionysius the Pseudo-Areopagite, writing perhaps in the latter half of the fifth century: a thoroughly apophatic approach can lead one to the transcendent. The center is in the dark, mean and nether regions where one can be touched by the light beyond all light.

11

The Stars of Mexico

Whether we live or die is a matter of absolutely no concern whatsoever to the desert. Let men in their madness blast every city on earth into black rubble and envelope the entire planet in a cloud of lethal gas—the canyons and hills, the springs and rocks will still be here, the sunlight will filter through, water will form and warmth shall be upon the land and after sufficient time, no matter how long, somewhere, living things will emerge and join and stand once again, this time perhaps to take a different and better course.

Edward Abbey

Today there is only junk mail . . . another appeal for the homeless—with statistics. That's a bit of information no different, in a sense, from all the innumerable bits of information available on the Internet—except that I have no access to all that. But whether it comes via junk mail or computer screen, the very same questions are raised: What is the character of information in a society? What am I to think about it? What am I to do about it? . . . for example, people with no roof over their heads. . . .

But the questions are not "out there." Sometimes, they don't even exist; they are a fabrication of the information itself; they have little reality beyond the news report or the computer hookup. Whatever their epistemological status might be, all questions must begin with me, with the particularities of my situation—living a quiet, isolated life, after having survived an extremely painful divorce. By choice, I have very little income, but I'm solidly settled in an idyllic rural land-scape, comfortable in a handsome passive solar house. Here I prepare my meals with food I've grown myself, on an elegant antique wood-burning cookstove that simultaneously supplies all the hot water I can use. The attached greenhouse, forming the south wall of the house, enlivens the main living areas even in cloudy weather, and provides me with fresh herbs and vegetables in the winter. Photovoltaics light a couple of small reading lamps at night. In the summer, freshly-cut roses delight my senses while, in the winter, bouquets of dried statice brighten the house with color. Various potted green plants add their flowers in season. In addition to a large, personal library, I have access to any book or article at the nearby university. One could characterize my life as quintessentially selfish.

Like everyone, I live with certain assumptions and beliefs. For example, value-free science does not exist; facts, ultimately, are to be understood by persons, not processed by machines; I think and act out of a moral self. Further, I assume that, in principle, one can know the truth, that is, roughly, the statement of a proposition can contain some meaning. To the extent I approach a meaningful truth, I am invited to act in accord with that truth. This is to be guided by a morally ontological vision. There is (should be) a strict correspondence between knowing and acting; a certain knowing demands a proportionate action. In this perspective, any information bit, fortuitous insight, acquired scientific knowledge, or unsought experience brings with it a vocation: I am called to fit my being into the truth of what has come to me. Therefore, reflecting on the news of homelessness in America, I cannot remain unmoved. I am asked to seek the truth of this information, allow myself to be affected by this truth and perhaps emerge from the encounter a different person, modified in my sense of who I am.

I immediately dismiss the idea of contributing money to a homeless cause, not because I have so little to spare but because I do not believe that one can overcome selfishness at a distance. A much more intimate act is necessary; I am flesh and blood. Love, whether of self or the other is, fundamentally, incarnate. Therefore, love is real if this truth is acknowledged and lived.

My original dream for the farm is dead. It was a family project—everything from the property purchase to the house design to the daily work schedule was thought out in terms of the family. Now that family is dispersed and I have to let this truth act on me. I can still believe in the dream, but in this place others will have to realize it. It is not fitting or proper that I remain here to enjoy the wealth of this property. For example, one visitor, a real estate agent, when entering the door, exclaimed, "This is the most visually exciting interior I have ever seen!" I must sell the place to a family with children.

Several years ago, the property—house, outbuildings, land—was appraised at about $60,000.00. The relatively low value derived from certain facts: the house was isolated in a poor area far from any population center, had no electricity or phone, and boasted only a composting toilet. Since then I had added various improvements, such as a small photovoltaic system. But anyone seeking a less commodity-intensive life would also be less deeply into the money economy. What kind of buyer could afford such a property? But why should I have any control over the buyer?

Memory then led me back through the histories that brought me here: the authors who awakened me to the evils of a society governed by out-of-control institutions and consumption; the wife responsible for much of the beauty and efficiency of the farm; the well-paid job that gave me the capital to begin a new life; the federal government that financed all my undergraduate and graduate education; my parents—the origin of my existence and moral sense. I saw that these histories manifested the character of a gift; my life, from its very beginning until today, is a literal succession of gifts. This truth partly defines me.

Looking further into the anthropological and theological truth of my past, I realized that, prior to the rise of industrial (modern) society, when men and women lived as gendered beings, what they gave one another were, ultimately, gifts. This was before the birth of *homo economicus*, before the hegemony of a market mentality, before scarcity. From Marcel Mauss, I learned something of the character and importance of gift-giving in a society, that there be a society. Within the faith tradition of the West, the universe is, strictly speaking, a gift, the original gift.

The conclusion was immediate and obvious: I should give away the house and land. This was the only way to act in character, to be faithful to my past. But that was not so simple. First of all, I had to discuss any such action with the children, now in their twenties. I had always refused to invest in life insurance, and this property would be their only inheritance.

Friends and family members raised all sorts of objections, judging me to have fallen somewhere between imprudence and insanity. The response of the two kids—the only ones who had a direct interest, the only ones who stood to lose—was quick and straightforward: I should do whatever I wished with the place. Their spontaneous generosity demonstrated that they understood something about gift-giving, that is, how to live in a society.

Some young people, neighbors who had grown up with our kids, heard that I was thinking of making a move, and asked about buying the place. I finally decided to sell it to them for about one-third its market value. It seemed good to charge something, and I would thus have an inheritance for the kids. The buyers did not have much ready cash, so we signed a contract for deed. They obligated themselves to pay me $300.00 a month until the property was paid for.

The universal practice on this kind of transaction in that area is for the owner to charge something around the prevailing rate of interest on mortgages. But I remembered an ancient text: "You must not lend on interest to your brother, whether the loan be of money or food or anything else that may earn interest" (Deut. 23:20). Thinking about this and making a quick historical study of usury in the West, I saw that I could not charge these young people any interest.

In the midst of working through the homelessness in America issue, I received a letter from an old friend, Ivan Illich, asking me if I could help him with the preparation of a book he was writing. Why not? No longer being responsible for that piece of land, I was free to wander. What better reason for travel than friendship? The children, independent, living far away now, had no need for me to remain fixed permanently in one spot.

But how do I travel from one place to another, from Southern Illinois to Mexico, where Illich was at that moment? Friendship calls me to make this journey, but how can I do it? Thinking about the various aspects of travel, I felt I could not get in another airplane. After many years and thousands of miles of air travel, I now found that each subsequent trip was more painful, more disorienting. The increasing discomfort brought me to ask some questions: How is it possible to move across the earth? What are the natural and cultural norms today? More basically, in what terms can I best ask the questions?

War and poverty, singly or in combination, continue to force many people to move. Others have been violently transported from one place to another as slaves or prisoners. Merchants and traders have covered great distances for many centuries. Gypsies are a unique example of a people who live on the road. In some cultures, people go on pilgrimage, walking to a place to transcend all place. But none of these kinds of travel helped me to clarify and state my questions, that I might come to give voice to my feelings, and then learn how to act well.

One way to begin the inquiry is to look at movement across the earth in terms of the extremes: to stay in one place, never traveling, or to be getting in and out of airplanes continually. In my life, at different times, I have experienced both. In the last few years, however, I have come to feel there is something fundamentally wrong with modern airplanes, with this kind of transport. I assume that if one were to invoke an ecological argument, they would be banned from the skies. But I am not looking at them from the perspective of the physical environment. A step toward a possible discussion in the terms that interest me here can be found in the last lines of a poem by Wendell Berry:

> To get back before dark
> is the art of going.

The title of the poem is "Traveling at Home." The lines themselves suggest that movement across the earth is an art, like the art of dancing or playing handball. I know that some people dance or play handball better than others, and I take pleasure in watching their artful motion or, better, practicing these arts myself. These lines also bluntly lay down what might at first seem a crude and simplistic rule for practicing the art of travel: One must return home before it becomes dark. Is that enough to constitute an art?

One must note that, as with all good poetry, these lines, too, contain more than is stated materially—and there are seven more lines in the poem. Berry believes in the possibility of home, in the reality of place. His poetry suggests that, in some way, to live on the earth is to be in a place, to make a home there. One can do this well or badly: well, if one practices the art of living in that place, the art of the *conversatio domestica*—moving gracefully in one's place. This does not mean to establish a "kingdom on earth" but, in terms of one's children, to give them the beliefs and forms of living, the foundational framework of a virtuous life. Berry also writes ("At A Country Funeral"),

> We owe the future
> the past, the long knowledge
> that is the potency of time to come.

This knowledge is kept in a *community* memory, handed on from generation to generation:

There is not only
no better possibility, there is no
other, except for chaos and darkness,
the terrible ground of the only possible
new start.

This is a difficulty with air travel: it continually—and falsely—promises a new start. But can anything good come from a procedure that begins by fearing that I am a potential criminal intent on destroying all my fellow passengers? Today, everyone must submit to the kind of body search formerly reserved only for those reasonably suspected of actually being dangerous criminals.

But quite apart from airplanes, there are many other serious questions that must be raised about the practice of modern movement across the earth. The kind of vehicle is important, in some sense crucial, but there is the more fundamental issue of the movement itself. I tried to find some single rule that would cut through both the technology and the resultant travel. At least for myself, I think I found one: friendship. Out of friendship, I could make this long journey, I could "violate" the art of living's maxim, "home before dark." But perhaps I did not have to get in an airplane and experience the loss of time and place, the sense of moving through a real space, which that kind of transport effects. Surely I could take a bus!

I looked at a map and saw that the Texas-Mexico border covers many miles. Where does one cross? Does the same bus continue on the other side of the border? Or does one change buses? What are the schedules? I then remembered that there were Mexican seasonal farmworkers in our area who helped with the fruit and vegetable harvests. They must use buses as the cheapest form of transportation to and from Mexico. I went to the local bus station, a small counter in a bicycle shop, and asked the agent the destination of the workers when they travel to Mexico. "They all buy tickets to Laredo," he answered. I bought a ticket, which turned out to be remarkably cheap. Since I would not make the trip until several weeks later, I was able to take advantage of a special offer. The agent knew nothing about connections across the border, so I decided to take my chances and not worry about it.

When the day of the great journey arrived, I packed enough food for a few days and got on the bus. From earlier bus travel in America, I had learned that bus stations are not good places to eat. Often, the only thing available is packaged junk food that comes out of machines, or miserably overcooked vegetables unappetizingly displayed in a warming counter. Further, I always thought the cost exorbitant. Most bus passengers, I had noticed, are clearly lower income people who travel for one of two reasons: to find a job or to visit family. Few tourists travel on buses. The great majority of people I have met are poorly dressed and carry their belongings in pasteboard boxes, plastic bags, or old beat-up luggage held together with a rope. I inwardly cringe each time I see them put their money in the machines and get such a rotten bargain.

I enjoyed the fatigue of many hours' sitting in the bus because I felt I was actually moving through a real space. The experience is not nearly so rich, so total as walking a great distance, but one has some attenuated sense of moving. At the bus stops, I was able to whiff the air of another place, to get some sense of the differences between places. In Memphis, for example, the bus station and its surrounding neighborhood are uniformly dreary. San Antonio, on the contrary, welcomes you with a pleasant atmosphere. After tasting the cities of four states, I arrived in Laredo. Sweating in the South Texas heat, I walked up to the counter in the small station, and learned that a bus was leaving for the border in a few minutes. I just had time to get some pesos at a nearby money exchange.

The Mexican bus station across the Rio Grande was not like the one in Texas. It was much larger, the buses were all older, there were many more people and, for a foreigner, a certain confusion seemed to pervade the place. But, knowing Spanish, I had no trouble finding the counter where I could buy a ticket to Mexico City. The bus was leaving almost immediately for the overnight trip; the timing was perfect; my good luck continued to hold.

As we left the city for the open country, I noticed a great difference from the American side. In Laredo, the city seemed to prosper from its position on the border. In Nuevo Laredo, on the Mexican side, the city seemed to suffer. This was especially evident in all public spaces, the common space. There was a certain urban beauty on one side, a definite urban ugliness on the other. Why was this, I wondered? The old question: How to live gracefully in a place?

At a rest stop, there was another striking difference: the great variety of food and drink available for the passengers. Traveling by public transport in America, one finds some choices, albeit expensive ones, only in the larger airports; the bus stations offer a few snack machines or a fast food chain. Mexican bus stations are always crowded; it seems that many people are constantly traveling. On our bus, every seat was taken, very unlike the partially-filled buses I rode to the border. Seeking a comfortable position in my seat, I fell asleep.

In the middle of the night, I was awakened by the bus stopping and everyone getting off. Sleepily, I followed. Although it was summer, the air was quite chilly. Shivering, I looked around—nothing to be seen. We were parked in lonely isolation in what appeared to be high desert. But why? Walking around the bus, I soon learned the reason for an obviously unscheduled stop—a breakdown. The driver was working on the engine while someone held a flashlight for him to see. But his only tools were a pair of pliers and a screwdriver!

A bus approached on the highway, slowed down, and then roared past. This happened several times, the buses going in each direction, north and south. Then one stopped . . . some conversation . . . it, too, continued on its way. Later, another, heading south, also stopped. From the talk, it appeared that the driver had two empty seats. What should I do? How would the fortunate travelers be selected? Being the only obvious foreigner on our bus, I was acutely conscious of my position—I did not want to be the ugly American who pushed himself forward for special treatment, but I was also alert to see what would happen. The driver offered the seats to two women with small children, and asked about their luggage. It turned out that, like many Mexicans coming from the border, they were traveling with huge pasteboard boxes, in addition to having suitcases. The driver explained that his baggage compartment was already filled with such boxes; he could only take people with little or no luggage. Turning to me, he asked what I had: only a small backpack that would easily fit in the overhead rack! He told me to get in. Without thinking to ask where the bus was going, I climbed in and found the empty seat. Then, noticing that the passenger seated next to me had been awakened by the commotion, I asked him where the bus was headed. "A México," he answered. Mexico City! Well, I was on my way again, with only a slight delay. I had always wondered, in admiration, when I got on and rode buses in Mexico. They usually seemed so old and used as to be unsafe or unfit for yet another trip over mountains and across deserts. But although I had often ridden on them, this was the first time I ever experienced a breakdown.

In the early morning hours, we approached Mexico City. They tell me that maybe twenty million people now live, rush about and work there. The city is very different from the one I used to know. In all my earlier arrivals, stretching back over thirty years, I came in on an airplane. Since the airport is more or less downtown, I often got a panoramic view of the city as the plane circled to land. I noticed the lower buildings spreading farther and farther out, while the single tall building downtown, La Torre Latinoamericana, was later joined by other skyscrapers scattered throughout the urban area. Over the years, something else changed—the air itself. To get into many cities of the world today, one must enter a dense, dirty, yellow-gray fog. In the years since I first came here, the poisonous miasma of Mexico City has thickened and darkened, always appearing more ominous, more threatening.

Today, entering the city at street level, I do not notice a sudden change from clear, country air to the leaden, dirty-white atmosphere of the streets. But knowing that there is a sun and not being able to see it, I again experience the dull depression I always feel when in such cities. We pass through a confused mingling of housing, factories, offices, and small businesses of every imaginable kind. No zoning rules here! On corners, early morning street vendors are selling juices, fruit, hot drinks, and a bewildering assortment of freshly cooked— over charcoal fires—and ready-prepared foods, together with various breads and rolls. Others, selling everything from calculators to underwear, are setting up their kiosks or spreading their wares on the sidewalk. All the streets are filled with the restless movement of buses, trucks, cars, and motorcycles. Can so many people have a place to which they are going? But I notice no casual movement—all seem nervous, determined, purposeful, in a hurry.

In a surprisingly short time, the bus pulls into the huge North Station, which serves all destinations north of Mexico City. It seems there are hundreds of buses here, some parked for loading and unloading, others arriving and departing. How quick and competent the drivers must be! In the station, as on the bus, I appear to be the only American. All the hundreds of other foreigners—tourists and businessmen—who arrive and leave every day, are at the airport.

Now I must travel across the expanse of this sprawling megalopolis to the South Station, which serves bus traffic to the South of the city. A great distance, but I know it will not take long to cover it. A few years ago, engineers directed the carving out of tunnels throughout the city so that now a rapid and efficient subway system reaches out in every direction. Each year or two, a new line seems to be added. Is this one of the pull-factors, attracting even more people to the city every year?

I make my way through the crowded station and out to the street. Never having been at the North Station, and not knowing if I shall have to ask for directions, I look around and, happily, spot a bright sign indicating a subway station directly across the street. When I first came to Mexico in 1962, I used to enjoy my occasional trips to the capital. I had a small VW and, once I learned the habits of local drivers, it was fun to drive in the city, with its wide avenues and frequent flower-filled *glorietas* (traffic circles). Today, I will miss all the colors and smells and sounds of the busy avenues and narrow side streets, but I know that there is nothing appealing in frustratingly weaving and jerking one's way across the vehicle-packed city these days, breathing the emissions. I descend the polished stone steps into the subway. I would prefer to wait until I'm dead before going underground, but I must be realistic: The subway is quiet, fast, clean, and costs about ten cents.

There is a clear and detailed map of the entire system on the wall—I see there are now nine lines—with a red arrow indicating where I am. From my memory of the city, I quickly orient myself and identify the lines I must take to reach my destination. There are two changes in the center of the city. I buy a ticket, go through a turnstile, and walk to the sparsely-peopled platform. In a few minutes, a train pulls up, almost noiselessly; I have heard that the large wheels are made of solid rubber. The doors open, a few get off, I enter and find an empty seat in the bright, metallic car. Gently, we start to move, then swiftly race along beneath what Cortéz knew as Lake Texcoco. When he and his fellow adventurers crossed the mountains and looked down on Tenochtitlán, marveling at the splendid city that lay before them, more wondrous than any they had known in Europe, they remarked on the purity of the air through which they saw the incredibly magnificent Aztec architecture reflected in the water of the lake. That was a long time ago. . . .

I check the simple line diagram above the windows to make certain I'm going in the right direction and that I change at the right station. In every country where I've been, these drawings are exactly the same and in the same place, contributing to the creation of yet more undifferentiated modern space; and raising troubling questions: Is where I sit today commensurate with what people formerly knew and experienced as space? How relate myself to these people that I might then come to see where I am today?

But in Mexico City there is one significant difference from other countries I know. Each station is named, but also identified by some recognizable symbol or simple drawing associated with that place. For example, the station near the most famous and visited shrine of the Americas, la Villa, where the centuries-old image of Our Lady of Guadalupe is displayed, is represented by a silhouette of the church. Not everyone among this amazing conglomeration of peoples can read the alphabet. I learned this one day while waiting for a bus. When each one pulled up to the stop, an older lady would ask the driver the bus's destination, although it was painted on the windshield in large letters. With a shock, I realized that she could not read! Spanish was probably her second language, and she possessed only a speaking knowledge of it.

Getting off the train at my first change, I see that I must descend even deeper into the earth to get the connecting line; signs and arrows clearly indicate the way. Nearing the platform, I find that I am indeed near one of the busy centers of the city. So many people are crowded together in front of me that I cannot get near the tracks. When a train arrives, some get off, slowly working their way through the mass of people waiting. Then we all press forward toward the open doors. I am carried along, almost up to a door. In a few minutes, another train arrives, and this time I am pushed into a car.

As with all my past experiences in the Mexico City subway, I see that people act with restraint, exercising a silent and gentle politeness. These passengers, almost universally from the "lower" sectors of the population, are a striking contrast with those I have met in airports, those who come from the middle and "higher" sectors. Among many of these, the rule seems to be: one always pushes forward aggressively, with a marked lack of civility and consideration for others. Children, young people and women—the worst offenders—appear to compete with one another for some prize in generally objectionable behavior. On the subway, however, young people carry themselves with a certain quiet politeness. . . . Will this change? Will city life harden them? Others are earning their living on the trains. Some sing and/or play a musical instrument, and then pass through the car, holding out their "hat." Others have something to sell, which they advertise by reciting its special qualities or attractive price. Once I saw a father-and-son act; they were dressed as clowns, complete with face makeup, and exchanged a spirited comic dialogue for the entertainment of the passengers. Ironically, the poor enjoy live local theater, while the rich are forced to look at inane foreign (Hollywood) movies in their airplanes.

My respect for these people, the people for whom the Mexican Revolution was ostensibly fought, the people who are forced to labor in the North, the people who do the work of Mexico, is renewed each time I enjoy this fleeting and superficial contact with them. Although I speak one of their languages, I know few of them personally; most of my friends and contacts are among the "upper" strata. In the subway, I am often startled and amazed by the strength and dignity of a face that radiantly expresses their ancient blood. I wonder. . . . Was it the faces in Diego Rivera's murals that opened my eyes to these sharp and noble features? Did I need his art to see this beauty?

My mind leaps back to some Aztec poetry I first read years ago. In translation to Spanish or English, the poems still retain great lyric power. When I first read them, I had no words to express what I had experienced; I could only say, What a fresh, original voice! But they were not that at all. We have no idea of their personal biographies. It appears certain, however, that poetry was a *societal* exercise for these people; all Aztec poets were, in a sense, poets laureate, singing the beliefs and joys, the perplexity and fears, of their people. Some believe that the following lines are part of a ghost-song ritual, and that the famous *voladores*, who slowly fly through the air, tied to a central pole, are a dramatic expression of the ghosts descending with their revelations.

> I'm to pass away like a ruined flower. My fame will be
> Nothing, my renown here on earth will be nothing.
> There may be flowers, there may be songs,
> but what might happen to this heart of mine?
> Alas, it's for nothing that we've come
> to be born on earth.
>
> Friends, be pleasured! Let us put our arms around
> each other's shoulders here.
> We're living in a world of flowers here.
> No one when he's gone can enjoy the flowers, the songs,
> that lie outspread in this home of Life Giver.
>
> Earth is but a moment. Is the Place Unknown the same?
> Is there happiness and friendship?
> Is it not just here on earth that acquaintances are made?

Over and over, in subtle and nuanced variations, the Aztec people celebrated three imaged experiences: flowers, music, and something akin to what is today called love or friendship. The flowers are still there, in Mexico, the flowers that gave them such fleeting pleasure. Bits of the music exist, too, thanks to the heroic efforts of a few people—among whom is counted a remarkable American, José Hellmer, a man who struggled alone for many years, searching out and attempt-

ing to help the musicians who, in remote mountain areas, had preserved these ancient instruments and their musical traditions.

But the third experience cannot be known by us. It is evident, from
the poetry itself, that the Aztecs did not have a notion of a modern
self. They were very different kinds of humans. Perhaps it is this unknown and unknowable aspect of their lives that imparts a mysterious
poignancy to their poetry. Today, as I sit in the subway, I wonder: What
are the connections between these people around me and their ancestors? Do they know this poetry? Do they gather regularly to enjoy it?
How many of them can read it in Nahuatl? Have they heard the ancient
music, *their* music? Or is the occasional Walkman I see drumming only
the latest U.S. pop import into their sensibilities?

In a short time, I'm out on the platform again, searching for the way
to the train that will take me to the South Station, Tasqueña, for I still
must cross some mountains to get to my final destination, Cuernavaca.
Following the signs with arrows, I find myself in a long tunnel, perhaps
fifty feet wide, divided in the middle by an iron railing, with people
hurrying along in opposite directions. After walking awhile—difficult
to judge how far down here, with no familiar markers—I notice that
the advertisements along the walls have been replaced by large, well-
lighted transparencies. I stop to examine one, then another. They are
satellite or space-vehicle photos, taken from various distances. There
are pictures of the earth, the moon, planets, stars, "space." A plaque
beside each photo identifies the object and its distance from the camera. All very exact, state-of-the-art, scientific.

I walk on, puzzled by these pictures, when suddenly the tunnel
darkens! But the people continue walking past me as if nothing has
happened. Then I notice tiny specks of light in the ceiling, which is
curved. I look up to see what this might be, and recognize an imitation
of the night sky. All the stars, of course, are in their correct places.
This must be some kind of educational exhibit, one of the fall-out fa-
vors of NASA technology. Then the tunnel becomes lighted again, and
there are more photographs. Some of them are surrounded by chatter-
ing school children, with characteristically black hair, shiny faces and
neat uniforms. All have notebooks and occasionally write something
down after looking at a picture and its caption.

I stop and wonder . . . What is the teacher's assignment? and, What
are they carefully writing? I start walking toward the children, to ask,
but hesitate . . . and then turn away. I realize that it really makes no
difference what they are writing. That is not the important question.
Further, the children could not answer the questions that should be

asked, nor could their teachers, nor could the officials at the Ministerio de Educación Pública who, I see from another large plaque, put up this exhibit for the instruction and scientific knowledge of the city's residents. With even less reason could the people at NASA speak to the issues that then assaulted my mind. To whom can I speak?

Bewildered, feeling a welling up of anger, I dumbly go along with the crowd to my train. After a stop or two, I find a seat, sit down, and stare at the ceiling. I don't have to worry about missing my station, it's at the end of the line. As happens now and then in these last few years, I feel sick, depressed . . . a dull ache in my imagination . . . violent, confusing thoughts criss-crossing my mind . . . feelings of quiet but desperate rage. I try to sort through the images and ideas, try to find some principle of intelligibility, try to begin *to think*.

The city itself—what to say about this swollen, stinking lake bottom with its immovable mass of choking smog and ever increasing number of belching vehicles and sickened people? I have heard that in 1985 or 1986 there were over three hundred days when ozone in the atmosphere exceeded safety levels set by the World Health Organization. Researchers found that newborn infants had toxic levels of lead in their blood, lead their mothers had breathed while the babies grew in the womb. This air is what the children I saw, all the passengers on the train, all the people of the city, breathe every day of the year. They are not just passing through, like me, temporarily feeling the acute irritation in my eyes and nose. How do I think of the horror?

Yet the city somehow works. There are ancient, majestic trees in Chapultepec Park that are still alive. On Sundays, the park is full of families with laughing, playing children. In the *artesanía* markets, one can buy some of the most beautiful handmade articles to be found anywhere on earth. The flower stalls are an extravaganza of colors and fragrances. The street musicians are a joyous and vital expression of song and celebration. Just as with the ugly, so with the beautiful—one can make a long, long list . . . leading to what?

Can it be said that NASA and the Ministry bureaucrats arrived just in time? The smog is now so bad, and the city's lights so bright, that people often can no longer see the stars. Is it then necessary to descend far below the surface of the earth in order to see what is high above? What I see as yet another grotesque monstrosity of technological hubris that sickens my soul as the fetid smog burns my lungs may be a last desperate attempt to save the heavens for the children.

I think of Teotihuacán, ancient ruins north of the city. It's called an archeological site and, I've heard, the government has turned it into another tourist attraction. In the 1960s, I visited the place several times. Dozens of scholars have studied it, attempting to learn its secrets. It's one of those places on earth where the air seems to have the quality or character I also feel at Monte Albán, a long way south in Oaxaca: a dry, lucid, lonely purity. When I was in Teotihuacán, I saw the two large pyramids—to the top of which I climbed—and the ruins of a few temples. Two thousand years ago, between 150 B.C. and 750 A.D., people built a city there, one that grew to contain maybe 200,000 inhabitants. The Aztecs gave a name to the place, but no one knows how these people were called, what language they spoke, or why their city was destroyed. In the eighth century, when the central section burned, it was the sixth largest city in the world. As I stood there, all was silent. The stones and sand said nothing to me. I could hear only the wind, but I heard nothing in it.

From the ruins, scholars have learned something of the two great pyramids and the temples, all designed, arranged, and built to serve as geodetic and astronomical markers. The structure of the city and its public buildings were made to place this people in their space and time, to fit them in their cosmos. All public space was symmetrically planned and executed. But aesthetics served the transcendent. Residential neighborhoods were constructed with the same cosmologically significant orientations as the public structures on the "Street of the Dead" (the principal avenue, named thus by the Aztecs).

> Many peoples see themselves at the center of the cosmos. What set Teotihuacan apart is that its leaders were able to act on that belief after the population concentration and to mobilize and motivate that population to realize the grandiose architectural vision that memorialized the city's unique significance. What might have been no more than a localized cosmic delusion centered on a parochial cult was transformed by charismatic leaders into the unique message of a triumphant religion and ideology when it was realized in material form.

No one knows the names of the city's rulers or sages, the engineers or workers. We can only meditate on the ruins of their magnificent achievement, on the place, a place where celestial mathematics were sculptured into geometric forms. Perhaps it should be called a holy city.

Once when I was at Teotihuacán, alone, feeling the silence of the ruins, seeing no living creature this side of the horizon, I sensed that yes, this was a special place, one of those sacred sites on earth where, I believe, something can happen, where an epiphany could occur. But I was unable to conjure up those ancient people who dreamed the design of the monumental buildings, who somehow elaborated the patterns of purification, worship, and celebration that the epiphany might burst forth, that the gods of the place might break through and reveal themselves.

It is now impossible to know how these people differed from me . . . what I might learn from them. But one supremely important fact I do know: They, together with all the pre-industrial peoples of whom we have any knowledge, looked at the heavens—thoughtfully, respectfully, as a people. Their architectural remains tell us this much. We would say that they studied the stars, but theirs was a *common* undertaking, not confined to the interests of specialists alone. Superficially, one might argue that the school children in the underground tunnel were still in this tradition. But the sickness I feel in my belly tells me that no, the children do something radically other.

The children see only what a camera "sees," they do not see the stars. And insofar as their vision is corrupted by mechanical or electronic images—which occurs inevitably, necessarily—they will never see the stars. To see the stars is to be moved, to be affected, to be changed, by the vision. This can only happen if one looks with an unclouded eye, through uncorrupted air, only if one actually feels the night sky enveloping the earth and all its creatures. Traditional peoples teach that one needs to be in a place like Teotihuacán for this to occur. But these places are becoming fewer and fewer. Recently, for example, the bureaucrats and engineers devised a light show for Teotihuacán at night; I assume, to attract tourists. The perversions to which the Mexican people are subjected know no limits.

The historical record is clear, unambiguous. Modern people, when specialists first began to "see" with their instruments, cut themselves off from this vital, living connection to the universe. As the electronic images multiply, as space exploration expands, as tourist travel increases, the separation widens, the night and its bright stars become more and more dead. The history of this rich intercourse with the heavens among ancient peoples is not a story of superstitious fables, but an account of true wisdom. This wisdom reveals, first of all, that what happens to people who see the stars is mysterious, not humanly comprehensible. The mystery begins with the fact that every society that truly sees the stars is strongly affected by the seeing. Places like Teotihuacán can suggest paths that lead to the experience of the mystery. But the school children, buried in the bowels of the earth, blinded by smog when they emerge from below, have been cut off from these, *their* ancestors, have been cut off from the cosmos itself.

But perhaps I can learn all I really need to know about these un-known people. I know that they were a sensible people, that is, they lived in their bodies, they exercised their senses. When they looked at the heavens, they did so as a people, a community, with their own eyes. And the clarity of their seeing directed them in the selection of their habitat site, the design of the structures, and the arrangement of spaces. Their senses and bodies, then, moved in certain rhythms in the search for communal harmony with the periodic movements of the celestial spheres. So they teach us much about place, architecture, public space, and common action. And, because I know so little about them, I cannot be tempted to look to them for easy recipes, formulas that, today, would be false.

Some might argue that they were a failed people—they were able to leave nothing behind except a few ruins. Therefore, they can have nothing to teach us. But what I see in those ruins impels me to ask certain questions. Are industrial images a lie? Can they finally destroy my ability to see and know? Do they trap me into believing that there is nothing more to public ritual than the sports stadium, the rock or religious spectacle, the shopping mall, the theater, the theme park?

A friend told me that when satellite television was introduced in Mexico, some people bought the dishes because they wanted to watch pornographic movies that were otherwise not easily available. I sup-pose government officials had tried to ban such movies on the grounds of wanting to protect children from "bad" images. The images are cer-tainly evil, not because of their content, but because of their falsity. All these images, whether of the heavens, of accident victims, of pop stars, of people feigning affection by exposing their naked, coiled bodies to a camera, are corrupting, deeply corrupting of my eyes. They act to question all my senses, to dry up my emotions, to dull my mind, to leave me more dead than alive.

The bus trip was yet another gift; it brought me to see my friend, and to learn that the next generation is being blinded. The world in-creasingly becomes a place where only the wide eyes of infants still see.

12

An Economy of Vision

There is no such thing as "Gandhism," and I do not want
to leave any sect after me. I do not claim to have
originated any new principle of doctrine. I have simply
tried in my own way to apply the eternal truths to our
daily life and problems. Truth and non-violence are as
old as the hills. All I have done is to try experiments in
both on as vast a scale as I could do. In doing so I have
sometimes erred and learnt by my errors. Life and its
problems have thus become to me so many experiments
in the practice of truth and non-violence.

M. K. Gandhi

With several hundred other passengers from the full Boeing 747, I made my way toward the customs officer, feeling just a hint of anxiety. I had landed in Bombay; images of dusty streets chock-full of people, animals, and assorted vehicles flickered across my imagination. How would I ever find my way from Bombay to Wardha, a city deep in the interior of the country? Preoccupied with my predicament, I glanced around the drab room and was shocked to see my name written in large letters on a sign held up by a strikingly beautiful young woman modestly dressed in a traditional sari. I identified myself as the person with that name, and she politely asked for my documents. With these in hand, she resolutely walked to the head of the line, with me following uncertainly. I then became the first person out of that huge crowd to pass through customs! Completely befuddled, I veered sharply from delight to embarrassment. I had not noticed any other foreigners among the passengers seated around me on the plane. What must these people think, seeing a nondescript American given such special VIP treatment? While following the young woman up to the customs officer, I tried to catch the expressions on others' faces. But no one seemed even to notice me!

This was only one of many experiences that bewildered me during this strange trip. Invited by followers of Mahatma Gandhi, my ticket paid for by some European agency, I had let myself be convinced to participate in a conference honoring Joseph C. Kumarappa, a Gandhian economist. A man associated with the conference met me in Bombay and put me on the proper train to Wardha. There I lived, busy each day with study and discussions, common prayer and meditation, with a group of Gandhians at the Centre of Science for Villages, established in the city of Wardha by Kumarappa many years before my visit. Outside the city, more workshops and installations carrying out other low-tech experiments were located—for example, bio-gas, paper making, beekeeping, irrigation systems, and house construction. An ashram where Gandhi had lived for just over fifteen years was also near the city.

One member of the Centre staff, although he never questioned me or spoke to me about it, apparently sensed that I would like to participate, and stopped by my room each morning to take me with him to common prayers. The men and women gathered early on the porch of Kumarappa's house, now part of a museum. Straw mats had been spread for us to sit cross-legged on the dirt floor. I could only listen to the chanting and reading, since I did not understand Hindi. However, that did not prevent me from participating in the ritual, from picking up the sense of the action. The liturgy set us in a place where we looked beyond ourselves, where we sought the good of this ancient society. The solemn inauguration of the day gave a definite tenor to all we did. I would not have understood the books I read and the conversations I enjoyed without this early morning exercise. After the ceremony, the director of the Centre, Devendra Kumar, my host, gave me a brief translation of the morning's reading—usually some anecdote or story from Gandhi's life. On January 1—of no significance to Hindus—he turned to me after the chanting and, without any previous warning, asked me to deliver a homily . . . at least, that's what I think he intended. Often, I was somewhat uncertain what was being asked me. It was continually evident to me that I moved in a very different culture.

At the ashram, named Sevagram, there were evening prayers that followed a ritual originally prescribed by Gandhi. Here, the prayer ground was a large leveled area covered with fine gravel and surrounded by a single-strand wire fence about six inches off the ground. All participants took off their shoes or sandals before stepping across the wire on the gravel. For prayers, mats were laid down in regular rows: men sat on one side, women on the other. More formal in their organization than the morning prayers at Wardha, these were also longer, and took place while the sun was setting. They began in the light of dusk and ended in darkness. Here, I was also asked to give a homily to the large crowd but had been warned the day before!

One day just after I arrived at the ashram, Devendra Kumar asked me if I had been to Gandhi's hut—a small dwelling, open, and preserved as he left it. Yes, I had visited it. He asked what the hut had said to me. Another puzzling remark that I didn't know what to do with. But I had already come to respect this man greatly, so I determined to explore the question. Before others were up and about, I arose early, went directly to Gandhi's hut, and sat there on the floor for an hour or two each morning. The early morning silence revealed secrets of the place, obviously a sacred place, a place marked by a holy man. Such places, I knew, can take one outside, beyond the limits of ordinary awareness and knowledge.

Although I had read several biographies of Gandhi, his autobiography and other writings, he meant nothing special to me. He was just another of the many people I admired, people who made sense, who had something to say, who lived well. Now I felt subtle but strong changes taking place inside me. I was not becoming a Gandhian, any more than I could become a Hindu or an Indian. Indeed, the better I came to know these unfamiliar and rather exotic people, and the more intimate I became with Gandhi's hut, the more strongly was I impelled to go deeper into my own tradition, to know my origins better—in order to be more faithful to their unsettling substance.

Every day, Gandhi became less an admired figure and more a revelation of truth, of truth I could not ignore, of truth I had to embrace. The greater the silence of his hut—because I had emptied myself of distracting images and thoughts—the more thoroughly was I imbued with Gandhi's vision. Immediately, in terms of the focus of my work in India, on questions surrounding economics. Remotely, I began to see the relationship between his vision and my own country. I understood that, if I let myself be led, I would see how he speaks as directly to Americans as Indians.

As a result, I can no longer think in terms of "the American economy." Every day, this conceptual entity becomes more and more false. I have to start with something called the worldwide or international economy. If I look at the power of the transnational economy today, it appears that most people on earth will soon be driven into one of two opposed enclosures. They will end up as prisoners of envy or prisoners of addiction. Perhaps so many people are already fenced in that one can speak about a historical threshold having been passed. There may be a greater proportion of people enslaved than at any time in the past. Because of the beguiling attractions that a versatile economy offers, and the weaknesses of human nature, it is especially difficult to live in such a way so as to be able to say truthfully, "I am free."

But this is not generally the kind of issue one hears discussed when the effects of the economy are studied, although nearly every comment on the economic situation, in the South or the North, is colored by worry and uneasiness, whether one is in India or America. The more fundamental of these anxieties may be traced to the appearance of three books: Rachel Carson's *Silent Spring* (1962), *Blueprint for Survival* (published in England by *The Ecologist* in 1972), and *Limits to Growth* (the first Club of Rome report, appearing also in 1972). Meetings and publications in the international centers of conventional power and prestige are expressing this mood in an ever more varied and confusing assortment of reports and prescriptions, worked out in response to the depredations produced by economic man. This central perspective analysis, promoted by the intelligent and responsible members of the most progressive circles in contemporary society, often takes on a character derived from the Club of Rome report.

That report was one of the very first studies to apply computer and systems analysis techniques to the world as a unit. Various scenarios were projected, given different assumptions about economic growth in one sector or another, using mathematical dynamic trend extrapolation and simulation techniques. The methodology itself contributed to the curious idea that one could construct models of societies or even of the world. In some circles, especially among academics, one heard a great deal of talk about a "no-growth," or "stable-state" economy. A few people even took E. F. Schumacher's delightful book, *Small Is Beautiful* (1973), seriously. But the discussions were mainly confined to articles and books. For most people in the West, the questions raised were, finally, only academic. Some would argue that these matters are still pretty much confined to the realm of talk, or only expressed in token-like and (empty) symbolic actions by public authorities. There are, however, individuals and groups all over America who attempt to scale back, to live much more simply.

But one feature inaugurated by the Club of Rome report can be observed in many published studies. It is a mindset, an overall approach, that finds its proper and immediate analogue in computer modeling. The meaning for you and me, for the entire society, in any country of the world, can best be seen when one looks at the end toward which this way of perceiving, conceptualizing, thinking, and proposing goes. The goal is never explicitly stated but can be inferred from a careful look at the studies, especially at the policy recommendations. The implicit thesis of many Western academics today is: the worldwide effects of economic behavior are such that only a technocratic, totalitarian, bureaucratically-organized, systems management of society is adequate to meet the seriousness and variety of the problems.

The world is made up of systems, the concerned intelligence tells us, natural and social. They—the responsible and knowledgeable experts—understand these systems, and can provide the technological means to change or maintain them, as necessary. The research programs producing this knowledge are organized bureaucratically, according to rational criteria of specialization and efficiency, and must be so structured because of their huge size. Their size is dictated by the magnitude and complexity of the problems. The proposals are produced by international teams of self-certifying professionals who then seek to impose their views on the world in a unilateral action. There is a great deal of "circulation of elites," that is, between government, industry and the academy—and between countries. Whenever any political authority takes up the policy proposals and acts on them—already happening in many parts of the world—these impositions become patently totalitarian. At times, there is a highly attenuated public discussion. Response and counterargument are often impossible because of the esoteric and specialized character of the knowledge involved, and because of the withholding and manipulation of information.

There is a promise, of course. The solicitous experts claim that if their proposals are implemented, the world will survive. Sometimes this is accompanied by a warning: if society does not accept their views, no one will survive. In most of the more serious literature, this seems to be the principal issue: survival. But one must look at this survival in the context of a careful examination of the probable scenarios resulting from the various expert positions. Generally, current proposals mean survival at the maximum possible limit of today's economic activity. The frame of reference is the mode of living found among the majority in affluent and the minority in "poor" countries. Survival, then, means living just on this side of the edge of environmental or social collapse, as defined by the specialists. Or living just at the point before the full panoply of necessary controls and therapies become the sole raison d'être of existence on the planet, again, as decided by the technocratic judges. One already sees that the more advanced a nation's economy, the more widely are social and psychological management techniques imposed. For example, through the standardization of schools for the masses, the legal defense of pornography, medical requirements, the diverse structures of caring services. In former times, some spoke about the world being "in God's hands." In the global modeling scenarios being elaborated and proposed in the international centers of research and development, the world and its inhabitants are placed directly in the hands of a few clever gamesmen, those who are the most successful players in the industrial-academic research sweepstakes.

It is necessary to see the social circumstances in which contemporary economic decisions affecting me, my community, the world, take place. Increasingly, many of these circumstances are the same, whether one speaks of New York City, Berlin, or Bombay. Cultural historians have pointed out and studied the effects of spectacles, games, circuses, and entertaining shows on the general populace—the various amusements and ephemeral satisfactions that work powerfully to keep a people distracted and quiescent. Not long ago, much of this was summarized and comically illustrated—from what I have seen in Germany and the United States—by the image of the "couch potato." Here, the public is portrayed as having been turned into a tuber: people seated before a television screen being slowly transformed into an inert mass, barely breathing. Modern communications systems have broadened and intensified a historically old experience. This fantastic assault on the mind and imagination complements the ancient practice of mitigating troubles by distorting or blunting one's sensibilities through drugs and drink. Today, the spectrum of temptation appears to be much broader, historically; affluence enlarges the opportunity and range of dissipation.

A new kind of anodyne is available throughout what has recently been called high culture. Social commentators have noted that the leisure class is in fact worrisomely harried. The pressures and tensions of modern living and working have produced a malady of universal impact, formerly unheard of: Stress. Every major city is well peopled by a wide range of psychological, "spiritual," listening, hand-holding, drug-dispensing, therapeutic services. This is one of the principal growth sectors in the Yellow Pages during the last fifteen to twenty years. But in addition to all these "healing" activities, the various cultural performances and artifacts—in the fine arts, serious music, dance and literature, the legitimate theater—operate in close concert with the popular entertainment and travel industries and, decisively, assisted greatly by the religious and academic industries to produce, among the so-called higher classes of both North and South, an especially pampered version of the common couch potato.

A new social configuration has emerged, affecting everyone enjoying modern diversions: the society of distraction, of amusement, of being entertained, of being lulled into insensibility. Marx's insight that certain social institutions act as opium finds a much wider application today. For example, in the Renaissance, only a few had access to paintings portraying Susannah and the Elders, thereby vicariously sharing in the lustful eyes of the two judges looking at the naked Susannah in her bath. Today, the more modern and sophisticated the city, the more widespread and varied the images of women in all stages and situations of undress—a small but pervasive example of society-wide experiences that dull and destroy peoples' sense of justice and propriety. Many years ago, a gendered society was destroyed. The sexist society that inevitably replaced it has exploded in a visual phantasmagoria respecting neither man, woman nor beast; no decent person would want to see or dwell on many of the images one finds, not only in museums but on every newsstand. The principal social effect of these images is to distract people from the stress of living as *homo economicus*. The principal effect on the individual is to distort one's sense of beauty.

In the perspective of this account of contemporary economic activities and responses to them, Gandhi appears to have thrown a brutal light on the scene. An examination of the economic aspects of his ideas illuminates not only the situation that India faces, but that of America and the world. First, I came to recognize, there in the hut, that Gandhi is not just another important figure on the historical stage, someone who affected his society, indeed, the world of his time. Gandhi is a holy man, one of those unique, enigmatic figures who appear from time to time, in one place or another, to challenge us, to upset our complacency, to give us confusing glimpses of what lies beyond our imagination and desire. Coming into contact with him, if only through the traces that remain, one is powerfully moved, frightened even by the splendor of his life. Second, Gandhi is recognized as a political actor of genius and extraordinary courage, one who "alone" confronted and defeated the most far-flung empire in the history of the world. Third, Gandhi thought about economics. What he had to say, together with the ways in which he acted on these thoughts, places him firmly among the most percipient of known economic theorists. In light of the last fifty years' economic experience in India—and of a much longer time in Europe and North America—one can now reach three conclusions about Gandhi, as an economic thinker:

1. His ideas constitute a coherent whole and these, taken together, present the very best "program" of any proposed for India. And, one might argue, they are the only set of ideas, among those discussed or known, which do make a coherent whole.
2. The ideas provide a marvelous source for those in the North interested in the possibility of a good society for the North itself, for the hyperindustrialized countries.
3. Gandhi's ideas are directly germane to any discussion of an alternative to ecological disaster, if one attempts to consider all the social, cultural, physical and spiritual aspects. I find no other body of economic thought that so directly counters the present slide into managed, that is, totalitarian, sustainability.

To place and understand Gandhi's thought, one should first look at something of the economic background in which he acted. This can be summed up in two sets of comments:

1. The major economic activity of India, for more than two hundred years, has been structured in a *colonial* mode. That is, most of the work of its people and the produce of its land have principally enriched foreign nations and a small native elite. This continues to be the situation today, although some would argue that the small affluent native sector has grown somewhat.
2. Independence—1947—changed this picture. That is, the colonial mode of organizing the economy was intensified and extended by a thoroughly foreign, cancerlike infection called development. The adoption of this ideology by the new government had two immediate and lasting consequences: the modernization of poverty and an ever-expanding creation of needs. Everything now came in large, industrial units: transportation, education, health care, agriculture, housing—which made the great majority poorer than before. This situation can only grow, that is, worsen. Secondly, people were taught that they had ever new and more needs in goods and ser-

vices, all to be supplied through an industrial mode of production. This, too, is a permanent growth sector.

Gandhi worked out his basic ideas on the economy long before the concept of development came to dominate the leading figures among India's political and academic elites. His secular genius lies in the fact that he recognized certain social truths that still hold today:

1. He saw that the experience of being a colonial—that is, thinking and behaving like a colonial subject—had been deeply internalized by many people in India's ruling and urban sectors.
2. Just as important, he saw that European economic theory and practice were profoundly foreign—so much so as to be totally inapplicable to the historical reality of India. India had to seek, not a third way but an altogether different way. One might almost say, to seek another world.

During Gandhi's lifetime, Europeans tended to look with some amusement at his traditional dress. But this was part of what I see as the overall coherence of his life and thought. In a paragraph often reprinted in the fronts of his books and collections of writings, he speaks of inconsistencies in his thoughts and positions—for which he had been criticized. He writes,

> In my search after Truth I have discarded many ideas and learnt many new things. Old as I am in age, I have no feeling that I have ceased to grow inwardly or that my growth will stop at the dissolution of the flesh.

Gandhi's dress, along with his daily devotion to prayer and work with the *charkha*, a traditional Indian spinning wheel, was an important part of his consistent rejection of a colonial way of thinking and acting. He dramatically showed that, to create an Indian economics, one must first abandon the impoverishing economic styles and patterns of Europe.

During all his life in India after his return from South Africa, Gandhi worked on the principles and details of his country's economy both through his writings and his daily actions. Just as he recognized that there could be no truth in living as a colonial subject, so he saw there was an absence of truth in western economic theory and practice. As I examine his economic thought and his behavior, I am especially impressed with their clarity and depth. He genuinely saw what lay before his eyes, India and its people, and he saw them in the light of the country's history and traditions. It would appear that his experiences in Europe actually sharpened his perceptions. For example, contact with the thought of Ruskin and Tolstoy helped him to see his own people and land in their truth, in the truth of their lives and places.

These insights into the reality of India, encompassing its economic, political, cultural and spiritual truth, are wonderfully captured in a statement Gandhi made in 1922, shortly before he was sentenced to prison. Speaking to his secretary at that time, he said,

> If the Government forces us to stop all other activities, then [pointing to a *charkha*] that is our work. I tell you it is my faith that all our duties, secular and spiritual, are embodied there. If you would closely scrutinize my activities you will find that the *charkha* is my only contribution to the world. Therefore, the wide acceptance of my message to India will be truly indicated only by the spread of the *charkha*.

This kind of insight represents a depth and breadth difficult to describe in Western conceptual categories. For example, extension— to use Gandhi's word, "spread"—in its perfection, is generally thought of as universal. For Gandhi, I believe, spread here refers to a way of thinking that would penetrate all aspects of Indian life. In addition to the physical use of a *charkha*, one would look at education, medicine, transport, and technology in general with a *charkha* mentality. The *charkha* would not only contribute to the making of cloth but, as a powerful symbol, to building a certain kind of society. After Gandhi's death, theoreticians of conventional development ideology pointed out that European economic thought was based on universalistic social concepts, which means, as can be seen today, that everyone will ultimately be treated as an interchangeable number by the social and political institutions. Gandhi believed that Indian society was made up of very diverse groups of people and that these diversities had to be respected. One had to find ways to face individual and cultural differences truthfully.

But the universalistic mind-set of Western economic theory and practice emphasizes an abstraction called output. This is measured not by the numbers of families and villages that have gained some measure of economic independence and dignity but by various social and economic indicators such as efficiency, productivity, GNP, or GDP.

These represent two very different worlds. In Gandhi's worldview, you look at the lives and situations of the majority of Indian people—men, women, persons of *all* ages—and you acknowledge their need to work, not to be worked *on*, their need to exercise some kind of autonomy in their personal and community lives. In the conventional Western worldview, you look at a series of abstractions and search for ways to manipulate them, believing that this will result in definable and measurable good for the society. In one world, you start with the person in front of you, in the other, with a concept in a computer.

Gandhi's thought differs from European economic theory principally in this: he looked at the "mass" of Indian society and saw individuals, families and communities in their spiritual, economic and cultural history. Economic theory looks at the "mass" and sees abstract concepts. Gandhi's thought leads to a vision of society where people can live in dignity and freedom, while today's economic theory, and its practice, lead to the totalitarian control outlined above. Gandhi's thought leads to this vision because he proposed two principles as being foundational:

1. The primary cultural character of subsistence agriculture and, concomitantly,
2. The primary cultural character of village-scale making of goods for use.

Some of the basic questions facing people who think about living well on this earth are: Is there a fundamental social unit (leaving aside the question of family)? That is, a basic social organization of people, out of which the individual acts, from which all larger units are composed? If so, what is its character, size, shape? It is not difficult to argue that the large modern city is not this unit; it is, in fact, a social monster. I think Gandhi spoke directly to these questions, and suggested answers.

India's leaders, with many in other parts of the world, have tended to accept an old idea dressed up in modern garb: the city is the center of progress and culture. Gandhi, however, saw that the modern cities of India had become a kind of metropolis, colonizing the rural areas of the country. He saw that India could not go on multiplying Calcutta and Bombay, the results of runaway urbanization. The huge majority of India, living outside the cities, were doubly colonized.

It is important to remember that the ugly, noisy, and foul-smelling urban areas that characterize India today were not nearly so well-developed when Gandhi made his proposals. A friend, showing me Hyderabad, told me that when Gandhi was alive it was still a beautiful city, marked especially by its Islamic architecture. No one today could possibly argue that the city is attractive, in spite of certain individual buildings and small, isolated pockets of urban elegance.

Gandhi saw the possibility of a graceful, moral-aesthetic form for human living on the earth in India's villages. His proposal was an *economic* initiative. He saw that the traditional Indian village could indeed be *the* social and economic unit of an independent India. The center of this unit was *khadi*, handmade, homemade cloth. All the aspects of making *khadi*, from growing cotton to sewing finished clothing, Gandhi proposed, would lead to economic freedom for the people of the villages. Greater equality would also result. With the development of various village-scale industries, people would learn, through all these experiences, that they can achieve greater and greater autonomy, more control over their lives. Individuals and their communities would experience, in themselves, a certain power over the shape of their lives, the power to form lovely lives, the power to choose a *good* life. Gandhi saw that modern employment, the economic basis of the city, was a strange historical bastard; it had no legitimate parentage. People *use* tools and *need* to work. With the *charkha* and associated village-scale tools—to the extent possible—the local community could create sufficient work to supplement and complement traditional farming. Such a way of life could start with one family, with ten, or with a million, and would require a ridiculously small investment of capital. As E. F. Schumacher said, "Anything people really needed could be produced very simply and very efficiently, on a small scale, with very little initial capital, and without doing violence to the environment."

As Gandhi well understood, in any conceivable social unit, there should exist the possibility to unite work, imagination, and intelligence. With agriculture practiced in a more subsistence mode, with the making of goods and the exchange of services reduced as much as possible to the village level, people would be able to work more autonomously, *and* would need to exercise both their imagination and intellect. Gandhi believed that, with decentralization and autonomy, together with the village educational plan he also proposed, village life would blossom. He believed that the *experience* of greater independence, of providing for their personal and common needs, would result in people acting to make their lives and surroundings attractive.

While Gandhi was alive, and since his death, critics have not been wanting, those who not only find fault with some aspects of his economic thought, but who dismiss him out of hand as a thinker in economic matters. It may be of some importance to note that, principally in the United States but in other countries, too, there exist thriving communities of people whose mode of life closely resembles what Gandhi advocates. These are the Amish, a religiocultural group of people whose ancestors emigrated from Europe. While using only horses to work their farms, eschewing modern "necessities" like electricity and higher education, they have continued to grow in numbers and communal prosperity. Tourists universally acclaim the charm of their communities and farms; those who frequent the local outlets where they sell surplus agricultural products attest to the quality of their offerings. If it is argued that Gandhi's ideas are impractical, the Amish people provide a strong, empirical counter argument, right in the middle of America.

If you look at India today you see, on the streets, in the homes, in the behavior of the people, an ever-increasing flood of foreign goods and services. Indians must work to earn the foreign exchange to pay for all of these imports. The resulting debt always increases. But the greatest loss suffered from this invasion is not economic but cultural, the destruction of the Indian spirit, the gradual elimination of Indian taste for things, ideas, ways, dreams that are truly Indian. Walking through the crowded streets of Bombay, Calcutta, Delhi today, Gandhi would weep. He believed that the reinvigoration of village life would strengthen a national taste among Indians. I would argue that this can extend much further. Just as there are different cuisines in different parts of India, so villages can each develop their own style and character. In this one sees the beauty of a people—in the variety of expressions in its ways of living. This could happen, in America as well as in India.

It is only now, perhaps, faced with some kind of ecological collapse and impending bureaucratic management of society, that one can appreciate the truth of Gandhi's views. If the village and its autonomy is the primary social reality, then there is no national, much less international, market. Any national or international trade would be secondary, auxiliary, only for those things each community judges useful for its well-being, as a community. There is no need to colonize peoples' lives to serve a national or international commerce ever more rapaciously devouring the goods of the earth and turning them into nondisposable trash. Peoples' loves and hatreds, all the essentials of a social life, begin and flourish in face-to-face relationships. One also sees Gandhi's genius in the proposal of an economic basis for living humanly. He was not an other-worldly mystagogue, but a practical dreamer.

Gandhi was wonderfully simple and direct in his explanation of the economic life he proposed for India. Writing of *khadi*, the central concept in this thought, he said,

> Let everyone try, and he or she will find out for himself or herself the truth of what I am saying. *Khadi* . . . means a wholesale *Swadeshi* [independent] mentality, a determination to find all the necessaries of life in India and that too through the labour and intellect of the villagers. That means a reversal of the existing process.

The final test of an economic theory is in the life experience of those who live by it. Gandhi throws down the challenge: live in this way, and feel, sense what your life is like. This is a test that requires neither a great investment nor a long time to see its effects. But it will require a certain self-denial, a certain asceticism. One cannot know the joy of this apparently austere life, and simultaneously squander one's sensibilities in distractions and consumption.

13

Yet Another War

Yurodiviy (Russian). A person who takes on an extreme
form of asceticism in which even the appearance of
sanity is abandoned and madness is feigned for the sake
of Christ. "Holy fools" like this were a fairly common
sight in Russia right up until Soviet times and can even
sometimes be seen today.

The Way of a Pilgrim

An enraged friend called the apartment to inform
us that President Bush had just ordered the
bombing of Baghdad. The dreadful news shocked and upset all of us—
a Swiss, several Germans, and me, an American. Because of our work,
research on the history of technology, and our personal inclinations,
no one of us was up-to-date on the current machinations of international political terror. We had no TV or radio, and read no newspapers
or news journals. But we all had some vague notion of what a murderous bombardment could do to the people of a city, in this case one
of the oldest cities in our tradition: more people killed; more buildings
razed; more possibilities for growth in the Gross Domestic Product.
Academic vultures would also profit—a new city where they could
study the effects of state-of-the-art bombing.

The bombing even touched me. I immediately noted a change in my
old friends' eyes, in their angry and frustrated voices. Their anguished
denunciations would suddenly halt in confused dismay. Seeing me,

they were reduced to silence. All of us suffered, each his own kind of pained embarrassment. I had witnessed, at a distance, protests against American political slaughter during the Vietnam War, but the protesters were unknown. Now, they were friends, here in the same room with me, in a quiet and orderly German city.

My friends were familiar with my story, how I had left America during the Vietnam War to live as an exile in Venezuela. At that time I came to feel a deep disgust for my country because of its action in that distant land. How could I continue to live in such a place? How could we raise our two infant children among such a people? For I felt that the rottenness went deeper, and was more extensive, than the current leadership. The government was a reflection of the populace, sharing the peoples' virtues . . . or vices. It was too easy, and false, to condemn Washington. The destruction of Southeast Asia somehow stemmed from the American people themselves. I felt I had to reject these people in order to be faithful to my nation, to the noble ideals of its Founders.

But life in Venezuela led to further questions. What *is* a nation? And in what sense is it mine? What is my true loyalty to it? How can I express this loyalty today? I came to feel that my decision to abandon America was a kind of running away, showing a lack of courage, a lack of imagination and, finally, a lack of truth. I had to go back. I had to face the task of making a good life in that place, the place of my birth. There is a nation, beyond the authorities and citizens who now live there, to which I owed allegiance, to which, along with God and my parents, I had to be grateful for my very being. This is part of the traditional virtue of piety. Instead, I had acted out of selfishness and cowardice, running away. Doing so, I had deeply hurt the children's grandparents, other family members, friends and all my fellow citizens. I had been totally absorbed in my own sincere but rather childish rebellion.

We had returned to America and I sought a job where I thought it would be possible to work for those ideals that would make the nation not great but good. Then, after seven years, after obtaining academic tenure, I moved again. Many aspects of my comfortable and secure existence troubled me when I reflected on them. Too many unanswered questions kept pressing. Often, the subject of my thoughts was my helplessness and complicity in the Cold War. The "billfold apostolate" was no longer adequate. Sending checks, signing petitions, speaking out, all the good, liberal activity was nothing more than an attempt to change *others*, to affect their behavior. Perhaps it was time to change myself. Finally, I could no longer live with the many conflicts in which I was immersed. Thinking about what institutions were doing to our children and to my sensibilities, my heart, I came to believe that I should leave the smothering embrace of job and consumption. I also saw that if I dropped out of the economy, I would no longer contribute to the violence, no longer pay the blood money.

I had thought about what Thoreau wrote in "Civil Disobedience,"

> I meet this American government . . . directly, and face to face, once a year—no more—in the person of its tax-gatherer . . . it then says distinctly, Recognize me; and the simplest, the most effectual, and, in the present posture of affairs, the indispens- ablest mode of treating it on this head, of expressing your little satisfaction with and love for it, is to deny it then.

I resolved to work in such a way that I would never again pay income taxes; I would no longer contribute to the making of yet more arms. I wanted to explore the possibilities of simplicity and poverty, a differ- ent way of being a modern American.

Now, years after those events, after moving out of the mainstream, I found myself temporarily working in another foreign country, and fac- ing another war. I had thought it good to assist my friends in their research and writing. We needed to probe more deeply the sources of the technological milieu, to understand better public fascination with extravagant and vainglorious artifacts. For example, are interpreta- tions like that proposed by Michel Serres true? He maintains that the space shuttle *Challenger* both is and is not the god Baal. The priests (technological experts) of the ancient Carthaginians constructed a huge metal statue of Baal. Inside, they placed their sacrifice, which included children, and set fire to the ensemble, creating a terrifying public spectacle. Some observers today say that the death of those inside the *Challenger* was a tragic accident. Serres points out that burning the victims alive was no more accident now than in the an- cient rite.

That day of the bombing of Baghdad, my work in Germany was over- taken by another technological holocaust. If our god is the work of our hands, the technological project, through which we flaunt our mastery over Creation, then the smart bombs need victims. We acknowledge that our god, like Baal, requires human sacrifice. But the Carthaginians were both less cruel and more courageous. They propitiated their god with a picked few of their own children; American technological wizardry immolated whatever lay in its path. Like the atomic bombs dropped on Japan, the demolition of Baghdad was more an act of hubris than of warfare; hence, more evil.

We heard about a demonstration planned for the early evening. As the hour for the public gathering drew near, we walked downtown. There we found hundreds of persons milling about confusedly, but then gradually getting organized for a quiet procession to an intersection of several streets, now blocked by the demonstrators. Using portable loudspeakers, the organizers made several short speeches against the war. There was a mood of expectancy, hope maybe, among the well-mannered crowd. All appeared rather young, no one past forty, solidly middle class. Many carried homemade signs, the most frequently seen reading, "Kein Krieg für Öl"—"No war for oil." The people stated their clear opinion about the reason for the war: to insure the smooth running of the economy in those nations that were most powerful today. I was impressed by the size of the crowd—a lot of people for Oldenburg, a comfortable, provincial city in the North of the country.

After the speeches, a procession formed again and moved to a large plaza in the middle of the city, filling it and the surrounding streets. Everyone appeared quite orderly and friendly; some marchers passed out printed flyers, people sauntered out of the expensive shops and salons to watch, the police efficiently re-directed traffic. Occasionally slogans were chanted, condemning German money and German arms for exercising such a baleful influence in the world.

There were more speeches, but people seemed uncertain what to do. What *could* they do? Tired and cold, feeling perhaps that we had said something about the world's business, my friends and I finally decided to return to the apartment.

What can *I* do? The passion of my friends pushed me to probe more deeply, to seek greater understanding, a more adequate response. Well, it is no news that leaders go to war. One should be surprised, rather, by the fact that the "great" powers have not bombed one another in the last fifty years. Maybe one should feel grateful that the world's rulers have been satisfied with sponsoring various surrogate wars and promoting "only" the murderous actions of their respective clients. But no, my sensibilities will not rest here. . . . I must attempt to understand better what is happening . . . and how I am involved.

Something very new, historically, seemed to be taking place before my eyes: people near the bottom, those without great wealth or power, believe they can affect the policies of the leaders at the top; or even change the regime. True, there have been slave and peasant revolts for a long time. But what I see here is something different. One might argue that at least since the time of the French and American Revolutions, there has been an ever stronger trend among the majority of people in Western countries, and significant minorities in others, that they have the right and the power to do something about the way they are governed. This historical movement has recently reached deep into societies where it was widely believed—outside those societies— that no such possibility existed: into Eastern Europe and the former Soviet Union. It would seem that people *are* affecting their destinies.

I am not so sure. One would have to study carefully the internal corruption and loss of confidence within the leadership of a regime, the various ways in which economics affects the legitimacy and authority of those in power, and the behavior of other actors in the international arena. The weight of all these factors raises serious questions about who influences what, long before "the people" voice any opinion through their actions from below.

But to judge the power of people today, one must consider the governing framework of all social and political action: the basic structure of advanced industrial societies. If these societies have indeed moved to a many-faceted organization based, ultimately, on a systems concept, that is, to the status of complex, interlocking systems, then the possibility of effective *action*, on the part of individual citizens or collections of persons organized into a social or political movement, must be seriously questioned. It appears that a society today, insofar as its economy participates in international consumption and the production of trash, is to that extent more thoroughly ordered and controlled through sophisticated systems, especially information systems. In such a situation, it is very difficult to find some individual or agency responsible for a specific policy or action. Further, the systems themselves take on a certain autonomy.

In the case of this war, for example, demonstrations and various other citizen actions in Germany and other countries *might* move the incumbent leaders to change some aspect of their policies. But such actions will have no effect whatever on the nature or character and basic direction of the respective societies. Indeed, if effective, such actions can only further legitimate what we live with, namely, the most destructive mode of living yet devised by men—now increasingly assisted by women—a way of being and acting that every hour makes the world less habitable, urban surroundings more poisonous and each of us more out of place. This is clearly evident in what occurs in the "new" societies of the East. The leaders work feverishly to incorporate their countries into the international economy. The people themselves break their backs or stretch the bounds of imaginative illegal activity to reach, if possible, the consumption level of the West. There is no indication, in any society of the world, of a significant movement away from a Western mode of extraction, consumption and waste. There are only individuals and, in some places, small groups who seek a more gentle and gracious way of life. All of these are, up to now, marginal.

The sign painters in Oldenburg—conscientious people of the society—attempted to express the truth about the war on their placards: "Kein Blut für Öl"—"No blood for oil." They understood well that the war was about oil. Oil is important, yes, in the origin of this war. But its greater significance is in its character of symbol; it is the symbol for a voracious worldwide appetite, a frantic seeking after more ways to suck more goods out of the earth, to exploit more places, to increase the productivity of workers. Each time I meet another person who is addicted to eating, drinking or sniffing, I am overcome by an ever heavier sadness—I see the sickness of the world in microcosm. As the addicted person cannot be satisfied by any amount of food, drink or drugs, so modern societies cannot stop consuming the latest offerings of the market. And each moment of every day technicians and entrepreneurs devote their talents to creating new articles and services to sell. The affluent who can afford these temptations live in a world that no longer has any connections with what has traditionally been understood as human need. Here, too, a historical threshold has been passed.

Every person exposed to contemporary media has now formed, inside themselves, a historically new need structure. Formerly, I could understand my inclinations toward evil in terms of the capital sins: pride, envy, anger, sloth, avarice, gluttony, and lust. These traditional sources of repulsive and destructive behavior have now been transformed. Formerly, I acted as an individual being tempted; I felt moved to vanity or anger, to greed or lust. Now, increasingly, I lose the possibility of yielding to a temptation, of sinning. Formerly, I stood alone before my neighbor's wife or new car, another pizza or beer, and either succumbed or resisted the temptation. The new character of needs has replaced, "May I do this?" with, "I must do this." The nonreflective person acts, feeling the need to comply with an internalized command. The reflective commentator explains the action: one must envy, must consume, because the continued operation of the economic system

demands that. Other systems also impose themselves with great impe-
riousness: You must choose whether to have a child; you must choose
the sex of that child; you must verify that the child has no defects
before letting it be born; you must eat this and do that exercise because you are responsible for your health; you must recycle this plastic because you are responsible for the environment; you must not
smoke because you are responsible for all life on the planet; you must
learn about this new threat to someone's rights; you must. . . .

The modern good citizen, in close touch with the media, is fast becoming the most miserable creature in history. Formerly, for example,
one could indulge in gloriously sensual eating and drinking to satiety
or sickness. Now, every bite or drink is accompanied by an accusatory
question: Do you know what this will do to your cholesterol count? to
your new diet's maximum daily caloric allowance? to keeping your
lover interested? The world of sin was a benign world: God was all-
merciful; the world of ecological/cultural/political correctness is tough
and implacable: future generations will not forgive. But the misery is
shared. The need and must structure have followed their inflexible
logic; they have eliminated the "I"—today, there is only an imperious
and aggrandizing "we" . . . we must be informed . . . we must save the
world. . . .

There is an element of truth in such thinking. One could trace a
connection between every person at the Oldenburg demonstration
and the war, just as one could identify a relationship between all people in the West and that war. As I am more involved in the economy of
the West, I am further implicated in that war. To the degree I participate in the mainstream institutions of the West, I am entangled in that
war. That is just "the way things are." No matter how vehemently I
might object, nevertheless I must acknowledge that I live in a Diet-
Coke society: candy without calories, steak without fat, pleasure without pain; now, war without American deaths. There, with my European
friends in Oldenburg, far from any sort of danger, I felt a constriction in
my chest. The news of the war corralled me into a we I wanted desperately to deny. But how escape?

The predicament is especially evident in the virulent contradictions
of marketing. Apparently, people feel impelled to insert themselves
ever more deeply in the economy in order to enjoy the thrills of shopping. What they find most alluring are the wildly offbeat or merely
attractive offerings of the worldwide tourist industry. Expenditures on
this form of escapism constitute the largest item in the international
market system. Modern travel, in all its varied forms, is also important

because in it one can see a sickness, a contemporary disorder of the spirit. The reasons for most travel among the affluent today can be reduced to two: business and pleasure or vacation. Business almost always means further despoliation of the earth and creating more trash. Travel for pleasure is to "get away," to leave the place where I am not satisfied, where I am bored, and to find a place that others have not already ruined or "discovered." This kind of travel is the admission of failure, the failure to be "at home" in my place on the earth. Historically, this is not an altogether new feeling. But in the past, such sentiments often led one to seek another, transcendent world. And it is instructive to reflect on the price—the suffering and pain—those who sought this other world were willing to pay. The vast pilgrimage literature colorfully chronicles the hardships and dangers ancient pilgrims faced. Today, most people are satisfied with "a place in the sun," meaning a travel resort, comfortable surroundings, good food and drink. For the more daring, there are packaged "exotic" tours. The dull shadow of the banal and mediocre, of the vapid and lukewarm, covers ever more people. . . .

Much has been written about modern shopping and the development of ever more spectacular shopping malls. The effort expended in the attempt to make them more attractive bears a direct relationship to their destructiveness, of both people and earth. In Germany, I see that the heart of large cities—the older section of the city, in the Middle Ages surrounded by a wall—has been turned into a huge shopping area, with all the streets made into sidewalks, and traffic confined to the perimeter. Shopping facilities, all over the North, *are* the heart of the society, but pumping a poisonous blood throughout the body.

Everything in the new, or refurbished old, shopping centers is designed with one view in mind: to give a pleasant tone, an attractive appearance, to the act of consumption. One does not see what can be found outside Catholic Worker houses in America: a disheveled young man, sitting awkwardly on the curb, struggling to stick the syringe in his vein; a filthy young woman, curled up in a doorway, sound asleep in the middle of the day. Every year, the street people appear younger . . . and more vicious. Although—at the end of the day . . . of the year . . . of one's life—the actions of consuming myriad commodities are no more satisfying than injecting the drug, business strategists make certain that they are done in seductive and glamorous surroundings. In this, Europe is more advanced than America. Very old buildings and cobblestone streets give a character to quaint boutiques and restaurants whose color and charm cannot be matched by modern glass and steel, nor by authentic reproductions.

But a new twist has appeared, the discount outlet center, and America appears to have regained the lead in catering to consumption. In comparison with the aesthetic tone of elaborate malls, the new centers concentrate on the basics: a huge inventory of merchandise stacked up with warehouse-like order, and no concern for taste or refinement of setting. Often situated near places known for tourism, such as Washington, D.C., or Niagara Falls, they now make shopping the most popular activity of vacationing Americans. Foreigners charter planes to reach them more efficiently and directly. They represent the fastest growing segment for both the retail and travel industries in the United States. Travel and tourism slide into naked consumption.

Everyone I knew and I would guess almost all the other persons at the demonstration were closely connected with the war, not by our protest but by our participation in the market economy—through our jobs and our way of life. But I think all of us also shared something else, a vague wish for a better world, a world where people are not awakened at night by the precision bombing of their homes. In this we joined countless others throughout history who have sought to flee war. Believing that demonstrations generally accomplish little more than to instill a momentary elation in their participants, I returned to the apartment thoroughly depressed. How understand this world in which I move with a complacency continually troubled? How accept the comforts when my claims appear more and more questionable? My eyes passed over the books on the shelf. Would they offer any answers?

Several comments, vaguely and imperfectly remembered from different times and occasions, came together and directed my hand to a novel first published in 1963, *Ansichten eines Clowns (The Clown)*, by Heinrich Böll. The story begins in postwar Germany with a professional clown whose girlfriend has left him to marry another, and who then starts drinking, foreseeing that he will end in the gutter. After a couple of hundred pages, the book stops: Hans, the clown, out of money, covers his face with white makeup, seats himself on the train station steps in his hometown, Bonn, and starts singing a ballad he has composed on the spot. It begins:

Catholic politics in Bonn
Are no concern of poor Pope John

> Let them holler, let them go,
> Eeny, meeny, miny, mo.

A passerby drops the first coin in his hat . . . about twelve hours have passed since the story began.

But the reader has come to know, through scathing satiric wit, that "respectable" German burghers kowtowed to and embraced the Nazis, that hypocrisy and inanity characterized several prominent Catholics, clerical and lay, that party politics could be a charade. Hans, the clown, dissects the jeweled flesh to reveal the festering stench. His artistry confers a license to offend pompous pretenders and sanctimonious Pharisees. But his truthfulness finally impels him to the life of an ignominious beggar in the city where his family lives at the summit of the social register. Irony and mockery incarnated in personal witness result in solitude and pain. Hans is revealed as a Holy Fool; a centuries-old tradition surprisingly sprouts anew in the burgeoning affluence of the new Germany. But now it's thirty years later, thirty more years of ever more glamorous commodity fetishism with ever widening hollowness behind the masques. Is there a Holy Fool weeping among us? Where can I look?

The war is a political and economic policy imposed by the State. In modern times, various persons and movements have opposed the State. Among the different initiatives and movements I found one impulse especially powerful and apropos, that of anarchism. According to a conventional and limited historical view, Proudhon stands at the origins of anarchism because he was the first person known to use the term as a virtuous mode of action in the world (in 1840). Others, such as William Godwin (d. 1836), had earlier described an anarchist response to the way European society was developing. Anarchism directly questioned, and rejected, the modern State. And most anarchist thinkers have also repudiated the modern economy. But since the time of Proudhon, anarchism, except for a few years in Spain, has not caught the imaginations of any significant number of people. While, on the contrary, the State has continually grown in power, and year by year encroaches ever further and more deeply into the lives of those whom it claims as its subjects. In places like Western Europe, supranational political decisions accompany the intrusions of the State.

I believe that a study of anarchist thought and action can help greatly to see through the false promises of state and economy and, more importantly, suggest a startling insight on what one can do, immediately, to face yet another war. I am not interested in anarchism, however, as a social or political philosophy with a complete alternative vision of society. I do not know how to think about society in this way, that is, in terms of universal prescriptive propositions defining or outlining a new social order. All such thinking assumes prescience unavailable to humans. All such action, requiring various kinds of social engineering, assumes power that I do not possess, nor that I would wish to exercise. Rather, I am thinking of myself and the *individuals* there in Oldenburg that night. How to avoid acquiescing in the horror of that war? What about the depth of my response? How to take the victims of that war into my heart? How to regard the beauty of our souls? of every soul in any way connected with that war?

Historians such as Staughton Lynd believe that among more radical forms of social thought, anarchism is the one most native to the American temperament. But I do not approach anarchism as an abstract body of thought; rather, I look to a person; I begin with him, with the story of specific anarchists. In this country, anarchism counts among its advocates figures with the stature of Whitman, William Lloyd Garrison, and Thoreau. For each person seeking to live honorably, virtuously, in hope, while facing the war, these men present an unnerving challenge.

Americans, thinking about their government—generally bereft of common wisdom, at times crazed with blood lust—can start with the example and writing of Henry David Thoreau. Just over a hundred years after his death, his words strike as clear and true as when he spoke them in Concord:

> O for a man who is a *man*, and, as my neighbor says, has a bone in his back which you cannot pass your hand through!

> How many *men* are there to a square thousand miles in this country? Hardly one.

Speaking of slavery, but his words are equally applicable to what I faced in Oldenburg:

> I know this well, that if one thousand, if one hundred, if ten men whom I could name—if ten *honest* men only—ay, if *one* HONEST man, in this State of Massachusetts, *ceasing to hold slaves*, were actually to withdraw from this copartnership, and be locked up in the county jail therefor, it would be the abolition of slavery in

America. For it matters not how small the beginning may seem to be: what is once well done is done forever.

Eventually, slavery ended, but in a way quite different than what Thoreau proposed. The war with Mexico, the other imperious action of government that he opposed, also ended, but only after the United States army killed many Mexicans. Yet the spirit of Thoreau did not die with him; on the contrary, his courageous life continues to appear in other Americans, even up to our own day. An outstanding example of a contemporary who lived and significantly enriched the ideas of Thoreau is Ammon Hennacy, who died in 1970. He died as he had lived, while acting out his anarchist philosophy in public witness. Walking up a hill in Salt Lake City, Utah, to begin another day of fasting and picketing, protesting the death sentence meted out to two men, convicted of murder, he collapsed on the sidewalk and died shortly thereafter.

Anarchism did not begin with the use of the term. Through a unique, intensely personal and solitary experience, Hennacy saw that anarchism is much more than a social and political position with a moral basis. It is, that is, it can be, a religiously transcendental stance; later, social and political consequences follow. Hennacy began to learn this in prison. In 1917, when he was twenty-four, he was arrested and sentenced to two years in the Atlanta federal penitentiary. He had refused to register for the draft, and had worked vigorously to dissuade others. While in prison, he successfully organized a nonviolent protest against the rotten fish served on Friday (the buyer had been pocketing most of the money). For this, he was stuck in solitary confinement, and charged with plotting to blow up the prison. During eight and a half months of isolation in the hole, he read the Bible, the only book permitted him. That reading changed his life, and transformed the nature of anarchism.

In a superficial sense, he noted what Weber, too, saw, and explained in his lecture, "Politics as a Vocation," written at almost the same time: There is a fundamental opposition between the teaching in the Sermon on the Mount and the world of politics. But Hennacy was not a modern academic; he had to act on what he understood; he had to choose, and he exuberantly lived with his choice, perfecting his commitment until the day he died.

As other anarchists in the tradition of Godwin, Proudhon, Bakunin, Kropotkin, and Tolstoy, Hennacy sought a better moral order here on earth, a good society. To achieve this he worked out his own "theory" of revolution, believing that the depth of political and societal corruption was such that it required nothing less than a genuine revolution, not an exchange of élites. One of his contributions to the history of modern anarchism is contained in the idea and practice of what he called the "one-man revolution." I can begin today, if I have the necessary courage, to live as I think one ought; I do not have to wait until the society is reformed. The way to change the world is to begin, oneself, to change. This is the "one-man revolution"; he believed there could be no other.

Of course, one of the principal acts of opposition to the State, important for every true anarchist, is to refuse to support the State through such acts as the payment of taxes. Finding that employers cooperated with the government in taking withholding taxes out of his salary, Hennacy began what he called a "Life at Hard Labor"—the title he also used for a newspaper column he wrote. For some years, he worked in the Western United States as a day-laborer, mostly in agriculture. He filled out his income tax forms carefully, noting exactly what he had earned and what he owed, and refused to pay, the government. Each year, on the last day for the tax payment, he conspicuously picketed the local post office, passing out leaflets describing his anarchist reasons for tax resistance. Since he also sent notices of this picketing and leafleting to the media, the tax people came to know him well. Some agents used to search for the place where he was working, to force the employer to withhold taxes from his wages. When the tax people found him, Hennacy simply moved on to a different farm. He continually and directly challenged both the State and his fellow Americans.

Every year before the anniversary of the atomic bombing of Japan, he fasted—one day for each year since the bombs were dropped. During this fast, he picketed the local federal government building, calling attention to his fast and passing out leaflets he had written against the arms race. Reflecting on Hennacy's actions, especially his fasts, one can begin to penetrate the mystery of anarchism in the economy of human action and suffering. Through an anarchist ethic, one can say "no" to the State, one can directly oppose the complex systems that more and more control the lives of all. I may not be able to change these myriad systems, but I can begin today to renounce their apparent comforts, securities, prestige and respectability. I can also just as directly unite myself with all those who suffer or die through the actions of states and their institutions. Hennacy sought to act in the truth. To the extent he achieved this, his actions live on; they can never be lost. Political tactics were not primary in his actions, worldly effectiveness of no importance in his thoughts. He understood where acts of self-transformation such as prayer and fasting would take him: to all those whom he wished to reach in his love, and to the center of his own being. He always insisted that there is really only one limiting factor in what can be accomplished: one's lack of courage. He believed courage to be the most needed virtue today . . . and the one most absent.

In his own life, I see two other salient characteristics: humor and imagination, often working together. In his confrontations with police, other state authorities and hecklers, he always evidenced a delightful sense of humor, of play almost. While picketing, he was asked if he was certain he could thus change the world: "No, but I am damn sure it can't change me." He understood that the enticing siren songs inviting one to the pleasures of dissipation are many and powerful . . . but their end is servitude. Freedom requires, not only vigilance, but repeated acts of resistance, and disciplines such as fasting. He continually dreamed up new ways to confound the authorities and thereby made his witness truly nationwide.

He admired Dorothy Day, and thought her the most courageous woman in America. In 1950, he visited the Catholic Worker house in New York, but soon went away critical of their meager efforts to feed bums on the Bowery. This piecemeal action was not going to change society; it was not revolutionary enough. He did not yet fully understand his vocation, the unique contribution he was to make to anarchism.

In 1952, he returned to New York, and lived in a Catholic Worker house for about eight years, participating in the work of giving soup and bread to society's outcasts, and helping with the paper. While he was there, one of his actions gained widespread publicity for his peculiar anarchist position. The Civil Defense Act required annual air raid drills; these began in 1953. In that year, and in 1954, Hennacy picketed against the drills when they were held. In 1955, people were required for the first time to get off the streets and into shelters. Hennacy organized a group of pacifists to remain on the street, picketing, in front of City Hall. Dorothy Day joined him, writing a leaflet, signed by her and Hennacy, in which she stated that one could not have faith both in God and the bomb. When the sirens sounded, the resisters were arrested, and the media coverage was broad and sympathetic. Each year, Hennacy and increasing numbers of others repeated their protest. In 1961, two thousand people joined him in his refusal to play the deceptive and deadly war game. No compulsory drills have been repeated in New York City since that day.

Leaving New York, he returned to the West, and founded a Catholic Worker house in Salt Lake City. He named it the Joe Hill House of Hospitality, and personally housed and served "tramps and bums" there until his death in 1970. Joe Hill, the anarchist labor leader and songwriter, was one of Hennacy's heroes. By this time, Hennacy had moved deeper into his vision of what he called a nonchurch anarchist Christian; he had come to stand more directly in the light of what he saw in the darkness of the hole in Atlanta.

Hennacy was no fool. His sharp logic-chopping intelligence displayed itself early in his understanding of capitalism and adherence to socialism while still in his teens. He realized, I believe, that the Sermon on the Mount made no more rational sense than the anarchism of Alexander Berkman, whose writings he knew and whom he met in Atlanta. But the genius of Hennacy, under the influence of Dorothy Day and The Catholic Worker movement, was to unite the Beatitudes to the absolute oppositionist position of a thoroughgoing anarchism. Hennacy came to see that a purely secular anarchism was useless; its historical moment had passed; the State was now but one element in a larger complex of tyranny. Further, the European tradition, emphasizing the inherent goodness of men and women, and the American tradition, emphasizing the freedom of the individual, were both incomplete and partially false. If people are good, why is society such a mess? If individualism is true, why do people regularly stretch it to extreme selfishness?

One can be a consistent, indeed, a great doctrinaire anarchist without practicing voluntary poverty, without living "a life at hard labor," without being a pacifist, without personally serving homeless and street people. But Hennacy saw that a life encompassing these four spheres, derived directly from the Gospel, together with the traditional practices of prayer and fasting, revived an otherwise dead ideological position. In New York, Hennacy had learned the necessity, the primacy, of the bums, that is, that *he* needed them.

Hennacy wrote a book, published posthumously, which contained seventeen biographical sketches of the people whom he admired. After attempting to live an exemplary life himself, he then wrote about such persons as Thomas Paine, John Woolman, Dorothy Day, Eugene Debs, Malcolm X, Clarence Darrow, and Yukeoma the Hopi, that young Americans might be moved by the truth and goodness of their lives.

He believed in the power of hagiography. They were the people who evidenced the courage he so much respected, and that he thought necessary for any genuine social change. Hennacy believed that actions to achieve such change are best taught, not by a rational theory of ethics, but by a skillful presentation of particular narratives. This approach has a long history, reaching back—for westerners—to the Greeks, Romans, and ancient Jews. Later, both Christians and Muslims recorded stories of good or holy persons for imitation and emulation. Hennacy felt that the attractive example of someone like Mother Jones who, fearlessly facing the violence of employers and government, helped organize unions, especially among coal miners, is more powerful than any abstract argument.

Thinking about that war in light of the remarkable life of this man, I see that what I face today is not a problem of war, nor the corruption of the political class in America, nor the pusillanimity of other foreign leaders, nor a problem of control over energy sources for the economy. If one can use the term problem at all, it can only refer to myself, to the way I live. Modern industrial/technological society is founded on the basic principle of exploiting the earth and its creatures to create an artificial universe. If I accept and enjoy the basic destructiveness of modern society as found in the economy, the State and their institutions, I am separated from Creation, from the real world. Hennacy believed in needs, too, not externally produced needs, those imposed by professional care-givers and marketing analysts, but internal ones, those one truly sets for oneself. Looking at the society about him, Hennacy thought that a fitting or proper response could be made only through resistance, and that one could resist only through the practice of virtue, the most important being courage. But looking back at him and the other anarchists he admired, and considering the changes in the society since he lived, I see that I must first stop and look. What am I seeing? What is out there? For example, in the perfectly programmed fields of Illinois, or in the latest status and fantasy object offered by the auto industry. What is this I see in front of me?

The youthful experience of Hennacy is aptly illustrative here, also; one can profitably reflect on what he achieved through extreme sensory "deprivation" in the hole at the Atlanta penitentiary. This initiatory cleansing rite, accompanied by a careful reading of the Scriptures, purified his senses, his sensibility, and sharpened his mind. Although he continued, all his life, to act *on* society, he also lived *outside* society.

Once, while the Communists were still in power, some work took me to Poland. At first, the countryside—it was winter—appeared barren

. . . there were no Marlboro billboards, no advertising signs at all. The streets of the cities were gray, dreary . . . no neon, no pictures of undressed men and women. Nothing called to me, nothing distracted me, nothing tempted me. There were no artful images, no beguiling illustrated promises. But there, precisely, my eyes were opened, my senses disinfected. I had the sudden and shocking feeling that I was seeing the real, in a way quite impossible in a "free" market city. The affluent style portrayed in *New Yorker* ads, or in a posh resort community of the Southwest, or a state-of-the-art shopping mall, are not real for they are at several removes from Creation. But this is not easily recognized. One no longer has eyes that grasp reality. Hence, one is not continually vomiting; sensibilities are thoroughly and safely dulled. Words, however, are inadequate to construct an argument to establish the real. One must find a way to see for oneself; one must find a path to vision.

Those who reflect on self and society today often raise the question of identity: Who am I in this place at this moment in history? The question was dramatically answered by Hennacy. After his experience in the hole, he saw his life as an intelligible narrative for which he was accountable. He kept the ending before his eyes at all times, thus forming a quest marking the shape of his narrative. All the actions enriching his biography contributed to that shape. Thoreau, too, was enlightened by his night in jail. He says that it was "a wholly new and rare experience . . . a closer view of my native town. . . . I never had seen its institutions before. . . . I began to comprehend what its inhabitants were about."

All modern theories and actions looking to society assume, basically, the possibility of change. With almost no exceptions, this change is viewed in terms of progress. But, finally, there is one overall condition, usually acting as a constraint—time. In Salt Lake City, Hennacy showed how to live fully committed to society—to specific individuals and to the nation at large—and, at the same time, jump outside time, leap over time. He did this principally through his evangelical/anarchistic rejection of power. Without fully realizing the reach of his insight, he saw through the third temptation in the desert (see Mt. 4:8–10). Walking through the streets of Salt Lake City in the early dawn hours, pushing his shopping cart from dumpster to dumpster, gathering the day's meal for the tramps sleeping in his house, perhaps Hennacy abandoned "even the appearance of sanity."

Church teaching and practice change. For example, the Church no longer accepts slavery, nor—at least in its teaching—torture. After a lifetime of clear, unambiguous writing and disciplined pacifism, Dorothy Day exerted an influence. Shortly before she died, the Church came to look on evangelical nonviolence differently. It is probable, one sincerely hopes, that Franz Jägerstätter, the Austrian farmer who, *because* he was a Catholic, refused to serve Hitler's National Socialism in any way whatsoever, would not have to go to his death alone today; he would now find priests and maybe a bishop to support him in his witness to the Gospel. Hennacy was greatly strengthened in his vision by Dorothy Day and the Catholic Worker. Although he ended in Salt Lake City as he began in Atlanta, as a nonchurch anonymous Christian, he presents the Church with a prophetic judgment: the Gospel forbids the use of power. The well-documented example of Hennacy's life is there for every believer to see.

Hennacy and his fellow anarchists in the Catholic Worker movement also show the way to another response. They answer all the enticements and smooth talk of a conventional good life with a profound skepticism. They refuse to be taken in by an ersatz creation; they are not satisfied with any bauble, but steadfastly seek the real thing. Their lives manifest a rare wisdom. The Latin word for wisdom is *sapientia*, and the verb form, *sapere*, also means "to taste," having the ability to sense subtle flavors and aromas. To be able to taste today, to see and embrace what is, to be alive in this age, to insert myself fully in the contemporary world, I must find the equivalent of Hennacy's hole, of Thoreau's jail cell. I need to plunge as deeply as possible into the anarchistic tradition, to speak a deep and resounding NO to the reigning affluence of liberal economics, which catches and paralyzes so many in its grasp; to search for all the places where I should say NO, no to the obscene institutions, practices and images. I need to construct a personal cell where I can seek to emulate the renunciation I find in the heroic and good people of this way; this is to reach toward total noncooperation with industrial and bureaucratic systems; to look for ways to share the pain of so many victims, while refusing the comforts, perquisites, and securities of modern myths. Hennacy is unique among political activists. He sought first to live as an anarchist, and only then to offer his insights and ideas to others. I imagine that Hennacy would have laughed till he cried, seeing one of Hans, the clown's skits. They would have recognized one another, and warmly embraced—it would feel good to be reminded that one is not alone, that the tradition lives. Now all of us can rejoice that fools are still among us, that their play makes the world visible.

Notes

Preface

Page ix ". . . Joseph Conrad." Letter to Stephen Crane, November 16, 1897, in *The Correspondence of Stephen Crane*, Stanley Wertheim and Paul Sorrentino, eds. (New York: Columbia University Press, 1988), vol. 1, pp. 312–13.

Page ix "'. . . reveals itself to us.'" Roger Shattuck, *Forbidden Knowledge* (San Diego: Harcourt Brace & Company, 1997), p. 9.

Chapter 1: The Practice of Patriotism

Page 1 ". . . Saint Thomas Aquinas." ". . . sicut religio est quaedam protestatio fidei, spei et charitatis, quibus homo primordialiter ordinatur in Deum, ita etiam pietas est quaedam protestatio charitatis, quam quis habet ad parentes et ad patriam." Thomas Aquinas, *Summa theologiae*, II II, q. 101, art. 3, ad 1.

Page 5 ". . . and what can be shown." Wittgenstein expressed the idea most clearly in a letter to Bertrand Russell. See Ray Monk, *Ludwig Wittgenstein* (New York: Penguin, 1991), p. 164.

Page 5 ". . . racist and imperialistic, respectively." Some information on the party can be found in Hugh Pearson, *The Shadow of the Panther* (Reading, Mass.: Addison-Wesley, 1994), pp. 149–51, 192–93, 252. Documents on the party are at the Bancroft Library, University of California at Berkeley.

Page 6 ". . . the Port Huron Statement." *The Port Huron Statement* (Chicago: Students For A Democratic Society, 1966).

Page 7 "'. . . murder as a method of social change.'" Daniel Berrigan, *Night Flight to Hanoi* (New York: Macmillan, 1968), p. 25.

Page 8 ". . . and questionable crusades abroad." Neil Middleton, ed., *The "I. F. Stone's Weekly Reader" Reader* (New York: Random House, 1973). See also C. Wright Mills, *Listen, Yankee!* (New York: McGraw-Hill, 1960).

Page 9 ". . . treatise on the virtue of justice. . . ." Aquinas's treatment of justice, one of the four cardinal virtues, can be found in the *Summa theologiae*, II II, qq. 58–122. In the Latin BAC edition (Biblioteca de Autores Cristianos, Madrid, 1952), this runs to 393 pages, small print, double column. The specific virtue of patriotism, *pietas*, is covered in the four articles of question 101.

Page 10 ". . . in a singular, even heroic, act." According to Aquinas, all virtues are habits, that is, one is disposed habitually in a certain way. See the *Summa*, I II, qq. 49; 55. Therefore, patriotism is what today might be termed not an action but a way of life.

Page 10 ". . . had little or no appeal for me." A play by Daniel Berrigan, *The Trial of the Catonsville Nine* (Boston: Beacon Press, 1970), dramatized the destruction of draft board files by Daniel and Philip Berrigan and others. Mary and I saw this play in downtown Los Angeles. It must have been one of many influences on me at that time.

Page 10 ". . . living in one's own land." One of the most dramatic, if disturbing, expressions of these ideas is implied in the words of Socrates toward the end of the *Crito*. He admits that he "could have proposed the penalty of banishment" at his trial. However, he "made a noble show of indifference . . . [toward death] and in fact preferred death . . . to banishment" (*Crito*, 52c; trans. Hugh Tredennick). A similar sentiment is found among the ancient Jews when they refer to the captivity in Babylon as their Exile.

Page 11 ". . . and their girl friends." Tad Szulc, *Twilight of the Tyrants* (New York: Henry Holt and Company, 1959), pp. 251–52. See also Philip B. Taylor Jr., *The Venezuelan Golpe de Estado of 1958: The Fall of Marcos Pérez Jiménez* (Washington, D.C.: Institute for the Comparative Study of Political Systems, 1968).

Page 12 ". . . a recipe for social disaster." Ivan Illich, *Toward A History of Needs* (New York: Pantheon Books, 1978), pp. 54–67; C. Douglas Lummis, *Radical Democracy* (Ithaca: Cornell University Press, 1996), chap. 2, pp. 45–78.

Page 17 ". . . at least a little." See, for example, the entries on chastity, Cathars, Dualism, Gnosticism, and Manichaeism in Charles S. Clifton, *Encyclopedia of Heresies and Heretics* (Santa Barbara: ABC-CLIO, 1992). Dietrich Bonhoeffer, living in the midst of Nazi intimidation and brutality, understood this. See Peter Berger, "Sociology and Ecclesiology," in Martin E. Marty, ed., *The Place of Bonhoeffer* (New York: Association Press, 1962), p. 70; and, H. Gaylor Barker, "Bonhoeffer, Luther and *Theologia Crucis*," *DIALOG* 34 (winter 1995): 10–17.

Chapter 2: New Beginnings in Illinois

Page 19 ". . . Simone Weil." Simone Weil, "Human Personality," in Siân Miles, ed., *Simone Weil: An Anthology* (New York: Weidenfeld & Nicholson, 1986), p. 78.

Page 21 ". . . Polanyi's research in economic history." For a good review of Polanyi's thought, together with bibliography, see Fred Block and Margaret R. Somers, "Beyond the Economistic Fallacy: The Holistic Social Science of Karl Polanyi," in Theda Skocpal, ed., *Vision and Method in Historical Sociology* (Cambridge: Cambridge University Press, 1984), pp. 47–84.

Page 25 ". . . and continued to be discussed." Allan Bloom, *The Closing of the American Mind: How Higher Education Has Failed Democracy and Impoverished the Souls of Today's Students* (New York: Simon and Schuster, 1987). In the spring of 1997, a conference on the issues raised by the book was planned at the University of Chicago, where Bloom taught before his death. See *The Chronicle of Higher Education*, January 17, 1997, pp. A 14–15. A short report on this meeting was published in the *University of Chicago Magazine*, August 1997, pp. 22–24.

Page 25 ". . . suggested reforms appear more ephemeral." For example, a recent book attempts to answer Bloom's criticism; see Lawrence W. Levine, *The Opening of the*

American Mind (Boston: Beacon, 1996). Some are concerned with retention rates of enrolled students (see *The Chronicle*, October 18, 1996, p. A 57) or arguing that higher education must accept its function as a mature industry (*The Chronicle*, January 31, 1997, p. A 48). One can judge the level and quality of the discussions through perusing the issues of *The Chronicle*.

Page 26 ". . . in nicely complemented studies . . . respectively)." Ivan Illich, *In the Vineyard of the Text* (Chicago: University of Chicago Press, 1993); Alasdair MacIntyre, *Three Rival Versions of Moral Enquiry* (Notre Dame: University of Notre Dame Press, 1990).

Page 27 ". . . in the universities of the West." MacIntyre, pp. 151–57.

Page 27 ". . . while I was at UCLA." Carlos Castaneda, *The Teachings of Don Juan: A Yaqui Way of Knowledge* (New York: Pocket Books, 1974), first published in 1968.

Page 31 ". . . it was another inconvenient historical detail." William D. Haywood, *Bill Haywood's Book* (New York: International Publishers, 1929)—an autobiography. J. Anthony Lukas, *Big Trouble: A Murder in a Small Western Town Sets Off a Struggle for the Soul of America* (New York: Simon and Schuster, 1997)—Haywood on trial. On the Haymarket event, see Page Smith, *The Rise of Industrial America* (New York: McGraw-Hill, 1984), pp. 241–57; Nick Salvatore, *Eugene V. Debs: Citizen and Socialist* (Urbana: University of Illinois Press, 1982); Waldo R. Browne, *Altgeld of Illinois: A Record of His Life and Work* (New York: B. W. Huebsch, Inc., 1924); Mary Harris Jones, *The Autobiography of Mother Jones* (Chicago: Charles H. Kerr, 1972); and Djuna Barnes, *Interviews* (Washington, D.C.: Sun and Moon Press, 1985), pp. 94–104, for the interview with Mother Jones.

Page 31 ". . . health standards established until 1969!" Maier B. Fox, *United We Stand, The United Mineworkers of America, 1890–1990* (Washington, D.C.: United Mineworkers of America, 1990).

Page 32 ". . . what Jacques Ellul called *la technique.*" Jacques Ellul, *The Technological Bluff* (Grand Rapids, Mich.: W. B. Eerdmans, 1990).

Page 33 "'. . . leap with joy.' (Ps. 96)." Scripture throughout is taken from the Holy Bible, New International version. Copyright © 1973, 1978, 1984 International Bible Society. Used by permission of Zondervan Bible Publishers.

Page 34 ". . . credential committees or watch-dog offices." There is a large and continually growing bibliography. One can start with Anne Klejment and Alice Klejment, *Dorothy Day and "The Catholic Worker": A Bibliography and Index* (New York: Garland, 1986).

Page 35 "'. . . the world would wish us to believe otherwise.'" Jeff Dietrich, "Compassion—A Radical Form of Criticism," *The Catholic Worker*, May 1992, p. 1.

Page 36 "'. . . who want to follow the lead . . . of the Lord?'" Robert Coles, *Dorothy Day: A Radical Devotion* (Reading, Mass.: Addison-Wesley, 1987), pp. 102–5.

Page 36 ". . . Helen and Scott Nearing's *Living the Good Life.*" Helen and Scott Nearing, *Living the Good Life* (New York: Schocken Books, 1970).

Page 37 "Wendell Berry's . . . *The Unsettling of America.*" Wendell Berry, *The Unsettling of America* (San Francisco: Sierra Club Books, 1977).

Page 38 "'. . . by which we proudly characterize ourselves as modern.'" Berry, *Unsettling*, p. 210.

Page 38 "'. . . our personal health is only a share.'" Ibid., p. 222.

Page 38 "'. . . of kindness to the ground, of nurture.'" Ibid., p. 191.

Page 38 ". . . Simone Weil's *The Need for Roots.*" Robert Heilbroner, *An Inquiry Into The Human Prospect* (New York: Norton, 1974); E. F. Schumacher, *Small Is Beautiful* (New

York: Harper & Row, 1973); Ivan Illich, *Tools for Conviviality* (New York: Harper & Row, 1973); Eldridge Cleaver, *Soul On Ice* (New York: Dell, 1969); Simone Weil, *The Need for Roots* (New York: Routledge, 1995), first translation, 1952.

Page 40 "'. . . is possible in a university.'" As quoted by MacIntyre, *Three Rival Versions*, p. 35. Nietzsche wrote the complaint in a letter to his dear friend Erwin Rohde in 1870. See Friedrich Nietzsche, *Werke in drei Bänden* (Munich: Carl Hanser Verlag, 1966), 3:1035.

Page 40 ". . . with a fight of this nature." C. Wright Mills, *The Power Elite* (New York: Oxford University Press, 1956).

Page 41 "'. . . It should be its spiritual core.'" Weil, *The Need for Roots*, p. 288.

Chapter 3: Life at the Margins

Page 43 ". . . Wendell Berry." Wendell Berry, *The Hidden Wound* (San Francisco: North Point Press, 1989), p. 82.

Page 46 ". . . *orare et laborare*." "To pray and to work." The Rule of the Master (RM, 86), on which Benedict drew for his Rule, forbids work in the fields as incompatible with a regular schedule of prayer and fasting. Benedict's Rule (chap. 48) speaks of both manual labor and prayerful reading (*lectio divina*). Benedict points out that the monks should not be distressed if they have to get in the harvest by themselves, "because then they are truly monks, living by the labor of their hands, just like our fathers and the apostles" ("quia tunc vere monachi sunt si labore manuum suarum vivunt, sicut et patres nostri et apostoli"). Timothy Fry, O.S.B., ed., *RB 1980: The Rule of St. Benedict in Latin and English with Notes* (Collegeville, Minn.: The Liturgical Press, 1981), pp. 248–53. A critical edition of the RM: A. de Vogué, *La Règle du Maître* (Paris: Les Éditions du Cerf, 1964–65). English translation: L. Eberle and C. Philippi, *The Rule of the Master* (Kalamazoo, Mich.: Cistercian Publications, 1977).

Page 54 ". . . eloquence born of heartbreaking experience." See the books of writers such as Wendell Berry, Wes Jackson, Gene Logsdon, Harry M. Caudill, and Edward Abbey.

Page 58 ". . . is higher, nobler." See C. H. Lawrence, *Medieval Monasticism* (London: Longman, 1989), 2d ed., pp. 274–90; Réginald Grégoire, Léo Moulin, and Raymond Oursel, *The Monastic Realm* (New York: Rizzoli, 1985), especially pp. 173–233.

Page 58 ". . . and the world's 'hidden wound.'" See Berry's *The Hidden Wound*.

Page 59 "'. . . in the sphere of work.'" Weil, *The Need for Roots*, pp. 93–94.

Chapter 4: The Last Farms in America

Page 64 "'. . . and gash gold-vermilion.'" W. H. Gardner and N. H. MacKenzie, *The Poems of Gerard Manley Hopkins* (London: Oxford University Press, 1967), p. 69.

Page 65 ". . . difficulty constructing a rational ethics." See Alasdair MacIntyre, *After Virtue* (Notre Dame: University of Notre Dame Press, 1984).

Page 65 "'. . . anarchy is loosed upon the world.'" William Butler Yeats, "The Second Coming," in Francis Turner Palgrave, ed., *The Golden Treasury* (London: Oxford University Press, 1964), p. 424.

Page 65 ". . . 'death of nature' in the West." Carolyn Merchant, *The Death of Nature* (San Francisco: Harper & Row, 1980).

Page 66 ". . . alone in the quiet of my remote home, . . ." During the time in the country, my wife and I were divorced. I continued to live on the farm.

Page 71 ". . . own blinders and prejudices." Among a few notable exceptions are Jane Adams, *The Transformation of Rural Life in Southern Illinois, 1890–1900* (Chapel Hill: University of North Carolina Press, 1994); Edith Bradley Rendleman, *All Anybody Ever Wanted of Me Was to Work: The Memoirs of Edith Bradley Rendleman*, Jane Adams, ed. (Carbondale: Southern Illinois University Press, 1996).

Page 74 "'. . . most precious part of a state.'" The quote and source are given by Berry, *Unsettling*, p. 220.

Page 77 ". . . for the Census Bureau to count them!" After forty-five years, the Census Bureau ended its annual report on the resident farm population with the publication of *Residents of Farms and Rural Areas: 1991*. Farm residents had declined from thirty-one million in 1940 to less than five million in 1991. But stopping the count was not due solely to dwindling numbers. Farm residence tells little about farmers today—93 percent of employed rural residents do not work in agriculture. See *American Demographics*, March 1994, pp. 21–22.

Chapter 5: From Science to Poetry

Page 81 ". . . Dorothy Day." William D. Miller, *All Is Grace* (Garden City: Doubleday & Co., 1987), p. 184. Dorothy Day refers to Dan. 3:23. The Canticle is counted among the Apocrypha in some Bibles (and may or may not be printed).

Page 81 ". . . my perception of the world." Rachel Carson, *Silent Spring* (Boston: Houghton Mifflin, 1962).

Page 85 ". . . then infected the Church." See, for example, Weil, *The Need for Roots*, pp. 134–35.

Page 85 "'. . . towards Bethlehem to be born?'" Palgrave, *The Golden Treasury*, p. 424.

Page 86 ". . . in a desire 'to serve' God." For a biblically inspired commentary on the demonic in modern American life, see Bill Wylie Kellermann, ed., *A Keeper of the Word: Selected Writings of William Stringfellow* (Grand Rapids, Mich.: William B. Eerdmans, 1994), especially pp. 187–292.

Page 86 ". . . to the principal world religions." Hans Küng, *Global Responsibility: In Search of A New World Ethic* (New York: Continuum, 1993).

Page 86 "'. . . Deus non daretur.'" "And we cannot be honest unless we recognize that we have to live in the world *etsi deus non daretur*. And this is just what we do recognize—before God!" Dietrich Bonhoeffer, *Letters and Papers from Prison*, Eberhard Bethge, ed. (New York: Macmillan, 1967), 3d ed., revised and enlarged, p. 196. The Latin, roughly, "as if God does not exist." The phrase *etsi deus non daretur* comes from the seventeenth-century legal philosopher Grotius. See William Nicholls, *Systematic and Philosophical Theology* (Middlesex: Penguin Books, 1971), p. 227.

Page 87 "'. . . the history of our species.'" Wendell Berry, *What Are People For?* (San Francisco: North Point Press, 1950), pp. 61–62.

Page 87 ". . . 'to save the planet.'" Wendell Berry, "Out of Your Car, Off Your Horse," in *Sex, Economy, Freedom & Community* (New York: Pantheon Books, 1993), pp. 19–26.

Page 87 ". . . for universal cataclysm." *The Bulletin of the Atomic Scientists. The Bulletin* was founded by men at the University of Chicago in 1945 with the aim to "frighten men into rationality." Between 1947 and 1990, the hands of the clock were changed thirteen times, from two minutes to midnight back to twelve minutes. In December 1991, the hands were set back again to seventeen minutes. But in December 1995, the board voted to set the clock forward to fourteen minutes before doomsday. See *The Bulletin*, January–February 1996, p. 2.

Page 88 ". . . to restrict the possibilities." Arthur Koestler, *The Yogi and the Commissar and Other Essays* (New York: Macmillan, 1946), pp. 3–14.

Page 93 "'. . . they are severally possessed.'" Plato, *Ion*, 534.

Page 94 "'. . . each day dies with sleep.'" Gardner and MacKenzie, *The Poems of Gerard Manley Hopkins,* p. 100.

Chapter 6: Word Roots

Page 97 ". . . Wendell Berry." Wendell Berry, *Standing By Words* (San Francisco: North Point Press, 1983), p. 150.

Page 98 ". . . seemed the only way to live." Cicero, *De officiis/On Duties*, Harry G. Edinger, trans. (Indianapolis: Bobbs-Merrill, 1974). See also Thomas N. Mitchell, *Cicero the Senior Statesman* (New Haven: Yale University Press, 1991), pp. 24–27.

Page 100 ". . . Art is not a therapeutic instrument, . . ." For the arguments on both sides, see Jerome Stolnitz, *Aesthetics and Philosophy of Art Criticism* (Boston: Houghton Mifflin, 1960), pp. 337–66. An especially enlightening discussion is presented by Isaiah Berlin, in the essay, "Artistic Commitment: A Russian Legacy," in his *The Sense of Reality* (New York: Farrar, Straus and Giroux, 1996), pp. 194–231.

Page 100 "'. . . connection between art and ethics.'" Ludwig Wittgenstein, *Notebooks 1914–16*, G. E. M. Anscombe and G. H. von Wright, eds. (Oxford: Blackwell, 1961), cited in Ray Monk, *Ludwig Wittgenstein* (London: Jonathan Cape, 1990), p. 143. Monk notes that Wittgenstein "adopts the Latin phrase used by Spinoza, *sub specie aeternitatis*" ("under the form of eternity"). The phrase is much older than Spinoza, and is perhaps better translated as "from the perspective of eternity."

Page 100 ". . . 'Poetry is power.'" Michael Ignatieff, "Whispers from the Abyss," *The New York Review*, October 3, 1966, p. 5.

Page 100 "'. . . rooted in the Russian past than Soviet power.'" Ibid. See also Peter B. Maggs, *The Mandelstam and "Der Nister" Files: An Introduction to Stalin-era Prison and Labor Camp Records* (Armonk, N.Y.: M. E. Sharpe, 1996), and Vitaly Shentalinsky, *Arrested Voices: Resurrecting the Disappeared Writers of the Soviet Regime* (New York: Martin Kessler Books, Free Press, 1996).

Page 102 "'. . . be able to acquire it.'" Simone Weil, *Waiting for God* (New York: Harper & Row, 1973), p. 116; translation originally published in 1951.

Page 103 ". . . anything at all!" While at the farm, we used to consult the *Bulletin of the Center for Children's Books*, sponsored by the Graduate Library School at the University of Chicago, to help us select books for the children to read. The *Bulletin* was available in the nearby university library.

Page 103 "So . . . some argue." See George Steiner, "Our Homeland, the Text," *Salmagundi*, no. 66 (1985), pp. 4–25.

Page 103 ". . . nothing more specific than in 'post-industrial.'" For an illuminating discussion based on the contemporary Jewish experience, see David Vital, *The Future of the Jews* (Cambridge: Harvard University Press, 1990), and David Vital, "Irreversible Loss," *Times Literary Supplement*, May 5, 1995, pp. 10–11.

Page 104 ". . . these were, in fact, Cities of Man. . . ." See Augustine's *City of God*. There are several translations; for example, that by R. W. Dyson, published by Cambridge University Press (1998).

Page 104 ". . . even before he was dead!" Julien Green, *God's Fool: The Life and Times of Francis of Assisi*, Peter Heinegg, trans. (San Francisco: Harper & Row, 1985), pp. 210–24. See also Adolf Holl, *The Last Christian*, Peter Heinegg, trans. (Garden City, N.Y.: Doubleday & Co., 1980).

Page 110 ". . . and that have almost disappeared." In June 1997, there were still seven members living in Maine. See *The Shaker Quarterly*, published by The United Society, Sabbathday Lake, Poland Spring, Maine, 04274.

Page 110 ". . . beautiful patterns and images." In the statement of the founder, Mother Ann Lee, "Do all your work as though you had a thousand years to live on earth and as you would if you knew you must die tomorrow." Quoted in June Sprigg, *By Shaker Hands* (Hanover, N.H.: University Press of New England, 1990), p. 33.

Page 110 ". . . systematic order and quiet piety. . . ." Meyer Schapiro, review of Lillian M. C. Randall, *Images in the Margins of Gothic Manuscripts* (Berkeley and Los Angeles: University of California Press, 1966), in *Speculum* 45, no. 4 (October 1970): 684–86. For many illustrations of this art, see Randall.

Page 111 ". . . 'Pied Beauty.'" Gardner and MacKenzie, *The Poems of Gerard Manley Hopkins,* pp. 69–70.

Page 111 ". . . merit such awe and respect." A somewhat similar argument is made by Roger Shattuck, *Forbidden Knowledge*, in the chapter "The Pleasures of Abstinence," pp. 109–36.

Chapter 7: The Beauty of Saying No

Page 113 ". . . Alasdair MacIntyre." MacIntyre, *After Virtue*, p. 121.

Page 117 ". . . living here at the turn of the century. . . ." John M. Synge, *The Aran Islands* (Marlboro, Vt.: The Marlboro Press, n.d.), first published in 1907.

Page 117 ". . . stories begun a generation later; . . ." Liam O'Flaherty, *Short Stories* (London: Hodder and Stoughton, 1992).

Page 117 ". . . *Man of Aran* (1934)." See Richard Griffith, *The World of Robert Flaherty* (New York: Duell, Sloan and Pearce, 1953), pp. 83–106.

Page 118 "'. . . a pain in his heart.'" Synge, p. xii.

Page 119 ". . . the young Antigone." Sophocles I, *Three Tragedies* (Chicago: University of Chicago Press, 1991), pp. 159–212.

Page 120 ". . . *Kristin Lavransdatter* . . ." Sigrid Undset, *Kristin Lavransdatter* (New York: Random House, 1987).

Page 126 ". . . common attribute of philosophical thought." The modern indictment reaches from Julien Benda, *The Treason of the Intellectuals* (*La Trahison des clercs*) (New York: W. W. Norton, 1956), first English publication in 1928, to Christopher Lasch, *The Revolt of the Elites* (New York: W. W. Norton, 1995).

Page 127 ". . . . One of the Seven Gifts . . . they named "understanding." According to the tradition, the gifts are understanding, counsel, wisdom, knowledge (*scientia*), piety, fortitude, and fear. See Aquinas, *Summa*, I II, q. 68, art. 4.

Page 129 ". . . his brother Ivan Karamazov." Fyodor Dostoyevsky, *The Brothers Ka-*

ramazov, trans. Constance Garnett (New York: Random House, 1950), Modern Library edition, pp. 292–312.

Page 131 ". . . I place myself myself *in* Creation." *Summa*, II II, q. 13, art. 3, corp.

Chapter 8: To Die My Own Death

Page 133 ". . . Ivan Illich." Ivan Illich, *Medical Nemesis* (New York: Pantheon, 1976), pp. 206–7.

Page 143 ". . . *Arbeit macht frei.*" Work makes (you) free.

Page 145 ". . . from the gas chambers." Thomas Keneally, *Schindler's List* (New York: Penguin, 1983).

Page 148 ". . . could exist for itself." See Aquinas, *Summa*, I, q. 29, art. 4, corp.

Chapter 9: Childhood as Addiction

Page 149 ". . . Saint Augustine." Augustine, *Confessions* (New York: Doubleday, 1960), p. 62.

Page 156 ". . . fragile treasure, slave, and super-pet." John Holt, *Escape from Childhood* (New York: E. P. Dutton & Co., 1974), p. 18.

Page 156 ". . . middle classes of seventeenth-century Europe." Philippe Ariès, *Centuries of Childhood* (London: Cape, 1962).

Page 156 ". . . appropriate male or female behavior." See Ivan Illich, *Gender* (New York: Pantheon Books, 1982).

Page 158 ". . . understood as a virtuous life." This is a theme that runs through much of his work. See, for example, *Recollected Essays* (San Francisco: North Point Press, 1981), pp. 174–83; *Home Economics* (San Francisco: North Point Press, 1987), pp. 162–78.

Page 160 ". . . 'better' books for them to read." See *Bulletin of the Center for Children's Books*.

Page 160 ". . . based on some anthropologist's interpretations." Jean Liedloff, *The Continuum Concept* (London: Duckworth, 1975).

Page 161 "'. . . guise of compulsory universal education.'" Holt, pp. 240–41.

Page 162 "'. . . exploit and prey upon each other.'" Ibid., p. 22.

Page 162 ". . . where they were truly needed." Berry, *The Hidden Wound*. See especially, pp. 80–85, 113–14.

Page 163 ". . . for which money is necessary, one is weak." Berry, *What Are People For?*, pp. 153–69.

Chapter 10: A Job to Find

Page 167 ". . . William Stringfellow." Kellermann, *A Keeper*, p. 321.

Page 168 ". . . taught prisoners at Sing Sing." Susan Cheever, *Home Before Dark* (Boston: Houghton Mifflin, 1984), pp. 169–72.

Page 168 ". . . true place . . . is also a prison." Henry David Thoreau, *Walden and Other*

Writings (New York: Bantam Books, 1989), p. 94. First Bantam edition, 1962; first published, 1854.

Page 171 ". . . did not greatly impress me." See, for example, C. Wright Mills, *White Collar Society* (New York: Oxford University Press, 1951).

Page 172 ". . . *Invisible Man*—invisible." Ralph Ellison, *Invisible Man* (New York: Random House, 1972), first published, 1952.

Page 172 ". . . account of such labor ever written." The essay published by Macdonald in his journal, *Politics* (December 1946), can be found in George A. Panichas, ed., *The Simone Weil Reader* (New York: David McKay, 1977), pp. 53–72.

Page 172 ". . . work quietly among the 'lower sectors.'" A biography of Foucauld: Anne Freemantle, *Desert Calling: The Life of Charles de Foucauld* (London: Hollis & Carter, 1950). The founder of the Little Brothers, René Voillaume, has written *Seeds of the Desert: The Legacy of Charles de Foucauld* (Chicago: Fides, 1955).

Page 179 ". . . *The Good Soldier Švejk.*" Jaroslav Hašek, *The Good Soldier Švejk and His Fortunes in the World War* (New York: Crowell, 1973).

Page 180 ". . . their respective experiences and insights." The two principal newspapers published at houses of the movement are *The Catholic Worker*, 36 East First St. New York, N.Y., 10003; and *The Catholic Agitator*, 632 North Brittania St., Los Angeles, Calif., 90033.

Page 184 ". . . can lead one to the transcendent." Pseudo-Dionysius, the Areopagite, *The Complete Works* (New York: Paulist Press, 1987).

Chapter 11: The Stars of Mexico

Page 185 ". . . Edward Abbey." Edward Abbey, *Desert Solitaire* (New York: Ballantine Books, 1971), p. 301.

Page 187 ". . . that there be a society." Marcel Mauss, *The Gift: Forms and Functions of Exchange in Archaic Societies* (New York: Norton, 1967).

Page 189 "'. . . is the art of going.'" Wendell Berry, *Collected Poems* (New York: North Point Press, 1984), pp. 216–17.

Page 190 "'. . . the only possible / new start.'" Ibid., pp. 158–59.

Page 196 ". . . descending with their revelations." John Bierhorst, trans., *Cantares Mexicanos* (Stanford: Stanford University Press, 1985), pp. 66–69.

Page 196 "'. . . that acquaintances are made?'" Ibid., p. 163.

Page 197 ". . . instruments and their musical traditions." I came to know Hellmer and his work while living in Mexico.

Page 198 ". . . while the babies grew in the womb." This was told to me by a friend in Mexico. He believes that the actual report was suppressed by the government and is not available.

Page 199 ". . . sixth largest city in the world." Rebecca Storey, *Life and Death in the Ancient City of Teotihuacán* (Tuscaloosa: The University of Alabama Press, 1992), p. 27. Susan T. Evans and Janet Berlo, "Teotihuacán: An Introduction," in Janet Berlo, ed., *Art, Ideology, and the City of Teotihuacán* (Washington, D.C.: Dumbarton Oaks, 1992), p. viii.

Page 199 ". . . named thus by the Aztecs)." René Millon, "Teotihuacan Studies: From 1950 to 1990 and Beyond," in Berlo, p. 392.

Page 199 "'. . . realized in material form.'" Ibid., p. 392.

Chapter 12: An Economy of Vision

Page 203 ". . . M. K. Gandhi." M. K. Gandhi, *Truth Is God* (Ahmedabad: Navajivan Publishing House, 1955), p. 6.

Page 204 ". . . Kumarappa, a Gandhian economist." His principal ideas can be found in two books: J. C. Kumarappa, *Why the Village Movement?* (Varanasi: Bhargava Bhushan Press, 1960), first published in 1936; Kumarappa, *Economy of Permanence* (Varanasi: Bhargava Bhushan Press, 1958), first published in 1945.

Page 206 ". . . Rome report, appearing also in 1972)." Edward Goldsmith et al., *Blueprint for Survival* (Boston: Houghton Mifflin, 1972); Donella H. Meadows, et al., *Limits to Growth* (New York: New American Library, 1972).

Page 211 ". . . is a permanent growth sector." Lummis, *Radical Democracy*, pp. 45–78.

Page 211 "'. . . dissolution of the flesh.'" Gandhi, *Truth Is God*, p. 2.

Page 212 "'. . . only by the spread of the *charkha*.'" Krishnadas, *Seven Months with Mahatma Gandhi* (Navijvan Publishing House: Ahmedabad, 1961), p. 78.

Page 214 "'. . . without doing violence to the environment.'" Fritjof Capra, *Uncommon Wisdom: Conversations with Remarkable People* (New York: Simon & Schuster, 1988), p. 218.

Page 216 "'. . . reversal of the existing process.'" M. K. Gandhi, *Constructive Programme* (Ahmedabad: Navajivan Publishing House, 1941), pp. 11–12.

Chapter 13: Yet Another War

Page 217 ". . . *The Way of a Pilgrim*." *The Way of a Pilgrim*, trans. Olga Savin (Boston: Shambhala, 1996), p. 136.

Page 219 "'. . . is to deny it then.'" Thoreau, *Walden and Other Writings*, p. 93.

Page 219 ". . . than in the ancient rite." Michel Serres, *Statues* (Paris: Éditions François Bourin, 1987), pp. 13–34.

Page 222 ". . . avarice, gluttony, and lust." A recent study that draws on the three moral traditions, Judaism, Graeco-Roman moral philosophy, and Christianity: Solomon Schimmel, *The Seven Deadly Sins* (New York: Oxford University Press, 1997). The bibliography contains a sampling of the classical sources.

Page 223 ". . . largest item in the international market system." World Tourism Organization, *Global Forecasts to the Year 2000 and Beyond* (Madrid: World Tourism Organization, 1994), vol. 5, pp. 1–2, 10.

Page 225 ". . . slide into naked consumption." Edwin McDowell, *The New York Times*, May 26, 1996, p. 1.

Page 226 ". . . since the story began." Heinrich Böll, *The Clown* (New York: McGraw-Hill, 1965), p. 244.

Page 226 ". . . that of anarchism." For anarchism, see Robert Nisbet, *The Social Philosophers: Community and Conflict in Western Thought* (New York: Thomas Crowel Co., 1976). For American anarchism, see David DeLeon, *The American As Anarchist: Reflections on Indigenous Radicalism* (Baltimore: Johns Hopkins University Press, 1978).

Page 227 ". . . native to the American temperament." Staughton Lynd, *The Intellectual Origins of American Radicalism* (New York: Pantheon, 1968).

Page 227 "'. . . Hardly one.'" "Civil Disobedience," in Thoreau, *Walden*, p. 90.

Page 228 "'. . . once well done is done forever.'" Ibid., p. 93.

Page 228 ". . . Hennacy, who died in 1970." Ammon Hennacy, *The Book of Ammon* (Baltimore: Fortcamp Publ. Co., 1994), originally self-published by Hennacy in 1965.

Page 228 ". . . and the world of politics." H. H. Gerth and C. Wright Mills, trans. and eds., *From Max Weber* (New York: Oxford University Press, 1958), pp. 122–26.

Page 231 ". . . until his death in 1970." See Patrick G. Coy, "The One-Person Revolution of Ammon Hennacy," in Patrick G. Coy, ed., *A Revolution of the Heart: Essays on The Catholic Worker* (Philadelphia: Temple University Press, 1988), pp. 134–73.

Page 231 ". . . people whom he admired." Ammon Hennacy, *The One-Man Revolution in America* (Salt Lake City: Ammon Hennacy Publications, 1970). The book was brought out by his wife, Joan Thomas.

Page 233 "'. . . what its inhabitants were about.'" Thoreau, "Civil Disobedience," p. 99.

Page 234 ". . . witness to the Gospel." See Gordon Zahn, *In Solitary Witness: The Life and Death of Franz Jägerstätter* (Collegeville, Minn.: The Liturgical Press, 1964).

Index

Abbey, Edward, 185
agriculture, 37–38, 50, 56–57, 59–60, 64–
    65, 67, 76–77, 80, 83, 97, 213–15, 229
Akhmatova, Anna, 100
Altgeld, John, 31
Amish, 37, 79, 138, 215
anarchist, 34, 41, 65, 226–32, 234
Antigone, 119, 127
Aquinas, Saint Thomas, 1, 9–10, 26, 101,
    126–27, 131
Ariès, Philippe, 156
Aristotle, xii, 10, 46, 52
Augustine, Saint, 104, 149
Auschwitz, 143

Bakunin, Mikhail, 228
Benedict, Saint, 104, 180
Berkman, Alexander, 231
Bernstein, Leonard, 8
Berrigan, Daniel, 7, 10, 36
Berry, Wendell, 37, 40–41, 43, 87, 97, 158,
    162–63, 182, 189
Betancourt, Rómulo, 12
Black Panthers, 5
Bloom, Allan, 25
Blueprint for Survival, 206
Bolívar, Simón, 12
Böll, Heinrich, 225
Bonhoeffer, Dietrich, 86
Borremans, Valentina, xi
Bunche, Ralph, 2, 6

Caldera, Rafael, 12–13
Camara, Helder, 12, 15
Carson, Rachel, 81, 206

Castaneda, Carlos, 27
Castro, Fidel, 12, 171
Catholic Worker, 11, 33–36, 41, 180, 224,
    230–31, 234
Cheever, John, 168, 170
Christ, 105, 129, 217
church, 7, 12, 17, 34, 48–49, 59, 69–71, 80,
    85, 90, 92–93, 133, 142, 157, 162, 233–34
Cleaver, Eldridge, 5, 38
Club of Rome, 206
Coles, Robert, 35
community, 5, 9–10, 32, 34, 37, 40, 44, 50–
    51, 55–60, 70–71, 73, 75–76, 79–80, 82,
    84–86, 88, 90–92, 97, 104, 108–9, 114,
    117, 138, 159, 189, 201, 213–15, 233
Conrad, Joseph, ix
Copei, 7, 12–13
courage, xii, 33, 36, 52, 65, 68, 95, 108,
    110, 119, 146, 162, 218, 229, 230, 232
Creon, 119
Czestochowa, 102–3

Dante Alighieri, 136
Darrow, Clarence, 231
Davis, Angela, 3
Day, Dorothy, 33–36, 40, 81, 230–31, 234
Debs, Eugene V., 31, 231
de Foucauld, Charles, 172
democracy, 6, 29, 79, 84, 99, 180
Dietrich, Jeff, 35
Dionysius the Pseudo-Areopagite, 184
Don Quixote, 102
Dostoyevsky, Fyodor, 8, 102, 129
drug, 3, 78, 108, 208, 222
Duden, Barbara, xi

Eisenhower, President Dwight, 2
Eliot, T. S., 8
Ellison, Ralph, 172
Ellul, Jacques, 32, 39, 41

family, 69–70, 75, 77, 79–80, 86, 88, 114,
    119, 159, 164, 170–71, 174, 186–87, 212–
    14
Flaherty, Robert, 117
flesh, 33, 79, 89, 93–94, 99, 164, 186, 211
Flores, Héctor, xi
fool, 90, 179–80, 217, 226, 231, 234
Francis, Saint, 104
friendship, 10, 44, 86, 94, 96, 129–30, 188,
    190, 196

Gandhi, Mahatma, 124, 203, 205, 209–16
Garrison, William Lloyd, 227
gift, 50, 98, 127, 131, 146, 148–49, 187–88,
    201
Ginsburg, Eugenia, 100
God, 1, 9, 80, 85–86, 93–94, 97, 100–102,
    105–6, 108, 111, 119, 130, 135, 138, 149,
    167, 182, 208, 218, 223, 230
Godwin, William, 226, 228
good, ix, 10, 13, 20, 22, 29, 30, 36, 38–39,
    45, 51, 79, 89, 98, 100, 102–3, 106, 109–
    10, 118–19, 121, 126, 137–38, 144–45,
    153–54, 159–60, 164, 167–68, 170, 176,
    204, 213–15, 218, 222
Gospel, 7, 48, 52, 231, 234
Grases, Pedro, 14–15
Guevara, Ernesto Che, 12

Hašek, Jaroslav, 179
Hayden, Tom, 6
Haywood, Big Bill, 31
Heilbroner, Robert, 38
Hellmer, José, 196
Hennacy, Ammon, 228–34
Hill, Joe, 231
Hitler, Adolf, 143, 234
Hoinacki, Ben, 45, 134, 163
Hoinacki, Beth, xii, 163
Hoinacki, Mary, 11, 13, 16–17, 37, 42, 45,
    162, 187
Holt, John, 150, 156, 161–63
Hopkins, Gerard Manley, 93, 110–11
Hutchins, Robert, 21

Illich, Ivan, xi, 12, 26, 38–39, 41, 188
individual, 9, 16, 39, 55–56, 68, 80, 86, 88, 100,
    129, 143, 213–14, 221–22, 227, 231, 233

Jägerstätter, Franz, 234
Jefferson, Thomas, 22, 36–37, 74, 79
Jehovah's Witness, 143
Jesus Christ, 102, 104, 109
John of the Cross, 107
Joyce, James, 8
justice, 8–10, 29, 31, 119, 125

Kafka, Franz, 169
Kennedy, John F., 6
Kennedy, Robert F., 6
Kevorkian, Dr. Jack, 135
King, Martin Luther, Jr., 6
Kropotkin, Prince Peter, 228
Kumar, Devendra, 204–5
Kumarappa, Joseph C., 204

labor, 57–59, 71, 75–76, 89, 105, 108, 133,
    141, 158, 172, 216, 229, 231
Laertes, 44
Larraín, Manuel, 12
Latin America, 3, 7, 10, 12–14, 23
Leo XIII, Pope, 13
Liedloff, Jean, 160, 163
Lombard, Peter, 126
Lyme disease, 163
Lynd, Staughton, 227

Macdonald, Dwight, 172
MacIntyre, Alasdair, 26
Malcolm X, 6, 231
Mandelstam, Nadezhda, 100
Mandelstam, Osip, 100
Marcuse, Herbert, 3
Maritain, Jacques, 8, 13
Marx, Karl, 32, 209
Maurin, Peter, 34–35
Mauss, Marcel, 187
meaning, ix, 41, 93, 126, 148, 177, 186
Méndez Arceo, Sergio, 12
Mills, C. Wright, 40, 171
Mitcham, Carl, xi
Monte Albán, 183, 199
moral, 6, 10, 26, 35, 37, 44, 52, 65, 74, 76–
    77, 79, 82, 85, 99–101, 106, 113, 119–23,

125–26, 128, 156, 167, 170–71, 179, 186–87, 214, 228
Mother Ann Lee, 108
Mother Jerome Nagle, O.S.B., xi
Munch, Edvard, 135

narrative, ix, 41, 232–33
NASA, 197–98
Nazi, 143–44, 226
Nearing, Helen and Scott, 36, 40–41
New Age, 27, 88
Nietzsche, Friedrich, 40
nonviolence, 203, 228, 234

O'Connor, Flannery, 127
O'Flaherty, Liam, 117
Our Lady of Guadalupe, 194

Paine, Thomas, 231
parents, 1, 9, 16, 18, 20, 44, 52, 146, 149, 153, 155–60, 162, 164, 181, 187, 218
Pasternak, Boris, 100
Paul, Saint, 144
Peace and Freedom Party, 5
Pérez Jiménez, Marcos, 11–2
pietas (piety), 1, 9, 16, 53, 110, 119, 218
Pirandello, Luigi, 8
place, 10, 21–22, 27, 39, 44–45, 47–50, 52–54, 57, 59–61, 67–68, 82, 89–91, 94–96, 98–99, 101, 105–6, 108, 111, 117–18, 125, 150, 159, 163–64, 172, 181–82, 186–89, 191, 193, 196, 199, 205, 218, 221–22, 224
Plato, 21, 25, 46, 65, 91, 93
poetry, 33, 81, 89, 91–96, 100, 127, 189, 196–97
Polanyi, Karl, 21
Port Huron Statement, 6
prayer, 33, 80, 94, 114, 137, 148, 180, 204–5, 230–31
progress, ix, 54, 95, 127, 129, 136, 213, 233
protest, 2, 4, 9, 10, 24, 218, 228
Proudhon, Pierre, 226, 228

reading, 26–8, 67, 91–92, 98–104, 106–8, 126, 129, 180–81
relatio subsistens, 148
religion, 1, 9, 53, 84–86, 102–4, 109–10, 120, 126, 128, 199, 201, 209
Rivera, Diego, 196

Rothko, Mark, 127
Roy, Rustum, xi
Ruskin, John, 212

Savio, Mario, 3
scarcity, 93, 174–76
Schumacher, E. F., 38, 41, 206, 214
science, 81–84, 86–88, 95–96, 114–15, 118, 120, 126, 128–29, 131, 136–37, 143, 186, 197–98
self, 30, 39, 51–53, 93, 101, 128, 138
Serres, Michel, 219
Sevagram, 204
Shakers, 108–11
Shakespeare, William, 107
Shattuck, Roger, ix
sin, 25, 86–87, 94, 106, 108, 131, 138, 142, 153, 222–23
Snare, Karen, xi
Socrates, 65
soil, 5, 21, 53–55, 57–58, 60, 63–65, 67, 70, 77, 79, 81–83, 87–90, 96, 103, 105, 108, 110, 117, 146
Solzhenitsyn, Aleksandr, 100
Sophocles, 119, 121
State, 34, 127, 153, 226, 229, 231–32
Steiner, George, 103
Stone, I. F., 8
story, ix, 14, 16, 18, 54, 60, 66–68, 78–80, 90, 106, 113, 115, 129–30, 140
stress, 208–9
subsistence, 41, 50, 54, 56, 61, 74, 117, 150–51, 159, 167, 213–14
sustainable, 56, 84, 210
Synge, John Millington, 117–18

technology, 32, 34, 37–39, 41, 43–44, 57, 59, 65, 67, 76, 88, 91–92, 114–15, 126, 129–31, 134, 136–38, 143–44, 190, 198, 207, 212, 217, 219, 232
Teotihuacán, 198–200
Teresa of Avila, 107
Thoreau, Henry David, 25, 164, 168, 219, 227–28, 233–34
time, ix, 61, 67, 70–71, 78, 89, 96, 98, 110, 114, 116, 118, 134–36, 138, 151, 185, 189, 233
toilet, 181–82, 184
Tolstoy, Count Lev, 212, 228
totalitarian, 84–85, 100, 207, 210, 213

truth, ix, 22–23, 30, 41, 43, 46, 53, 60, 67,
78–80, 86, 91, 93, 96, 98, 100–101, 103–
7, 109–10, 114, 129, 138, 140, 158, 168,
170, 179, 182–83, 186–87, 203, 205, 211–
12, 218, 223, 229, 231

Undset, Sigrid, 120
university, 4, 6, 15, 19, 21, 24–34, 36–38,
40–42, 47, 49, 53–54, 67, 70, 73, 78, 98–
99, 101–2, 115, 120–22, 126–27, 146,
159, 168–71, 173, 175, 178–81
usury, 188

Van Herik, Judith, xi
Vietnam, 2, 7, 22, 218
virtue, xii, 10, 20, 26, 29, 34, 52, 65–66, 78,
91, 96, 101, 103, 119–21, 123–25, 127–
28, 130, 158, 165, 189, 218, 230, 232

war, 2, 10, 155, 188, 217–27, 232
Weber, Max, 74, 228
Weil, Simone, 19, 38–39, 41, 58–59, 85,
102, 127, 172
Whitman, Walt, 227
Winsor, Philip, xi
Withey, Barbara, xii
Wittgenstein, Ludwig, 5, 100–101
Woolman, John, 231
work, 43–44, 46, 48–51, 58–60, 63, 69–70,
72, 75, 78, 80, 91, 99–100, 106, 111, 133,
138, 141, 147, 151–59, 162, 167–68, 176,
180–82, 186, 212–14, 217

Yeats, William Butler, 85, 107
Yukeoma the Hopi, 231

Zinn, Howard, 7